Translated Tex

C000044911

This series is designed to meet the ne
history and others who wish to broaden their study by the
material, but whose knowledge of Latin or Greek is not sufficient to allow
them to do so in the original languages. Many important Late Imperial and
Dark Age texts are currently unavailable in translation and it is hoped that
TTH will help to fill this gap and to complement the secondary literature in
English which already exists. The series relates principally to the period 300-
800 AD and includes Late Imperial, Greek, Byzantine and Syriac texts as
well as source books illustrating a particular period or theme. Each volume is
a self-contained scholarly translation with an introductory essay on the text
and its author and notes on the text indicating major problems of
interpretation, including textual difficulties.

Editorial Committee

Sebastian Brock, Oriental Institute, University of Oxford
Averil Cameron, King's College, London
Henry Chadwick, Peterhouse, Cambridge
John Davies, University of Liverpool
Carlotta Dionisotti, King's College, London
Robert Markus, University of Nottingham
John Matthews, Queen's College, Oxford
Raymond Van Dam, University of Michigan
Michael Whitby, University of St Andrews
Ian Wood, University of Leeds
Jan Ziolkowski, Harvard University

General Editors

Gillian Clark, University of Liverpool
Margaret Gibson, St Peter's College, Oxford
Mary Whitby, University of St Andrews

Front cover drawing: Detail of Ezra miniature (Codex Amiatinus, fol. V), drawn by Gail Heather.
Book titles after R. L. S. Bruce-Mitford, `The art of the Codex Amiatinus', *Journal of the Royal
Archaeological Association*, 32 (1969), p. 10.

For a full list of published titles in the Translated Texts for Historians series, please see pages at the end of this book.

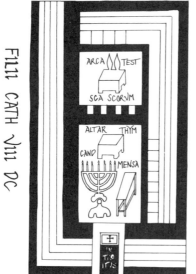

drawn by Gail Heather

NOTE TO FRONTISPIECE

Codex Amiatinus, fol. IIr-IIIr. Wearmouth-Jarrow, late seventh century. Plan of the tabernacle of Moses, perhaps based on a diagram in the sixth-century Codex Grandior of Cassiodorus. (See the discussion in this volume on p. 92, n.1.) A doorway (INTROITUS) on the east leads into an outer chamber which contains a seven-branched lampstand (CAND), the table (MENSA) of showbread and the altar of incense (ALTAR THYM). Inside the holy of holies (SCA SCORUM) stands the ark of the covenant (ARCA TEST) surmounted by two winged cherubim. In front of the tabernacle stand a bronze laver (LABRUM) in which the priests wash themselves and the altar of burnt offerings (ALTARE HOLOCAUSTI), below which are inscribed the names of Moses and Aaron. The four cardinal directions are given in Greek words (ARCTOS = North), the initial letters of which spell ADAM. On three sides of the tabernacle are written the names of the sons of Levi (Gershon, Kohath and Merari) with the enumeration of their clans as in num. 3. Not pictured here is an outer colonnade surrounded by the names and numbers of the twelve tribes of Israel.

Translated Texts for Historians
Volume 18

Bede:
On the Tabernacle

Translated with notes and introduction by
ARTHUR G. HOLDER

Liverpool
University
Press

First published 1994 by
Liverpool University Press
PO Box 147, Liverpool, L69 3BX

British Library Cataloguing-in-Publication Data
A British Library CIP Record is available
ISBN 0 85323 378 0

Printed in the European Community by
Bell & Bain Limited, Glasgow

CONTENTS

ACKNOWLEDGEMENTS

The first draft of this translation was produced in preparation for the writing of my doctoral dissertation at Duke University. I wish to thank my teachers Franklin Young, Roland Murphy, David Steinmetz, Charles Young, Richard Pfaff, and especially my advisor Robert Gregg, for guiding my research in the history of exegesis in late antiquity and the early Middle Ages. For financial and moral support during my years in graduate school, I am grateful to the Center for Medieval and Renaissance Studies at Duke, the Episcopal Diocese of Western North Carolina, parishioners and friends at the Church of the Holy Cross, Valle Crucis, and above all my mother, Mary Ruth Holder. More recently, a sabbatical grant from the Conant Fund of the Episcopal Church's Board for Theological Education has made it possible for me to see this project through to completion. The administration at the Church Divinity School of the Pacific and my faculty colleagues there have unfailingly encouraged me in my conviction that the study of Bede's pastoral theology is not irrelevant to the education and training of priests and teachers for the Church in our own day. In addition, I am greatly indebted to Margaret Gibson, whose careful reading and gracious editorial advice have improved this volume immensely, and to M. R. Ritley for her expert assistance in preparing camera-ready copy. As always, my deepest appreciation goes to my wife Sarah and our son Charles, whose love and support have sustained me beyond measure.

ABBREVIATIONS

ACW   *Ancient Christian Writers*
ANF   *Ante-Nicene Fathers*
CCCM   *Corpus Christianorum, Continuatio Medievalis*
CCSL   *Corpus Christianorum, Series Latina*
CSEL   *Corpus Scriptorum Ecclesiasticorum Latinorum*
FOTC   *Fathers of the Church*
GCS   *Die Griechischen Christlichen Schriftsteller*
LCL   *Loeb Classical Library*
MGH AA   *Monumenta Germaniae Historica, Auctores Antiquissimi*
NPNF   *Nicene and Post-Nicene Fathers*
PL   *Patrologia Latina*
SC   *Sources Chrétiennes*

INTRODUCTION

Most of what we know about the life of the Venerable Bede (673-735) is derived from the brief autobiographical account at the end of his *Ecclesiastical History of the English People*, completed in 731. Born in Northumbria on lands that would later belong to the monastery of Saint Peter and Saint Paul at Wearmouth and Jarrow, he came to Wearmouth as an oblate at the age of seven and soon thereafter moved to Jarrow, where he spent the remainder of his life. He received his early monastic training under Benedict Biscop (the founding abbot of the monastery) and Benedict's successor at Jarrow, whose name was Ceolfrith. At the age of 19 he was ordained a deacon by John of Beverley, bishop of Hexham, and eleven years later he became a priest. His daily routine was given over to the fulfillment of a religious vocation which he described as follows:

> I have spent all my life in this monastery, applying myself entirely to the study of the Scriptures; and amid the observance of the discipline of the Rule and the daily task of singing in the church, it has always been my delight to learn or to teach or to write . . . . From the time I became a priest until the fifty-ninth year of my life, I have made it my business, for my own benefit and that of my brothers, to make brief extracts from the works of the venerable Fathers on Holy Scripture, or to add notes of my own to clarify their sense and interpretation.[1]

Although Bede is remembered today chiefly for his work as a historian, it is clear that he thought of himself as a Christian teacher who specialized in the interpretation of the Bible. When he appended a catalogue of his own writings to the autobiographical statement quoted above, he grouped all the scriptural commentaries together and placed them at the head of the list, as if to suggest that they took pride of place. In all periods of his life, even while writing the *Ecclesiastical History* and to the end of his days, Bede continued to be engaged in the work of exegesis.[2] As a result, anyone who wishes to understand the history of Anglo-Saxon England as recorded by Bede must also take account of the commentaries which illuminate so many of his characteristic phrases and patterns of thought. These exegetical works

---

1 Bede, *Hist. eccl.* 5, 24 (ed. and transl. Colgrave and Mynors, 566-7). The best comprehensive treatments of Bede's writings in the context of his life are Hunter Blair (1970), Brown (1987), and Ward (1990).

2 For introductions to Bede's exegesis, in addition to the relevant chapters in the works mentioned in the preceding note, see Jenkins (1935), Willmes (1962), Ray (1982), Holder (1990), and (on his exegesis of the New Testament only) de Margerie (1980-), 4: 187-228.

are also rich sources of information for students of early medieval literature, art, theology, spirituality, education, and culture.

BEDE'S AUDIENCE AND PURPOSE IN WRITING

The primary audience for Bede's biblical commentaries was that select group of preachers and teachers which included the members of the ordained clergy as well as all others holding some form of spiritual authority. Like his master Gregory the Great, Bede envisioned these 'doctors of the Church' as the principal means by which the English people would be instructed in the Christian faith and guided in its practice; thus he fervently hoped that they would be moved to implement the program of ecclesiastical reform set forth in his writings.[1] Most of these contemporary readers would have been monks, but we should not imagine them as cloistered contemplatives dwelling in solitude behind their monastery walls. In Bede's time, and throughout the early Middle Ages, monks were extensively involved in giving pastoral care to neighbours near and far; this explains why Bede was as much concerned for their ministry as missionaries and pastors as for their monastic life of prayer and worship.[2]

Recognizing Bede's underlying pastoral motivation helps us to understand how all of his prodigious literary output in a variety of genres was in fact directed to a single purpose. The historical works offered worthy examples for Christian teachers to emulate and to commend to others, while the didactic treatises gave them the basic tools of grammar and calendrical calculation which would enable them to carry out their liturgical and pastoral duties. In the biblical commentaries, these same teachers could grasp the essential doctrinal and moral truths of Scripture as transmitted through the great tradition of patristic authors, but suitably adapted for the local situation. For Bede was ever mindful of the needs of his readers, and of the limitations of their training; little or nothing in his exegesis could be called speculative or constructive theology. His work may best be described as a form of pastoral theology—not in the narrow sense of the theology of pastoral care (although that is certainly included), but in the wider sense of a theology that describes and informs the ministry of those charged with the cure of souls. As Henry Mayr-Harting put it, 'Bede's great strength was in this sphere where doctrine and the practical life of the Christian meet.'[3]

---

1 Thacker (1983 and 1992); McClure (1985)

2 In addition to the works cited in the previous note, see Constable (1982), Amos (1987), and Foot (1989).

3 Mayr-Harting (1972), 219

ON THE TABERNACLE: SUBJECT, COMPOSITION, AND SOURCES

Henri de Lubac, writing of several twelfth-century commentaries on the tabernacle of Moses, referred to this particular kind of treatise as 'the genre previously inaugurated by Bede in conformity with a tradition which had arisen in the earliest times of the Church.'[1] As this remark implies, Bede's commentary *On the Tabernacle* was the first work of Christian literature entirely devoted to an allegorical exposition of this topic; it was also the first verse-by-verse commentary to cover Exod. 24:12-30:21. Along with a subsequent companion treatise on the temple of Solomon and several shorter expositions of Old Testament houses of worship, *On the Tabernacle* is a prime example of what Charles Jones once called 'Bede's rather exceptionally architectural approach to Revelation'.[2] Indeed, there seems to have been something about the balance, harmony, and regularity of architectural design that appealed to Bede's imagination and stimulated him to formulate a comprehensive theological and pastoral vision in relation to the various sacred structures described in the Bible.

As Bede was well aware, the tabernacle of Moses was a portable shrine that served as the principal sign of God's presence among the ancient people of Israel during their years of wandering in the wilderness and for some time after their settlement in the land of Canaan. From the giving of the law on Mount Sinai until the time of Solomon, the tabernacle was the primary location of both divine revelation and cultic worship. Unlike the later temples of Solomon, Zerubbabel, and Herod, this tabernacle was not a grand stone edifice but rather a tent constructed out of fabric curtains erected on a wooden frame and covered with animal skins. It housed a number of sacred objects such as the ark of the covenant containing the tablets of the law, the table of showbread, a seven-branched lampstand, and the altar of incense; outside the tent stood an altar for burnt offerings and a bronze laver in which the priests performed their ritual ablutions. Although the description in Exodus is incomplete and not altogether clear in details, it indicates that the tabernacle was similar to tent shrines known from other Semitic cultures in the Ancient Near East.[3] According to 1 Kgs. 8:4, the tabernacle

---

1 de Lubac (1959-64), 2, 1: 406

2 Jones (1969-70), 169. See also *De templo* (*CCSL* 119A: 144-234); *De sch. et trop.* 2, 2 (*CCSL* 123A: 168, 265 - 169, 273); *In Gen.* 2 (*CCSL* 118A: 107, 1220-4; 109, 1285 - 110, 1314); *In Ezr.* 1 (*CCSL* 119A: 241, 1-21, and *passim*); *In Apoc.* (*PL* 93: 141D, 162A); *In Reg. XXX quaest.* 12 (*CCSL* 119: 304, 18-21); and *Hom.* 2, 1; 2, 24; 2, 25 (*CCSL* 122: 184-92; 358-67; 368-78).

3 Cross (1961); Friedman (1992)

was brought to Jerusalem by Solomon and set up inside the temple there; presumably it was destroyed along with the latter in 587 BCE.

Allegorical interpretations of this Mosaic tabernacle can be found in both Jewish and Christian writings of the first century CE. The Jewish authors Philo and Josephus understood the tabernacle as a symbol of the cosmos, while the Epistle to the Hebrews in the New Testament saw it as a copy of the true heavenly sanctuary into which Christ entered as high priest after his ascension. Later Christian authors continued both of these themes, sometimes repeating cosmological symbolism and sometimes setting forth expositions of the tabernacle as a figure of the virtuous soul, the incarnate Christ, or the Christian clergy. Prior to Bede, exegesis of the tabernacle appeared in selected writings of patristic authors such as (in the East) Clement of Alexandria, Origen, Methodius, Ephrem Syrus, Gregory of Nyssa, Theodore of Mopsuestia, Cyril of Alexandria, Theodoret of Cyrus, Procopius of Gaza, and Cosmas Indicopleustes, and (in the West) Ambrose, Jerome, Augustine, Eucherius of Lyons, Gregory the Great, and Isidore of Seville.[1] None of these authors, however, offered an extended commentary on the tabernacle of the sort found in the work Bede himself named as *De tabernaculo et vasis eius ac vestibus sacerdotum, libros III*, or *On the Tabernacle and Its Vessels and the Priestly Vestments, Three Books*.[2]

Although it has no prologue and no topical references that point to a specific date of composition, *On the Tabernacle* can probably be assigned to the period *c.*721-5; it was certainly prior to both *On Mark* and *On the Temple*, for it is mentioned in both of those works.[3] There is no indication of its having been revised over the space of a number of years (as was Bede's commentary on Genesis, for example), and since there are a number of other commentaries that must be dated to roughly the same period we may conclude that *On the Tabernacle* was composed within a fairly short amount of time. The principal sources Bede employed were a Latin translation of the *Jewish Antiquities* of Josephus, Jerome's *Letter* 64 to Fabiola on the subject of the priestly vestments, and the *Book of Pastoral Rule* written by Gregory the Great. He derived useful bits of information from Jerome's book *On Hebrew Names*, Pliny's *Natural History*, and the *Etymologies* compiled by Isidore of Seville; on one occasion, he also made reference to a drawing of the tabernacle that Cassiodorus caused to be placed in the Codex Grandior. Compared with some of his other more derivative biblical

---

1 For bibliographical references and a brief survey of this exegesis, see Holder (1993).

2 Bede, *Hist. eccl.* 5, 24 (ed. Colgrave and Mynors, 568)

3 Laistner and King (1943), 70; see Bede, *In Marc.* 1 (*CCSL* 120: 464, 1060-2); *De templo* 2 (*CCSL* 119A: 232, 1575-7).

commentaries, this treatise on the tabernacle shows Bede as a creative and original exegete working without the benefit of extensive patristic models to follow.[1]

BIBLICAL INTERPRETATION IN THEORY AND PRACTICE

On the Tabernacle contains several explicit statements of exegetical theory which are interesting for the light they shed on Bede's approach to biblical interpretation, even though they cannot always be harmonized with one another and do not represent anything like a systematic program which was rigidly applied in practice. The commentary begins with a clear statement of the method that Bede intended to follow:

> Since with the Lord's help we are going to speak about the figure of the tabernacle and its vessels and utensils, first we ought to examine and attentively consider the topography of the place and the circumstances that obtained when these things were commanded to be made. For *all these things*, as the Apostle says, *happened to them in figure but were written down for us.* 'All these things' [includes] not only the deeds or words that are contained in the Sacred Writings, but also the description of the locations and hours and times and the things themselves, as well as the circumstances under which they were done or said.[2]

Despite the appeal to 1 Cor. 10:11 as warrant, the example of Saint Paul was not the only precedent standing behind Bede's methodological principle here. As Roger Ray has pointed out, Bede's focus on the *circumstantiae* recorded in the biblical narrative links him with the classical rhetorical tradition of *inventio*, in which details of person, place, and time furnished the basic material for discussion of any historical topic.[3]

It would have been utterly foreign to Bede's way of thinking to have considered any person, object, or event mentioned in the Bible as merely a datum of historical fact. After all, had Saint Paul not stressed that all things in the Old Testament had happened in figure and were recorded for the benefit of future Christian generations? When Bede read the description of

---

1 Detailed information on Bede's sources in this commentary appears in Holder (1989b) and in the index of patristic and classical sources in this volume.

2 *De tab.* 1, Prol. (*CCSL* 119A: 5, 1-9)

3 Ray (1982), 16-18. He is convinced that Bede had studied Cicero's *De inventione* or some other manual of Roman rhetorical theory; see Ray (1987).

the intricate details of the construction of the tabernacle, he was of course aware that it had reference, in the first place, to a concrete, physical architectural reality. But that sacred structure had long since been destroyed, while the inspired text which had both commanded and recorded its existence still continued to stand fast. The demise of the literal tabernacle must have sustained Bede in his conviction that the deeper (and ultimately more significant) meaning of the text had to do with the edification of the Christian Church.

How did Bede understand the relation of this deeper spiritual meaning to the letter of the biblical text? It is customary to discuss this question under the heading of the 'senses of Scripture', and there are several passages in *On the Tabernacle* in which Bede uses this kind of language. The first, and most often quoted, is Bede's comment on the four feet of the table described in Exod. 25:26. This was the passage that prompted Henri de Lubac to speak of Bede as the first writer to give us a fully developed account of what came to be the traditional medieval understanding of the fourfold sense of Scripture as revelatory of historical, allegorical, tropological, and anagogical truth.[1] Elsewhere in the same commentary, however, Bede expounded a threefold formula of biblical interpretation.[2] And in practice, it seems that he actually distinguished only two senses, one literal or historical and another that he named variously as 'spiritual', 'typic', 'sacramental', 'mystical', 'figurative', or 'allegorical'.[3]

In *On the Tabernacle*, it was the spiritual sense which occupied most of Bede's attention. His usual procedure was simply to quote a verse or two from the biblical text, perhaps provide a brief paraphrase of it, and then proceed to develop the allegorical meaning. There were a few instances, however, in which Bede found it necessary to investigate the literal sense in some detail. In each of those cases, he made it plain that his treatment of the letter was preliminary to the allegorical exposition it was meant to serve, and from which it was carefully separated. For example, a concise summary of the description of the tabernacle and its furnishings at the beginning of Book 2 is both prefaced and concluded by Bede's remarking that it was necessary to reflect upon the letter of the text for a while so that the spiritual sense could be better understood.[4] In some of his other commentaries Bede dealt at length with textual, historical, and archaeological questions, but

---

1 *De tab.* 1, 6 (*CCSL* 119A: 24, 776 - 25, 811); de Lubac (1959-64), 1, 2: 422
2 Ibid. 2, 13 (*CCSL* 119A: 91, 1956-60)
3 This is the case in Bede's other commentaries as well; see Barrows (1963), 179-98, and Jones (1969-70), 135-55.
4 *De tab.* 2, 1 (*CCSL* 119A: 43, 70-1; 44, 96-9; cf. 56, 578-82; 65, 914-15)

here his curiosity about such matters, though evident, was thoroughly subordinated to a search for spiritual edification on the allegorical plane. From her study of Bede's commentary on the Song of Songs, Mary Barrows concluded that

> Bede's methods include all the elements that had come to him through the rich tradition of patristic and earlier thought. He uses interpretations based on etymologies, on the meaning of numbers, on the nature of the image under consideration, and on testimonies from all parts of Scripture. Further, he follows what he conceives to be the sense of the story in both its literal and allegorical contexts, and the sense of the entire history of salvation.[1]

All of these exegetical approaches can be found in *On the Tabernacle* as well, along with the structural use of wordplay which Lawrence Martin has identified as a distinctive feature of Bede's exegetical style.[2] In a verse-by-verse commentary on a biblical text largely composed of lists and descriptions of architectural detail, Bede naturally devoted most of his attention to the interpretation of individual persons, objects, measurements, and materials. It would be wrong, however, to suppose him insensitive to the larger context in which the individual verses appeared. When commenting upon the introductory narrative account of Moses' ascent up Mount Sinai to receive the tablets of the law from the Lord, for example, Bede was highly alert to the elements of character, plot, and setting. Since he understood Moses' ascent as a typological event instructing Christians how they ought to approach divine wisdom, he interpreted all the elements that figured in the story—whether they were natural images like the mountain, the cloud, and the burning fire, or human beings like Joshua, Aaron, and Hur—in relation to this typology.[3]

Perhaps the most striking use Bede made of his comprehensive sense of the biblical narrative was his contrast between the tabernacle and the temple. He treated these two structures as types, respectively, of the Church militant and the Church triumphant (because the former was carried through the wilderness while the latter remained stationary in the promised land) or as figures of the Old and New Testament communities (because the former was built by Jews alone but the latter was constructed by the cooperative

---

1 Barrows (1963), 205-6
2 Martin (1986)
3 *De tab.* 1, 1-2 (*CCSL* 119A: 5, 10 - 10, 211)

efforts of Jews, proselytes, and Gentiles).[1] But even when commenting on
the detailed descriptions of particular objects contained in the tabernacle,
Bede never lost sight of the larger context of the biblical narrative. Whether
he was discussing Aaron's vesture, or the altars of holocaust and incense,
or Solomon's role in building the temple, what he had to say was very much
informed by his understanding of such Old Testament institutions as
priesthood, sacrifice, and kingship. Bede did not derive these under-
standings from any one verse, or even from the series of chapters in Exodus
on which he was commenting. He read the Bible as a unified whole, and he
always constructed his interpretation in relation to the entire story of the
people of God, of which he believed the tabernacle to be an epitomizing
symbol.

BEDE'S THEOLOGICAL TEACHINGS

Modern readers unfamiliar with the ancient Christian practice of allegorical interpretation may be tempted to suppose that such exegesis followed a
rather mechanical process of deciphering arcane signs according to a
predetermined code. It is true that with some authors the procedure could
at times result in a dry and lifeless collection of symbolic identifications—
as it does, for example, in Eucherius of Lyons' *Forms of spiritual intelli-
gence*, which is nothing more than a catalogue of exegetical
commonplaces.[2] Bede's commentaries, however, are altogether different.
His exegesis derived not only its categories but also its dynamic movement
from a Christian theology of history that Bede inherited from the Latin
church fathers, especially Saint Augustine.

Like the Bishop of Hippo, Bede believed that all human beings created
by God had sinned in Adam, that God had predestined the elect to be saved
by the blood of Christ offered as a sacrifice for sin, and that these elect,
along with the angels who had never fallen away, constitute the true
Catholic Church in communion with the apostles and with the bishops who
have succeeded them. Some of the faithful elect already reign with the Lord
in heaven, while others continue to pursue their pilgrim way here on earth.
The visible Church, in which the sacraments are celebrated as signs of
redemption and means of grace, is the company of those who profess faith
in Christ, hope for a resurrection like his in both soul and body, are united

---

1 *De tab.* 2, 1 (*CCSL* 119A: 42, 1 - 43, 50); cf. *De templo* 1 (*CCSL* 119A: 147, 34 - 148,
53). Bede seems to have been the first Christian author to contrast the two Old Testament
houses of God in this way.

2 Cf. Eucherius' exposition of the tabernacle in *Form. spir. intell.* 9 (*CSEL* 31: 51-4).

to one another in a fellowship of love, and perform good works with the aid of the Holy Spirit. Not all members of this visible Church, however, can be counted among the elect; some are false Christians who outwardly seem to belong to Christ but inwardly continue to rebel against him through impenitent pride. At the last judgement, these false Christians and the rest of the reprobate will be consigned to unquenchable fire, but the elect will enjoy the vision of God in heaven forever—their enjoyment being in proportion to the merits they have earned by divine grace. All of human history, Bede thought, should be understood as the working out of this divine plan of salvation, which is clearly proclaimed in the pages of Holy Scripture.

Throughout *On the Tabernacle*, and especially in his discussion of the priestly vestments of Aaron, Bede stressed the practical implications of this theology for the moral conduct and pastoral ministry of those eighth-century Anglo-Saxon monks and missionaries who were his intended audience. On several occasions, however, he was careful to note that the spiritual message of the Bible was addressed to the whole people of God. 'Therefore,' he wrote, 'we admonish all the faithful to be known by the mystical name of priests, inasmuch as they are members of Christ, that is, of the eternal Priest.'[1] For clergy and laity alike, Bede unfolded his characteristic teachings on a number of favourite themes: the unity which is manifest in the rich diversity of the Church, the definite and discernible stages through which the faithful pass as they make progress in the Christian life, the humble obedience in action which is prerequisite for the exercise of any kind of authority, and the blessedness of eternal rest which awaits those who labour actively in good works.[2]

ON THE TABERNACLE IN THE MIDDLE AGES

The Latin patristic tradition contained relatively little exegesis of the Mosaic tabernacle. It is not surprising, therefore, that a commentary on this topic by the foremost biblical scholar of the early Middle Ages should have been in great demand. We know that Bede himself sent copies of the companion treatise *On the Temple* to Bishop Acca of Hexham (at whose request many of his commentaries were undertaken) and to Abbot Albinus in Canterbury.[3] He must have assumed that Acca and Albinus would have had access to *On the Tabernacle* as well, since he felt free to refer readers

---

1 *De tab.* 3, 14 (*CCSL* 119A: 138, 1756-8)
2 For a full treatment of these themes in *De tabernaculo* and *De templo*, see Holder (1991).
3 *De templo*, Prol. (*CCSL* 119A: 144, 55-9); *Ep. Alb.* (ed. Plummer, 1: 3)

of *On the Temple* to the earlier work, with no further explanation.[1] Thus it
is apparent that Bede intended for his commentaries to be read by those
beyond the confines of his own monastery, but he can hardly have imagined
just how far beyond Northumbria, and England, his audience would extend.
Laistner's compilation of information from medieval library catalogues
and extant manuscripts indicated that as early as the ninth century copies
of *On the Tabernacle* were to be found at Fleury, Saint Martin's at Tours,
Saint Emmeram, Saint Gall, Reichenau, Lorsch, Salvatorstift at Würzburg,
and Freising; it is safe to say that there must have been many others in
addition to these.[2] Presumably, Bede's works were widely distributed in
England as well, but the evidence there is quite thin as a result of the
destruction wrought by the Danish invasions. It was primarily, then, the
Anglo-Saxon missionary centers on the Continent, not the besieged or even
ruined English monasteries, that preserved, copied, and distributed Bede's
commentaries during the Carolingian period. From the rest of the Middle
Ages, and especially from the twelfth century, we possess numerous
English and Continental manuscripts and library catalogues that contain *On
the Tabernacle*, so we know that this text continued to inform, instruct, and
console Christian readers eager to understand the mysteries of the sacred
page.[3]

Besides circulating under Bede's name as an independent treatise, *On
the Tabernacle* was sometimes taken up, in whole or in part, into the
writings of later medieval exegetes. Rabanus Maurus (d. 856) included a
somewhat abbreviated version in his commentary on Exodus, and over a
dozen quotations from *On the Tabernacle* appear in the *Office Book* of
Amalarius of Metz (*c.*780-850/1), who used Bede's comments on the Old
Testament liturgy in his own allegorical interpretation of the rites of the
Christian Church.[4] When the *Ordinary Gloss* was compiled early in the
twelfth century, Bede's commentary provided the great bulk of the material
used in the tabernacle section of that most influential of all medieval biblical
commentaries.[5] So much of *On the Tabernacle* appears in the *Gloss*, in fact,
that it is often difficult to tell whether or not later writers were quoting from

---

1 *De templo* 2 (*CCSL* 119A: 232, 1575-7)

2 Laistner and King (1943), 10-13, 70-4

3 To the entries given in Laistner and King (1943), 10-13, 70-8, add those noted in Ker
(1944).

4 Rabanus Maurus, *In Exodum* (*PL* 108: 136-218); Amalarius of Metz, *Liber officialis* (ed.
Hanssens, 2: 19-565; quotations from Bede's *De tabernaculo* are listed in the index found in
vol. 3: 348).

5 *Glossa ordinaria* on Exod. 24:12-30:21 (ed. Froehlich and Gibson, 1: 161-90). On the
origins and development of the *Glossa*, see Gibson (1992).

the *Gloss* or from the original work. Andrew of Saint Victor (*c.* 1110-75) quoted several passages from Bede's treatise in his commentary on the Heptateuch, but the large chunks of this work that the twelfth-century compiler Robert of Bridlington copied into his commentary on Exodus came straight out of the *Ordinary Gloss.*[1]

Medieval exegetes were not content merely to copy or summarize Bede's work. They often incorporated his ideas into their own treatment of the tabernacle, and sometimes they took up where he left off and developed new interpretations of the same subject.[2] A number of twelfth-century exegetes followed Bede's example by devoting entire treatises to the subject of the Mosaic tabernacle. The two commentaries on the tabernacle by Peter of Celle (*c.* 1115-1183) and the one written by Peter of Poitiers (1193-1205) are dependent on Bede for much of their material; the second treatise *On the Tabernacle* by Peter of Celle is little more than an abbreviated paraphrase of Bede.[3] Like their eighth-century predecessor, both of these two authors concentrated on allegorical interpretation of the tabernacle as a figure of Christ and the Church.

Other writers sought to supplement or correct Bede by giving attention to those senses of interpretation which he was thought to have neglected. Richard of Saint Victor, for example, composed no fewer than three works on various aspects of the tabernacle. In the opening lines of the treatise commonly called *Benjamin major*, which contains Richard's interpretation of the ark of the covenant as a figure of six different degrees or kinds of contemplation, he explicitly declared that he aimed to supplement the allegorical expositions given by other learned writers (surely including Bede) with a tropological interpretation of his own; an appendix joined to it deals in similar fashion with other parts of the tabernacle as well.[4] A third work addresses certain 'difficulties' Richard perceived in the exposition of the tabernacle, including the problem presented because Bede (whom Richard discreetly avoided naming) had dared to claim that the allegorical meaning of the curtains over the tabernacle in Exod. 26:12-13 was obvious, even though the literal sense was difficult to explain.[5]

---

1 Andrew of Saint Victor, *In Exod.* 25, 17 - 28, 22 (*CCCM* 53: 142, 1624 - 153, 2028). The commentary by Robert of Bridlington is still unprinted, but see the reference to his quotations from Bede in Smalley (1944), 230.

2 See Chenu (1957), 192-6, and de Lubac (1959-64), 2, 1: 403-18.

3 Peter of Celle, *De tabernaculo I* and *De tabernaculo II* (*CCCM* 54: 171-219; 220-43); Peter of Poitiers, *Allegoriae super tabernaculum Moysi* (ed. Moore and Corbett).

4 Richard of Saint Victor, *Benjamin major* (*PL* 196: 63-192) and *Nonnullae allegoriae tabernaculi foederis* (*PL* 196: 191-202)

5 Richard of Saint Victor, *Expositio difficultatum suborientium in expositione tabernaculi*

Bede's treatment of the outer curtains made of goats' hair in Exod. 26:9 occasioned further controversy, because the reason he gave for the doubling of the sixth curtain did not agree with that of Josephus.[1] Both Andrew of Saint Victor and Peter Comestor (c.1100-c.1180) readily accepted Josephus' opinion, implying that ancient Jewish tradition carried more weight than Bede's conjectures with twelfth-century exegetes who were interested primarily in the literal sense of the biblical text.[2] On the other hand we have Adam of Dryburgh (d. 1212), who in 1176 took up this troublesome question in a lengthy treatise On the Tripartite Tabernacle.[3] Adam professed great respect for Bede's exegesis, declaring in his preface that his own exposition diligently followed Bede in every respect without contradicting him at all.[4] On the controversial matter of the sixth curtain, he quoted the opinion of his master Andrew of Saint Victor in full, but Adam went to great lengths to defend the trustworthiness of Bede's account.[5]

These varying assessments by twelfth-century exegetes delineate the limits of Bede's authority in the High Middle Ages, and beyond. His commentary on the tabernacle was read and studied by virtually every medieval exegete who ventured to address this topic, and he was regarded as an allegorist par excellence for his profound application of Scripture to the sacramental, ascetical, and pastoral dimensions of the Christian life. But when it came to speculative theology (such as the precise delineation of the various kinds of contemplative prayer) or to the satisfaction of historical curiosity about architectural details, his exegesis was sometimes found wanting. For four centuries, Bede's On the Tabernacle had stood uncontested as the definitive treatment. By the end of the twelfth century, however, it no longer occupied that singular position, although it continued to be widely read, copied, and appreciated for many years to come.[6]

This change in status would probably not have come as much of a disappointment to Bede. His efforts had always been intended to stimulate

---

foederis (PL 196: 211-22); cf. Bede, De tab. 2 (CCSL 119A: 56, 578-82)

1 Bede, De tab. 2 (CCSL 119A: 56, 571-8); cf. Josephus, Ant. Jud. 3, 6, 4 (ed. Blatt, 235, 5-9)

2 Andrew of Saint Victor, In Exod. 26, 9 (CCCM 53: 146, 1837-40); Peter Comestor, Hist. schol., Lib. Exod. 55-6 (PL 198: 1177-8)

3 The three books of Adam of Dryburgh's De tripartito tabernaculo (PL 198: 609-796) deal with three aspects (literal, allegorical, and tropological) of the significance of the tabernacle.

4 Adam of Dryburgh, Epistola Joanni Kelchou de materiali fabrica tabernaculi Moysi transmissa 8 (PL 198: 632C)

5 Adam of Dryburgh, De trip. tab. 1, 14 (PL 198: 651-3)

6 For an example of the continuing influence of Bede's De tabernaculo, consider John Ruysbroeck's borrowings from it in the fourteenth century, as noted by Krabben (1935).

and support the learning of others rather than to make their scholarship unnecessary. Richard of Saint Victor was simply taking Bede's renowned humility at face value when he sought to justify his own temerity in challenging this venerable authority (whom he readily acknowledged as a father of the Church) by quoting Bede's concluding words about the obscurities he recognized in regard to the interpretation of the tabernacle curtains:

> In so far as we have been able to understand them, we have taken care briefly to explain these things concerning this most difficult subject, but we are ready to learn more accurate information about these matters if anyone wishes to instruct us.[1]

Coming from the pen of another early medieval author, such words might have been just the obligatory repetition of another worn-out literary commonplace. But one senses that Bede, who so often urged Christian teachers to practice what they preach, sincerely intended to defer cheerfully to any new insights that the future might disclose, even as he had cherished, preserved, and (as far as he was able) extended the traditional wisdom of the past. No scholar of his day or ours could do more, or should do less.

MODERN EDITIONS AND THE PRESENT TRANSLATION

The first publication of *On the Tabernacle* was in the Basel edition of Bede's collected works printed by John Heerwagen in 1563. Another edition by J. A. Giles appeared in his collection of the complete works published in London in 1843-4; this was the text reprinted by Migne in *PL* 91. The present translation is based on the critical edition prepared by David Hurst for *CCSL* 119A; page references to that volume are provided in the margins. A few of the most significant variant readings given by Hurst are indicated in the notes.

Although Bede's Latin has often been praised for its lucidity, modern readers would find it difficult to follow if rendered directly into English. It has seemed advisable, therefore, to break many of his long complex sentences into two or more shorter ones, to change some passive constructions into active ones, and occasionally to repeat nouns, pronouns, and verbs that appear only once in the Latin text but serve in several successive clauses. Common nouns of masculine gender such as *homines* or *filii* have

---

1 Bede, *De tab.* 2, 3 (*CCSL* 119A: 56, 578-81), quoted in Richard of Saint Victor, *Expos. diff. tab.*, Prol. (*PL* 196: 211B).

been translated as 'people' or 'children' when it seems apparent that Bede's reference was intended to include persons of both sexes, but as 'men' or 'sons' in references to the ordained clergy of Bede's time, the Old Testament patriarchs, or other obviously male figures. Following the same reasoning, singular masculine pronouns have sometimes been translated in an inclusive sense by rephrasing, or by changing singular to plural forms.

Biblical quotations are in the style of the *New Revised Standard Version*, but translated afresh so as to reflect Bede's usage, which customarily follows the Vulgate but sometimes reflects his acquaintance with Old Latin versions. Citations of biblical references are given according to the NRSV numbering, with the Vulgate numbering in parentheses in cases where it differs. When Bede is quoting another author directly, the quotation is printed in italics; allusions and parallels remain in roman type but are indicated in the notes. The Select Bibliography includes all primary sources and secondary works cited in either the Introduction or the notes. Indices of Bede's biblical quotations and allusions and of his patristic and classical sources are provided at the end of the volume. The section headings are Bede's own *capitula*, which are given here at the beginning of the individual sections instead of being listed all together as a table of contents, as they were in the manuscripts and in the printed editions.

ON THE TABERNACLE

BOOK ONE

Since with the Lord's help we are going to speak about the figure of the   *[5]*
tabernacle and its vessels and utensils, first we ought to examine and
attentively consider the topography of the place and the circumstances that
obtained when these things were commanded to be made. For *all these
things*, as the Apostle says, *happened to them in figure but were written
down for us.*[1] 'All these things' [includes] not only the deeds or words that
are contained in the Sacred Writings, but also the description of the
locations and hours and times and the things themselves, as well as the
circumstances under which they were done or said.[2]

1.   MOSES GOES UP ONTO THE MOUNTAIN OF GOD WITH
     JOSHUA AND LEAVES AARON AND HUR BEHIND TO
     GOVERN THE PEOPLE

24:12 [The Book of Exodus] says: **The Lord said to Moses, 'Come up
to me on the mountain and remain there, and I will give you tablets of
stone, and the law and the commandments, which I have written for
you to teach them.'** When the Lord is about to give the law to Moses he
first summons him to the top of the mountain, so that by tarrying with [the
Lord] on high he can more easily hear the precepts that he is to teach to the
people when he returns below. And at the same time, he can deduce from
the height of the place how lofty is the law which he is receiving, and how
far removed from human teaching. For it can be perfectly understood or
kept only by those who have separated themselves from earthly contagions
by living more sublimely and more perfectly. Hence [the Lord] also
commands the people to wait below until Moses should return, that he might
suggest by means of a type that while the secrets of his law are indeed
heavenly things grasped only by the more perfect, even so the weak do not
lack an opportunity for salvation, if they will eagerly and humbly listen to
the wisdom of the elders.

---

1 1 Cor. 10:11
2 As noted in Ray (1982), 16-18, Bede here shows his familiarity with the classical
rhetorical tradition by using the *circumstantiae* of the biblical narrative as the basis for his
commentary.

Similarly, in the gospel the Lord called the new heralds of grace together on a mountain when he taught them with salutary precepts,[1] so that it might be evident even from the topography of the place that he was giving them lofty things, whether commandments to live by or rewards by way of recompense.[2] This accords with that [saying] of the psalmist, *'Your right-eousness is like the mountains of God.'*[3] And after the resurrection he appeared to them again on a holy mountain when he sent them to preach not only to the one people of Israel but to the whole world, saying, *'Go teach all nations, baptizing them in the name of the Father and of the Son and of the Holy Spirit, teaching them to observe all that I have commanded you.'*[4] Consequently, the Lord gave the precepts of both the law and the gospel on a mountain, so that he might in this way commend the sublimity of both testaments.

[6]

But since at that time the Scripture of the law was being committed solely to the people of Israel, while the grace of the gospel was going to reach all nations throughout the world by the preaching of the apostles, it was suitable for Moses to go up onto a mountain alone to learn and to receive the law, but the apostles heard the teaching of the gospel when all of them together were with the Lord on a mountain, along with the crowds who were listening [to him] as well.[5] Nor was it the apostles alone who received the gift of the Holy Spirit by which this same grace-filled truth[6] of the gospel was given more manifestly to the Church, but a very great company of the faithful who were gathered together in an upper room on Mount Zion, and this [took place] with a distribution of diverse tongues,[7] so that by this particular kind of miracle it might be signified that the Church was going to be praising God in the tongues of all the peoples throughout the world.

He says: **And I will give you tablets of stone, and the law and the commandments, which I have written for you to teach them.** This is like that [verse] from the gospel that we cited above: *'teaching them to observe all that I have commanded you'*.[8] Consequently, neither Moses nor the apostles nor any one of the teachers ought to teach the people of God any precepts other than those that the Lord himself taught, [those precepts] which in the eternal decree of his counsel he has directed us to observe, and

---

1 Matt. 5:1; Mark 3:13

2 Augustine, *Serm. dom. in monte* 1, 2 (*CCSL* 35: 2, 33 - 3, 46)

3 Ps. 36:6 (35:7)

4 Matt. 28:19-20

5 Matt. 7:28

6 literally, 'grace and truth', but treated as a singular subject.

7 Acts 1:15, 2:1-11

8 Matt. 28:20

in the observation of which he has willed that we should have eternal life. Nor should the teachers omit any of the things that he has ordered to be performed, for they are obliged to commit to their hearers everything that he has commanded them. Furthermore, he wrote these things on tablets of stone because he has established that they are to be kept and preserved by faith with a fixed purpose in the steadfast hearts of the elect. When he set forth the statutes of the law written in stone, it was just as if he was displaying examples for us to imitate. For Daniel also saw how the Lord, in the form of a stone hewn from a mountain not by hands, destroyed the pomp of a worldly kingdom so that his own kingdom alone might endure without end,[1] and Peter admonishes the faithful, saying, *And, like living stones, let yourselves be built up into spiritual houses.*[2]

24:13 **Moses rose up, and his servant Joshua.** Moses' servant Joshua designates the Lord Saviour both by name[3] and by deed. Rightly is he called Moses' servant, because when he appeared in flesh he deigned to submit himself to the ceremonies of the Mosaic law, since he came not to abolish but to fulfill the law.[4] He follows Moses' footsteps in all things, because   *[7]* if he is properly sought, [Jesus] is to be found in everything that Moses says or writes, being designated either by means of a type or openly, as if he were [Moses'] inseparable companion. For this reason also he says to the Jews, *'If you believed in Moses, perhaps you would also believe in me; for he wrote about me.'*[5]

24:13-14 **And as Moses was going up onto the mountain of God, he said to the elders, 'Wait here until we return to you. You have Aaron and Hur with you; if any question arises, you should refer it to them.'** Aaron is interpreted as 'mountain of fortitude', Hur as 'fire' or 'light'.[6] Hence Aaron designates the Lord Saviour and Hur the Holy Spirit, since Isaiah says of the one, *And in the latter days the mountain of the house of the Lord shall be established on the height of the mountains,*[7] and the other appeared upon the apostles in fiery light.[8] Therefore, when Moses went up to the Lord he left Aaron and Hur (that is, 'mountain of fortitude' and 'fiery

---

1 Dan. 2:34-5

2 1 Pet. 2:5

3 The name of Jesus is a Greek form of the Hebrew יהושע ('Joshua'), of which the usual Latin form is *Josue*. However, the Vulgate sometimes refers to Moses' assistant as *Jesus*; see Sir. 46:1, Acts 7:45, and Heb. 4:8.

4 Matt. 5:17

5 John 5:46

6 Jerome, *Nom.* (*CCSL* 72: 73, 6; 77, 5)

7 Isa. 2:2

8 Acts 2:3-4

light') on the plains to govern the people. And if we are unable to follow our teachers to the height of divine contemplation, let us take solicitous care lest temptation should somehow draw us far away from the mountain of God. Instead, let us persevere in [good] works according to the measure of our powers, cleaving with unwavering heart to the sacraments of our Redeemer, into which we have been initiated, and taking care to preserve undefiled in us the grace of his Spirit, with which we have been sealed. And if by chance we should be disturbed by the problem of adversities, then let us call upon the aid of our same Redeemer, who is accustomed to protect his faithful from every evil and to deliver them through the gift of the Holy Spirit. Nor should we have any doubt that if we continue steadfastly in what we have begun, our weakness and lowness[1] will be strengthened and raised up by the mountain of fortitude, and empowered against the attacks of every enemy. Furthermore, our ignorance will be illuminated by the light and fire of the Holy Spirit, as our soul is enkindled with love for that same benevolent Maker.

24:15 **And when Moses had gone up, a cloud covered the mountain.** Just as the mountain upon which Moses received the law designates the height of the perfection that was written down in that law, so does the cloud which covered the mountain suggest the grace of divine protection, which is enjoyed more and more the higher one ascends in order to search out the wonders of God's law, as the eyes of one's heart are opened. For surely the cloud covered not only the mountain upon which Moses went up, but also the people who were travelling through the wilderness. They were by no means able to ascend to the higher regions, but the cloud sent from heaven

[8] overshadowed them nevertheless.[2] Hence it is written that *he spread out a cloud for their protection,*[3] since the Lord surely protects with heavenly benediction *all those who fear him, both small and great.*[4]

2.   ON THE SEVENTH DAY [MOSES] IS CALLED TO THE
      SUMMIT OF THE MOUNTAIN, WHERE HE REMAINS
      WITH THE LORD FOR FORTY DAYS AND NIGHTS

24:16 **And the glory of the Lord dwelt upon Sinai, covering it with a cloud for six days; and on the seventh day he called to [Moses] from the midst of the cloud.** Not only the height of the mountain on which the

---

1 *humilitas*
2 Exod. 13:21-2
3 Ps. 105:39 (104:39)
4 Ps. 115:13 (113:13)

law was given, but even its very name as well, figuratively announces the perfection of that law. For Sinai is interpreted as 'my capacity' or 'my measure'.[1] Consequently, it was arranged by divine providence that the mountain on which the law was given should be called 'my measure', as if the Lord himself was signifying by this name that his law teaches the perfect rule of life for everyone and renders to all people in accordance with their works.[2] This agrees with what he himself said: *'For with the judgement you pronounce you will be judged, and the measure you give is the measure with which it will be given back to you.* [3]

Now it is properly said that when Moses went up [onto the mountain] a cloud and the glory of the Lord covered the mountain for six days, and on the seventh day [the Lord] called him to the summit of the mountain. For surely we are commanded in the law to work for six days and to rest on the seventh.[4] And when he went up on the mountain Moses was covered by the cloud and the glory of the Lord for six days, so that it might be mystically suggested that anyone who fulfills the commandments of the Lord with righteous works is surely worthy of divine protection. Now the same Lord who ordered Moses to go up onto the mountain also surrounded him with his own cloud and splendour while he was on the way up, because the one who bestows upon us the gift of doing well also illumines us while we are doing well, lest we should falter, and shields us, lest we should be burned up by the temptations of the ancient enemy as if by the boiling heat of the sun.

The Lord called Moses to the summit [of the mountain] on the seventh day because the law promises us eternal rest after we have completed our works, so that we who have taken care to stand by the Lord on the height of right action will then deserve to go up to see and speak with him, in accordance with that [saying] of the psalmist, *For he who gives the law will give a blessing. They will go from strength to strength; the God of gods will be seen in Zion.* [5] Even in this life, it is certainly true that some of the elect have been permitted to ascend to the grace of divine contemplation once they have perfected the active life. After a fashion and to some slight degree, this can be achieved by persons who are still clothed in flesh; it was granted to many of the patriarchs and prophets, and above all to Moses himself, of whom it was specifically said that he spoke with God *face to face, as one*

---

1 Jerome, *Nom.* (*CCSL* 72: 77, 1)
2 Ps. 62:12 (61:13)
3 Matt. 7:2
4 Exod. 20:9-11
5 Ps. 84:7 (83:8)

[9]   *speaks to a friend.*[1] Hence it is also possible to understand why this man in
particular was covered with the cloud and with the glory of the Lord for six
days on the mountain, and climbed up on the seventh day, when he was
called to talk with [the Lord] on the summit of the mountain. For on account
of the good works that he had received from the Lord's favour he doubtless
merited to be further enlightened by him, and to be sheltered from all
assaults of the evil ones, and so he attained to the higher gifts of seeing and
talking with [God]. For surely the midst of the darkness, from which he is
said to have been called, does not signify that there are any shadows in
God,[2] but rather that he dwells in light inaccessible. As the Apostle also
says, *No human being has seen him, or ever can see him.*[3] For that darkness
is the obscurity of the heavenly mysteries.[4] It is indeed inaccessible to
earthly hearts, but when disclosed by divine grace it can be penetrated by
Moses and the rest of the blessed who are pure in heart, to whom it is said
in the psalm, *'Come to him and be illuminated.'*[5] For his light is indeed
inaccessible to our human strength; nevertheless, by his munificence one
can draw near to it. Here there is aptly added:

24:17 **Now the appearance of the glory of the Lord was like a burning
fire on the top of the mountain in the sight of the children of Israel.**
Surely the appearance of the glory of the Lord looked like a burning fire
because it both enlightens the hearts of the elect with the gift of heavenly
knowledge and inflames them with the fire of his charity. Consequently,
the glory of the Lord appeared in a cloud, in darkness, and in fire: in a cloud,
because it protects us from the heat of temptations; in darkness, because the
power of his majesty can be wholly comprehended by no creature, for *the
peace of God surpasses all understanding;*[6] and in burning fire, because it
both illumines the minds of the faithful with the knowledge of supernal
blessings and enkindles them with hope and love.

The children of Israel behold this glory of the Lord from afar and from
below, but Moses enters into it by ascending higher. For the perfect
doubtless see the hidden things of the divine mysteries perfectly and
sublimely, while we who are mindful of our frailty and indolence, although
we are unable to enter therein by comprehending, can at least take care to
stay nearby and to observe by believing, hoping and loving.[7] For it is as if

---

1 Exod. 33:11
2 1 John 1:5
3 1 Tim. 6:16
4 *archarnorum*
5 Ps. 34:5 (33:6)
6 Phil. 4:7
7 1 Cor. 13:13

the children of Israel look from afar toward the mountain of God and toward the sight of his glory whenever those weak ones in the Church who earnestly desire to see God himself diligently keep their minds' eyes fixed on the recollection of eternal splendour. It is as if they stay near to the mountain of God, upon which they know that Moses has ascended, whenever they confine themselves upon it by living temperately, so as never to divert the course of their action very far away from the imitation of the highest men,   *[10]* although they are not yet fully able to follow their footsteps to perfection.

24:18 **And Moses, entering into the midst of the cloud, went up onto the mountain, and he was there forty days and forty nights.** Moses enters into the midst of the cloud and goes up onto the mountain when the preachers of the divine law, among whom Moses himself was preeminent, are invited and led by the Lord to penetrate the heights in order to contemplate *the ambiguities and secrets of divine wisdom.*[1] Now Moses was with the Lord forty days and forty nights so that he might learn from this amount of time that the only ones who are able to fulfill the Decalogue of the law which he, with his people, had received are those whom [the Lord] assists with the grace of evangelical truth, which was to be recorded in four books; for four times ten makes forty. Or perhaps [it means] that the time would come when those same teachings of the Decalogue, which he then received with the one people of the children of Israel, would be spread abroad through the generosity of divine grace and would be made known to all the races contained in the four parts of the world, and that by observing them all nations would come to eternal salvation. And because Moses arrived so quickly in his miraculous ascent to receive the law, we have learned that even at this moment we ought to direct our ears to hearing what he heard and our minds to expounding those same commandments of the law, as far as we are able.

3.   THE CHILDREN OF ISRAEL ARE COMMANDED TO OFFER
        FIRSTFRUITS TO THE LORD AND TO MAKE A SANCTUARY

There follows:

25:1-2 **And the Lord spoke to Moses, saying: Tell the children of Israel that they should bring me firstfruits; from every person who offers voluntarily, you shall take firstfruits for me.** We bring the firstfruits of our possessions to the Lord when, if we do anything good, we truthfully attribute it all to divine grace. Acknowledging from the inmost heart that we are unable even to begin a good action or thought without the

---

1 Ps. 51:6 (50:8)

Lord, we must confess that our misdeeds, although instigated by the devil, are always begun and brought to completion by us ourselves, nor can they be undone unless the Lord forgives. The Pelagians are unwilling to bring the firstfruits of their possessions to the Lord but retain whatever they own for themselves, because with foolish presumption they allege that they have something good from themselves apart from the grace of God.[1] And Moses was well advised to take firstfruits from every person who offers voluntarily, *for God loves a cheerful giver*, and the Apostle commands us to do good [works] *not reluctantly or under compulsion*, but from a intention that is heartfelt.[2] Knowing that he is to do this, the prophet takes pride in saying to the Lord, *'Of my own accord will I sacrifice to you.*[3]

[11]   25:3-8Now these are the things you must take: gold and silver and bronze, blue and purple and scarlet twice dyed and fine linen, goats' hair and rams' skins dyed red, blue skins and acacia wood, oil for preparing lamps, spices for ointment and for sweet-smelling incense, onyx stones and precious stones to adorn the ephod and the rational. And they shall make me a sanctuary, and I will dwell in the midst of them. All these things that the Lord directed to be offered to him in a material fashion for the making of a sanctuary by the people of earlier times should also be offered with spiritual understanding by us who desire to be the spiritual children of Israel (that is, imitators of the people who saw God[4]). For it is through freewill oblations of this sort that we may merit for him to make in us a sanctuary for himself and that he may deign to abide in our midst, that is to say, that he may consecrate a dwelling place for himself in our hearts.

---

1 Pelagius (*c*.350-*c*.425) was a British monk who taught in Rome, North Africa, and Palestine. His affirmation of human freedom and his denial of original sin, which brought him into conflict with Augustine of Hippo, were later developed by others such as the Italian bishop Julian of Eclanum (*c*.380-485) against whose teachings Bede directed the preface to his commentary on the Song of Songs (*CCSL* 119B: 167-80). Harsh condemnations of Pelagianism appear throughout many of Bede's works; see the list of citations in Plummer (1896), 1: lxii-lxiii. Controversy surrounds many aspects of the development and demise of Pelagianism in Roman Britain. Myres (1960) and Morris (1965) argued that the Pelagian heresy originated in Britain (not, as generally supposed, in Rome) against the background of Roman withdrawal early in the fifth century. They were opposed by Liebeschuetz (1963 and 1967) and Brown (1968). More recently, Markus (1986) has suggested that the theological orientation of British Christianity may well have tended toward a 'pre-Pelagian' position before the controversy arose, and maintained an ill-defined mixture of Pelagian and orthodox elements well into the sixth century.

2 2 Cor. 9:7

3 Ps. 54:6 (53:8)

4 The etymology is found in Jerome, *Nom.* (*CCSL* 72: 75, 21; 139, 22; 152, 15-16; 155, 20), and *Quaest. heb.* (*CCSL* 72: 41, 8-23).

We offer gold to him when we shine brightly with the splendour of the
true wisdom which is in right faith; silver when with our mouth we *make
confession unto salvation*;[1] bronze when we rejoice in spreading that same
faith by public preaching; blue when we lift up our hearts; purple when we
subject the body to suffering; scarlet twice dyed when we burn with a double
love (that is, for God and neighbour); fine linen when we shine with chastity
of the flesh; goats' hair when we put on the habit of penitence and
lamentation; rams' skins dyed red when as leaders of the Lord's flock we
see ourselves baptized in his blood; blue skins when we hope to be clothed
after death with spiritual bodies in heaven; acacia wood when the thorn-
thickets of sin have been cleared away and we serve the Lord alone, pure
in body and in soul; oil for preparing lamps when we shine brightly with
the fruits of charity and mercy; spices for ointment and sweet-smelling
incense when our reputation for good deeds spreads far and wide among
the multitudes as an example of living well.

We offer onyx stones and precious stones to adorn the ephod and rational
when with the praise that is due we extol the miracles which adorn both the
thoughts that the saints have devoted to God and their virtuous works, and
when we use these [miracles] to support our faith whenever there is the
need. For since we are accustomed to bear burdens on [our] shoulders, it is
fitting for the ephod (which is [worn] on the shoulders[2]) to suggest the
works of the righteous and their devoted labours for the Lord. And since
the seat of thought is in the chest, it is fitting for the pure thoughts of the
elect to be portrayed in the rational, which is the vestment for the priest's
chest. Both onyx stones and precious stones adorn the ephod and the
rational when miracles are joined like insignia to the outstanding acts and
thoughts of the most excellent fathers. Nor is there anything to prevent us   *[12]*
from understanding the onyx stones, which are said to be the colour of
blood,[3] as the merits of martyrdom which are added to good works. With
the assistance of God's grace, we shall discuss all of these things more fully,
each one in its own proper place.

---

1 Rom. 10:10

2 literally, 'that is, the superhumerale'

3 *Onyx*, which derived its name from the Greek ὄνυξ ('fingernail'), was usually said to be
yellowish in colour. However, the late fourth-century Greek Christian author Epiphanius
explained that some forms of onyx were so called 'because the nails of refined men are like
marble somewhat reddened with a mixture of blood'; see *De XII gemmis* 34 (ed. Dindorf, 4,
1: 193, 19 - 194, 2). Kitson (1983), 80-8, has shown that Bede knew a Latin version of
Epiphanius' work, which he used in composing his commentary *In Apocalysin* (*PL* 93:
129-206).

25:8-9 He says: **And they shall make me a sanctuary, and I will dwell in the midst of them, in accordance with every likeness of the tabernacle that I will show you, and of all the vessels for its service.** The Lord showed Moses the tabernacle on the mountain and the vessels consecrated for its service because while he kept [Moses] there with him for such a long time he certainly must have indicated to him the great piety, humility, and purity with which the angelic powers rejoice to obey their Creator. They are his perfect tabernacle in every way, for the one by whom they were made never ceases to remain and to dwell in them. A life like theirs and a share in their conversation in the Lord's presence is promised to us also in the resurrection, provided that we strive, while we are on earth, to leave the contagions of this world behind and to imitate their life by praising and loving God, by loving the neighbour in God, and also by even helping our enemies, through acts of kindness calling to the love of God people such as those to whom the Apostle said, *'But you, brothers, are not in the flesh but in the spirit.'*[1]

Thus the tabernacle that was shown to Moses on the mountain is that heavenly city and celestial homeland which we believe to have existed at that time for the holy angels alone, but which after the passion, resurrection, and ascension into heaven of the Mediator between God and humankind[2] [now] receives the countless multitude of radiant and holy souls. Surely the vessels of that tabernacle are all the individual persons of those blessed spirits for whom that Jerusalem which is the mother of us all[3] stands in true peace and unity. And we should take care to note that the children of Israel were ordered to make for the Lord a sanctuary that was not to be similar only in part, but was to be according to every likeness of the tabernacle that he showed to Moses, and of all the vessels for its service. Now if we aspire to fellowship with the angels in heaven, we who are on earth should always imitate their life, *to the degree that sinful bodies do not hinder* [us], *nor earthly limbs and mortal members make* [us] *dull.*[4]

Perhaps you are asking how you, a fleshly human being born from the [13] earth, can possibly imitate this celestial tabernacle which is spiritual. They

1 Rom. 8:9
2 1 Tim. 2:5
3 Gal. 4:26
4 Vergil, *Aen.* 6: 731-2 (*LCL* 1: 556); Bede may have come across these lines quoted in Augustine, *De civ. Dei* 14, 3 (*CSEL* 40: 5, 25-6). Hunter Blair, in Bonner (1976), 250, suggested that all of Bede's quotations from Vergil were taken from other writers, and that Bede had no knowledge of Vergil in the original. But Wright (1981) has argued persuasively that Bede's Vergilian quotations were more extensive than those recognized by Hunter Blair and that he must have had access to all that poet's works.

love God and their neighbours; imitate this. They come to the aid of the unfortunate (not to angels who are altogether blessed, but surely to humans); imitate this. They are humble, they are gentle, they are peaceable toward one another, they obey the divine commands; how well would you do to imitate this! They neither speak, nor do, nor think anything that is evil, or useless, or unjust, but assist at the divine praises with speech and thought that are unwearied; as far as you are able, imitate this. Build a sanctuary for the Lord in accordance with the pattern that was shown to Moses on the mountain, and when our Lord and Saviour comes he and the Father will make a home with you, and then after this life he will bring you into that blessed tabernacle which you have always imitated. There follows:

25:9-10 **And you shall make it in this way: build an ark of acacia wood.** It is appropriate that the ark, which is the first of all the things ordered to be made in the tabernacle, designates the incarnation of our Lord and Saviour, *in whom are hid all the treasures of wisdom and knowledge.*[1] It is easy to see that the ark is properly ordered to be built out of acacia wood, for they say that acacia wood is light and incorruptible in nature, not very different in quality from whitethorn.[2] Consequently, the ark was made of acacia wood because the Lord's body is composed of members free from every stain of imperfection. And this same wood is quite similar to that of a thorn, because though he came not in sinful flesh, nevertheless it was in the likeness of sinful flesh, as the Apostle said.[3]

4.   THE DESCRIPTION OF THE ARK

There follows:
25:10 **The length of [the ark] shall be two cubits and a half; the width, a cubit and a half; and the height also, a cubit and a half.** Someone is bound to ask how we should reckon the length of the cubit that Moses employed [in describing] both Noah's ark and the making of the tabernacle. This question is easily answered if we look at the words of Josephus, for we must not suppose that a Jewish man of priestly descent, most excellent in ability and most learned in literature both secular and divine, could be mistaken in any way about such a matter. Now this is what he says: *The*

---

1 Col. 3:2
2 Jerome, *In Es. 12 (CCSL* 73A: 474, 51-7); *In Ioel.* 3, 18 *(CCSL* 76: 207, 349-52)
3 Rom. 8:3

ark was made five hands in length and three in width.[1] From this it is obviously quite clear that [Moses'] cubit designates the span of two hands. Mystically, however, the length of the ark suggests the long-suffering patience with which our Lord and Redeemer lived among humankind; its width suggests the amplitude of that love with which he was willing to come to us and dwell among us; its height suggests the hope of future sublimity,

[14]   in which he foresaw either that he himself would be glorified after his passion or that we shall be glorified.[2]

Hence it was also fitting for the ark to be two cubits long, because of the teaching and the deeds with which he shone brightly in the world. On this account the evangelist Luke declared that he had [previously] written a treatise concerning those things *that Jesus began to do and to teach,*[3] and [Jesus'] fellow citizens marvelled, saying, *'Where did he get this wisdom and these powers?'*[4]—obviously meaning by 'wisdom' those wonderful things that he was saying, and by 'powers' those that he was doing. But in addition to these two cubits, the length of the ark contained another half-cubit; we can ascribe this to the slowness of human frailty, which could never worthily grasp the sublime words and deeds of the Saviour.[5] For this reason also it was plainly said of some of his mystical actions: *His disciples did not understand these things at first, but when Jesus was glorified;*[6] and in like manner of his more sublime words: *But this saying was hidden from them, and they did not understand what was said.*[7] The ark, therefore, was two cubits long because when the Lord appeared in flesh he was brilliant both in word and in deed, and it was a half cubit more because of the long-suffering with which he bore the slowness of the disciples who could never perfectly grasp either his words or his deeds.

The width of the ark was one cubit on account of the dispensation of the Lord's own charity, with which he took care to unite his elect in God. For

---

1 Josephus, *Ant. Jud.* 3, 6, 5 (ed. Blatt, 235, 15-17). As a Jewish priest with firsthand experience of worship in Herod's temple before its destruction in 70 CE, the Jewish historian Flavius Josephus (*c*.35-100) was able to provide important information supplementing the biblical description of the tabernacle cult. Bede employed the Latin translation of Josephus' *Antiquitates Judaicae* that Cassiodorus had arranged to be made at Vivarium. It was suggested in Laistner (1935), 246-7, that Bede may have made use of a copy of the Greek original as well, but this remains only a conjecture.

2 Gregory the Great, *Hom. in Ezech.* 1, 6, 18; 2, 3, 11; 2, 9, 9; 2, 10, 17 (*CCSL* 142: 78, 371-3 and 380-1; 243, 209-10; 363, 284-6; 392, 432-3)

3 Acts 1:1

4 Matt. 13:54

5 Gregory the Great, *Hom. in Ezech.* 2, 9, 9 (*CCSL* 142: 363, 286-93)

6 John 12:16

7 Luke 18:34

this reason also, when he prayed to the Father on their behalf he said: *'Now I ask not on behalf of these only, but also on behalf of those who will believe in me through their word, that they all may be one, just as you, Father, are in me, and I in you, that they also may be one in us;* '[1] and a little later: *'And I made your name known to them, and I will make it known, so that the love with which you have loved me may be in them, and I in them.* '[2] After the one cubit, there was another half cubit in order to signify our frailty, for while we are in this life we never manage perfectly to love God for his own sake, or to comprehend the love that God has towards us.[3] Indeed, just as the Apostle bears witness that *we know in part and we prophesy in part,*[4] it is evident in the same way that we also love in part. Therefore the ark was one cubit and a half because the Lord loves us with a singular affection, uniting us to himself and to the Father, and with an equally affectionate kindness he also accepts our capacity to love, however limited it may be in this life, until we are worthy to come to that vision of him in which we shall love him with all our heart, all our mind, and all our strength.[5]

Quite aptly, the height of the ark was also one cubit and a half. [The one cubit] obviously signifies the singular hope with which the Lord himself, when he was with us in the flesh, was awaiting the event of his future resurrection and subsequent glory; [the half cubit] reminds us who are amidst the adversities of the world that we should always rejoice on account of the rewards of future blessings. Therefore the ark was a full cubit in height because our Lord and Saviour (although he was corruptible as long as he was still dwelling in the flesh) knew full well how much glory was laid up for him in the future, whether in himself or in his members, which we are. It was another half cubit in height because he has also willingly accepted into his body those of us who piously strive to love the future homeland with humble devotion. Although we are as yet unable to grasp perfectly what its felicity may be, nevertheless what we do grasp here, that we have from him alone.

[15]

25:11 **And you shall overlay it with the purest gold inside and outside, and you shall make a golden crown over it all around.** The ark is overlaid with the purest gold inside and outside because the human nature assumed by the Son of God was full of the power of the Holy Spirit on the inside, and on the outside it openly displayed the works of the Holy Spirit to [all]

---

1 John 17:20-1
2 John 17:26
3 Gregory the Great, *Hom. in Ezech.* 2, 9, 10 (*CCSL* 142: 364, 321-4)
4 1 Cor. 13:9
5 Mark 12:30

people. The top of that ark is doubtless properly ordered to be encircled with a golden crown, because when he appeared in flesh and came to redeem the human race, the Son of God was anticipating a certain time and hour when he would overcome the death he had borne for us (along with the author of death himself), and ascend victorious to the Father in heaven. Of this crown the Apostle says: *But we see Jesus, who was indeed made a little lower than the angels, crowned with glory and honour because of the suffering of death.*[1] Of this crown John in the Apocalypse says: *And I looked, and behold, a white horse! And the one who was sitting upon it had a bow, and a crown was given to him, and he went out conquering that he might conquer.*[2] Surely the white horse is the Church; the rider who was commanding it is the Lord; he had a bow because he was coming to make war against the powers of the air; and a crown of victory was given to him because by dying he overthrew the reign of death.

25:12 **And there shall be four golden rings, which you shall put at the four corners of the ark; two rings on one side, and two on the other.** The four golden rings are the four books of the gospels, which are deservedly golden on account of the splendour of the wisdom with which they glisten. They are deservedly compared to rings because the very wisdom of God which they preach is the eternal divinity received by the human Christ, which neither began in time nor will ever cease to be eternal. For this reason, when the hour of his passion was near he prayed to the Father, saying: *'And now, Father, make me shine in your own presence with the splendour that I had with you before the world existed.*[3]

[16]

Now the ark has four corners because the sacrament of the Lord's incarnation never ceases to be celebrated throughout all the regions of the world into which the Holy Church is spread. And four rings were put at those four corners because the gospel of Christ is preached to the ends of all the world, so that the hearts of the faithful might be saved.[4] And there are two rings on one side and two on the other, either because two of the evangelists became disciples of the Saviour when he was in the flesh preaching and doing miracles and the other two came to faith in him after his resurrection and ascension into heaven,[5] or because in the figure of the four living creatures the two designated by the man and the calf display the tokens of his passion and death, but the two prefigured by the lion and the

---

1 Heb. 2:9

2 Rev. 6:2; 'bow' = *arcus*, which is similar in sound to *archa* = 'ark'.

3 John 17:5

4 Gregory the Great, *Reg. past.* 2, 11 (*SC* 381: 254, 25-8)

5 Matthew and John became disciples of Jesus during the period of his earthly ministry (Matt. 4:21; 9:9), while Mark and Luke became Christians only after his ascension.

eagle reveal the signs of the victory in which he destroyed death.[1] For the man represents the Lord as he was made mortal through the incarnation; the calf stands for him as he was offered for us upon the altar of the cross; the lion portrays him when he bravely conquered death; the eagle when he ascended into heaven. And thus there are two rings on one side and two on the other because the figures of two evangelists doubtless suggest the Lord's assumption of human frailty, and the two others suggest the victory in which he triumphed over the same frailty that he had assumed, and over death as well. For just as the left side of the ark had two rings since two evangelists are figures of the Lord's incarnation and passion, there were similarly two rings on the right side because two evangelists likewise figuratively represent his resurrection and ascension, which pertain to the glory of the life to come.

25:13-15 **You shall also make poles out of acacia wood, and overlay them with gold. And you shall insert them through the rings that are on the sides of the ark, so that it may be carried on them. They shall always be in the rings; they shall never be taken out of them.** The poles with which the ark is carried are the holy teachers who carry the Lord to the hearts of their hearers by preaching.[2] It is prescribed that these poles are always to be in the rings because it is doubtless necessary that those who preach the heavenly sacraments to others must never inhibit their minds from the recollection of the Sacred Scriptures, nor their hands from the observance of the divine commandments.[3] And there properly follows:

25:16 **And you shall put in the ark the testimony that I will give you,** because we ought to speak and to believe about the incarnate Son of God only those things that the Lord himself has deigned to reveal to us through the authors of Sacred Scripture. And if you want to know what that *[17]*

---

1 Rev. 4:7; cf. Ezek. 1:5-10. Although there was general agreement in the early church that the four living creatures symbolized the authors of the four gospels, there were diverse opinions about which creature represented which evangelist. According to Irenaeus, *Adv. Haer.* 3, 11, 8 (*SC* 211: 160, 175 - 170, 236), Matthew, Mark, Luke, and John were figured by the man, the eagle, the calf, and the lion, respectively, while Jerome, in the preface to his *In Matth.* (*CCSL* 77: 3, 55 - 4, 84) and in *In Ezech.* 1, 1, 6-8 (*CCSL* 75: 11, 191-206), preferred the order man, lion, calf, and eagle, which is that found in most medieval art, including the illuminations of the Lindisfarne Gospels and the Book of Kells. Bede, however, consistently followed the order lion, man, calf, eagle, which had been advanced by Augustine in *De cons. evang.* 1, 6 (*CSEL* 43: 9, 3 - 10, 14). As a result, some readers of the prologue to his early commentary *In Apocalypsin* (*PL* 93: 144A-B) accused Bede of being an innovator; his reply, which appeals to the authority of Augustine, is found in the prologue of *In Lucam* (*CCSL* 120: 6, 68 - 10, 220).

2 Gregory the Great, *Reg. past.* 2, 11 (*SC* 381: 254, 28-32)

3 Ibid. (*SC* 381: 254, 38 - 256, 55)

'testimony' might be that Moses received from the Lord to be put into the ark, listen to the Apostle, who says: *And behind the second curtain was a tabernacle which is called the holy of holies, containing a golden censer and the ark of the covenant covered on all sides with gold, in which there was a golden urn holding the manna, and Aaron's rod that budded, and the tablets of the covenant.*[1] Now the golden urn in the ark holding the manna is the holy soul in Christ which contains in itself all the fullness of Divinity.[2] Aaron's rod that budded although cut off [from the tree] is the invincible power of his priesthood, concerning which the prophet says: *'The rod of your kingdom is a rod of equity.*[3] Even after it seemed for the time being to have been cut off through death, in the dawn of the resurrection morn it was found to have blossomed again all the more vigorously, and it became clear that it would remain forever imperishable and unfading. For *Christ rising from the dead will never die again; death no longer has dominion over him.*[4] The tablets of the covenant in the ark indicate that all knowledge of the Father's secrets and all power of judgement are in Christ. For on the tablets of the covenant were inscribed the faith of the eternal Divinity which creates and rules the world, and the commandments through which one ought to serve God, and the discerning judgement with which he rightly condemns those who hate him and with due mercy rewards those who love him. This, then, is the testimony that the Lord gave Moses to be put into the ark. It indicated the truth that we ought to confess in Christ about his flesh, his soul, and his word; it showed that after the passion of death the same flesh would be glorified in the resurrection and lifted up to the eternal dignity of a king and priest; it taught that he alone is privy to the Father's secrets, just as truly as he is the judge of all worlds, of one and the same majesty with the Father.

5.   THE PROPITIATORY AND THE CHERUBIM

25:17 **You shall also make a propitiatory of the purest gold; two cubits and a half shall be its length, and a cubit and a half its width.** People often ask about the propitiatory, with which it says the ark was to be covered. But since he orders it to be made of gold and to be of the same length and width as he had commanded the ark to be made, it is established beyond a doubt that he wanted the board to be made with the same amount

---

1 Heb. 9:3-4
2 Col. 2:9
3 Ps. 45:6 (44:7)
4 Rom. 6:9

of gold as it took to cover the ark. From this it is clear that the propitiatory is nothing other than the Lord Saviour, but it especially designates the heart of compassion[1] that is in him, concerning whom the Apostle says: *God put him forward as a propitiation through faith in his blood.*[2] For this reason also is it placed up above, because he exalts mercy over judgement. For this reason the psalmist also says: *The Lord is sweet to all, and his mercies are over all his works.*[3]   *[18]*

25:18-21 You shall also make two cherubim of beaten gold, at the two ends of the mercy seat.[4] Let one cherub be on the one side, and the other on the other. Let them cover both sides of the propitiatory, spreading their wings and covering the mercy seat,[5] and let them look toward one another, their faces being turned toward the propitiatory with which the ark is to be covered, in which you shall put the testimony that I will give you. The prophet Ezekiel clearly declares that 'cherubim' is the name of the angelic powers[6] which he describes as having appeared to him with wings, according to the pattern in which they are orderded to be deployed here. For he indicates that those others had appeared to him when he says: *And the sound of the wings of the cherubim was heard as far as the outer court, like the voice of God when he speaks.*[7] In the singular number it is indeed called a 'cherub' and in the plural 'cherubim', and it is a noun of the masculine gender, but according to Greek custom it is put in the neuter gender as 'cherubin', the letter *m* being changed to *n*. But our translator, following the Hebrew idiom, puts it in the masculine gender: *'You shall also make two cherubim of beaten gold,'* not 'two cherubin of beaten gold'. This [latter reading] I believe to be a corruption in his translation arising from the negligence of scribes, so that 'cherubin' was written instead of 'cherubim' in the manner of the ancients.

Now 'cherubim' or 'cherubin' is interpreted as 'multitude of knowledge' or 'understanding of knowledge',[8] because it is evident that the name is quite rightly appropriate to the angelic powers inasmuch as they perfectly adhere to the vision of their Maker, free from every impure impulse of thought. And on that account also the painters' fancy is accustomed to depict wings in the figure of the cherubim Moses is ordered to make, and

---

1 *viscera pietatis*; literally, 'bowels of piety'
2 Rom. 3:25
3 Ps. 145:9 (144:9)
4 *oraculi*; literally, 'of the oracle'
5 *oraculum*
6 Cf. Bede, *De templo* 1 (*CCSL* 119A: 178, 1269)
7 Ezek. 10:5
8 Jerome, *Nom.* (*CCSL* 72: 74, 20-1)

in that form of them that the prophet testified that he had seen. In this way it is signified that the angels have their dwelling place on high and are able to hasten everywhere as if with nimble flight; nor do they suffer any delay, but rather appear immediately wherever they wish. This same thing is certainly promised to us also after the resurrection, for we shall then be clothed with spiritual bodies. Therefore the cherubim spread their wings and cover the propitiatory because the angels dedicate to their Maker's service every power of their nature, by which they deserve to dwell on high and to enter by a smooth and joyful way all the regions of that supernal homeland. And when they contemplate the propitiatory it is as if they cover it over (that is, they adorn it with honour by veiling it), because they regard every rank of perpetual felicity that they attain as coming from the grace of him from whom they have received the power to will no evil.

[19]   Now there are two [cherubim] to signify the peaceful fellowship of the angels, because *it is not possible for charity to be exercised among any fewer than two.*[1] Then they are also ordered to look towards one another and to face the propitiatory, doubtless because they agree with one another in glorifying the Divine Vision. In addition, the two testaments can be figured through the two cherubim; one of them proclaims the incarnation of the Lord as future, the other as having been accomplished. They look toward one another because they do not disagree with one another at all in the attestation of truth which they preach. They turn their faces to the propitiatory because they vigorously commend the Lord's mercy, which is the world's only hope. For this reason they are on each side of the mercy seat,[2] because they fill the times preceding the Lord's incarnation, as well as those that follow, with the preaching of spiritual knowledge.

The name 'multitude of knowledge' or 'knowledge multiplied'[3] is also appropriate for them, because Sacred Scripture is clearly filled with spiritual and divine knowledge, and the same knowledge from which Scripture itself was originally composed is always increased and never ceases to be multiplied. Hence the angel also said to Daniel, *'Many shall pass by, and knowledge shall be manifold.'*[4] Surely the Lord himself bears witness that Moses acquired more knowledge than the patriarchs, for when he appears to him he says: *'I am the God who appeared to Abraham, to Isaac, and to Jacob as God Almighty, but my name Adonai I did not make known to*

---

1 Gregory the Great, *Hom. in evang.* 17, 1 (*PL* 76: 1139A)
2 *oraculi*
3 Jerome, *Nom.* (*CCSL* 72: 63, 11; 74, 20)
4 Dan. 12:4

them.'[1] Therefore the understanding of divine knowledge was multiplied from the time when the Lord showed Moses this thing concerning his own self, which he had not made known to the patriarchs.

Let us consider whether David, who was meditating on the law of the Lord day and night, might have perceived himself to have understood something more about the Lord than had Moses who wrote the law. He says: *'How I have loved your law, O Lord; it is in my meditation all the day;'*[2] and he immediately added: *'I have understood above all my teachers.'*[3] Hence he also glorifies the Lord elsewhere, saying: *'You have made known to me the hidden things and the secrets of your wisdom.'*[4] Likewise the Lord himself declares the apostles to have known greater things than the prophets, for he speaks to them, saying: *'Many prophets and righteous people desired to see the things you see, and did not see them, and to hear the things you hear, and did not hear them.'*[5] But he also promises them still greater grace of knowledge after his resurrection and ascension, saying: *'I still have many things to say to you, but you cannot bear them now; but when the Spirit of truth comes he will teach you all truth.'*[6] He also assures them that in the future he will reveal to them greater things than all those that they are able to know in this life, saying: *'And those who love me will be loved by my Father, and I will love them and manifest myself to them.'*[7] [20]

Rightly, then, does 'cherubim' mean 'knowledge multiplied', because in both testaments knowledge of the truth became known to the faithful more and more as time went by. Rightly are the cherubim said to cover the propitiatory of glory, because as knowledge grows through time and is multiplied, the testaments preach to us the propitiation of the Lord Saviour and do not cease to honour it always with grateful voices, as if they were spreading their wings to fly. For since the words of those who talk come from the speakers' mouths into the hearts of their hearers as if they were flying through the air, they can deservedly be designated by the cherubim with spreading wings, who are, as it were, prepared to fly.

---

1 Exod. 6:2-3. The sacred name that God revealed to Moses was given as יהוה ('Yahweh'; the Tetragrammaton) in the Hebrew text, which the Greek translation known as the Septuagint rendered as Κύριος ('Lord'). The Vulgate reading *Adonai*, which Bede gives here, is the transliterated Latin form of the Hebrew אֲדֹנָי ('Lord'), which was substituted in Jewish tradition for the Tetragrammaton when the text was read aloud because the Divine Name itself was considered too holy to be pronounced.

2 Ps. 119:97 (118:97)
3 Ps. 119:99 (118:99)
4 Ps. 51:6 (50:8)
5 Matt. 8:17
6 John 16:12-13
7 John 14:25

25:22 **I will speak to you from above the propitiatory, and from the midst of the two cherubim, which shall be upon the ark of the testimony, and from there I will enjoin all the things that I will command the children of Israel by you.** From above the propitiatory the Lord speaks to Moses all the things that he commands the children of Israel by him because through the grace of God's propitiation it happened that he deigned to appear to humankind after the crime of transgression and to show them the way of truth after they had gone astray. He speaks from the midst of the cherubim because the Lord appeared and spoke to Moses through an angelic vision and not in his own substance, as the Apostle attests that *the law was put forth because of transgressions, until the offspring should come to whom he had made the promise; and it was ordained through angels by the hand of a mediator.*[1] Or, alternatively, the Lord speaks from the midst of the two cherubim because through the words of the two testaments he instructs us in the true faith with one harmonious voice; or perhaps he speaks from the midst of the cherubim because God the Father deigned to manifest his will to the human race through his Only-begotten who appeared in flesh between the two testaments. What Habakkuk said can also be taken in this sense: *'In the midst of two living beings you will be known.'*[2]

The ark can also be taken figuratively as the Holy Church which is constructed from incorruptible wood (that is, from holy souls). Extended throughout the four quarters of the world, with faith in the holy gospel [the Church] expects from God the eternal crown of life.[3] It contains in itself the tables of the covenant by continual meditation on the law of God; it also contains the golden urn with the manna as a guarantee of the Lord's incarnation, and Aaron's rod that budded as a sharing in the kingship and priesthood of the Lord; for the apostle Peter says: *'But you are a chosen race, a royal priesthood.'*[4] Up above, it has the propitiatory to remind it that every good thing it possesses it has received from the generosity of divine grace; and on the propitiatory it has the glorious cherubim, signifying

---

1 Gal. 3:19

2 Hab. 3:2. Bede quotes from the Old Latin version, which reads *in medio duorum animalium innotesceris.* Jerome, in his commentary *In Hab.* 2 (*CCSL* 76A: 619, 52 - 621, 114), expressed a preference for the reading *in medio annorum* ('in the midst of the years'), which he had used in his own Vulgate translation. At the same time, however, Jerome recorded several possible interpretations of the older version, including those referring to the cherubim and to the two testaments which Bede gives here. In his own commentary *In Hab.* 3, 2 (*CCSL* 119B: 383, 60 - 384, 77), Bede interprets the phrase *in medio duorum animalium* as referring to the manifestation of Jesus, either between Moses and Elijah at his transfiguration or between two thieves at his crucifixion.

3 Jas. 1:12

4 1 Pet. 2:9

either the angelic assistance with which it is always aided by a gracious   *[21]*
God, or the testaments in which it is taught how it ought to live and in what
manner it ought to seek the aid of divine propitiation so that it may live
properly. Now the cherubim were set over the propitiatory in this way just
as the city of Christ (that is, the Holy Church) is said to have been built
upon the mountain[1] (that is, upon Christ himself); not that his city can be
higher than he, but because it derives support from his assistance. The ark
has cherubim over the propitiatory because both the angelic ministries and
the Divine Eloquences surely give aid to the Church in so far as they
themselves stand firm upon the foundation of the highest truth.

6. THE TABLE

25:23 **You shall also make a table of acacia wood, two cubits in length,
and a cubit in width, and a cubit and a half in height.** The table made
from acacia wood is the Holy Scripture composed out of the bold words
and deeds of the holy fathers. In showing us what the joys of eternal
blessedness might be and how they might be attained, it surely supplies us
with the food of salvation and life. This [table] has length, because it
suggests to us perseverance in religious undertakings; width, because it
suggests the amplitude of charity; height, because it suggests the hope of
everlasting reward. And it is properly two cubits long because our active
life is comprised of two virtues in particular, namely mercy and innocence,
as the apostle James says: *But religion that is pure and undefiled before
God and the Father is this: to visit orphans and widows in their distress,
and to keep oneself unstained from this world.*[2] For by commanding us to
visit orphans and widows in their distress he indicates that we ought
mercifully to do all things that are needful toward our neighbours, and by
admonishing us to keep ourselves unstained from this world he expresses
all the ways in which we ourselves ought to live uprightly.

The Lord himself also declared that these two cubits of good action are
in the table of his own words, for he said: *'Let your loins be girded and
your lamps burning.'*[3] Evidently, our loins should be girded so that we may
remain free from the contamination of this world, and our lamps should be
burning so that through works of mercy we may shine bright before the
Lord. For what follows, *'and be like people who are waiting for their master*

---

1 Matt. 5:14; Eph. 2:19-20; Heb. 12:22
2 Jas. 1:27
3 Luke 12:35

when he returns from the wedding, [1] pertains to the height of that same
table, that is, to the hope of future recompense.

[22]   The table is one cubit wide, figuratively indicating the unity of that same
love which the entire sequence of the Old and New Testaments commends
to us. For charity is indeed one (that is, piety is simple[2] and pure in heart),
inasmuch as we are commanded to love God and neighbour and even our
very enemies, although with a considerable difference in quality and a most
proper distinction of that same love. We ought to love God in the first place,
enemies in the last; and the measure of love that ought to be weighed out
to our neighbours will vary according to the diversity of their merits, just
as we know that the patriarch Jacob, although he loved all his sons,
nevertheless loved Joseph more than the rest because of his singular
innocence, as Scripture bears witness.[3] Hence the Church says pleasingly
of Christ in the Song of Songs: *'He brought me into the wine chamber, he
set charity in order in me.* [4]

Furthermore, since [the table] was a cubit and a half high, the cubit (just
as the cubit in width) suggests the unity of our heavenly hope, with which
we expect that our Lord when he returns from heaven will reward those
servants whom he will find keeping watch with their loins girded and their
lamps of good works burning. For although there are many mansions in the
Father's house[5] on account of the diversity of merits, there is nevertheless
one kingdom of heaven into which all the elect are received.

The additional half [cubit] indicates the beginning of the contemplative
life, which some of the saints merit to enjoy even while still remaining in
the flesh. To them it is granted not only to hope for heavenly rewards but
also to have a foretaste [of them] by seeing in part, as did Isaiah and Micah
and the rest of the prophets, who saw the Lord sitting upon the throne of
his glory surrounded by the host of heaven;[6] as did Peter, James, and John,
who saw the Lord glorified between Moses and Elijah on the holy mountain;[7] as did [Paul] the teacher of the Gentiles, to whom it was granted before
he paid the debt of the flesh[8] to be caught up to Paradise and the third heaven
and to hear secret words which human beings are not permitted to speak.[9]

---

1 Luke 12:36
2 *simplex*, cf. the English 'simple', which can also mean 'without guile'.
3 Gen. 37:3
4 S. of S. 2:4
5 John 14:2
6 Isa. 6:1; 1 Kgs. 22:19; 2 Chr. 18:18
7 Matt. 17:1-3
8 i.e., before he died.
9 2 Cor. 12:4

In these, then, and in other such servants of Christ, the table of the tabernacle (that is, the Divine Scripture from which the Holy Church is refreshed without ceasing) adds unto us beyond the cubit in height another half [cubit] of our common hope, because to them it reveals the joys of celestial blessedness which are foreshown before they are given. Surely this fore-showing, since it appears to the minds of the saints fleetingly and only in passing, is rightly figured by a half cubit and not by a full cubit.

25:24 **And you shall overlay it with the purest gold.** The table of the tabernacle is overlaid with the purest gold because Sacred Scripture shines brightly with the perception of heavenly knowledge, and because those who produced it were prophets resplendent in life and in speech. *[23]*

25:24-5 **And you shall make for [the table] a golden lip all around, and on the lip itself an embossed crown four inches high.** A golden lip is made all around the table because the doctrine of Sacred Eloquence is taught to us through the most pure mouths of faithful preachers. Those who delivered the divine secrets to us did not allow their speech to be defiled in any way whatsoever with words of human conversation; rather, they took care to spurn and contradict not only hurtful human words but idle ones as well. Or perhaps a golden lip is made all around the table because Sacred Scripture, if rightly understood, resounds to us with the clarity of heavenly wisdom from every part of its speech.

To this lip, evidently, a crown is added because the tongues of those who are preaching promise their hearers the reward of life eternal. And that crown is properly ordered to be made four inches high because the eminence of the eternal crown is shown to us by the four books of the holy gospel, or because it is necessary for us to attain the crown of life by keeping the evangelical faith and work. And the books are pleasingly designated by inches, doubtless because the tablets of the law are reported to have been written by the finger of God, [1] and because in the gospel the Lord, when he was going to temper the punishment [prescribed by] the law, *wrote with his finger on the ground,* saying to the Pharisees and scribes concerning the adulteress whom they were accusing: *'If any one of you is without sin, let that one be the first to cast a stone at her.'* [2] Now the finger of God is understood to be the Spirit of God; hence when Luke reports that the Lord said, *'If then by the finger of God I cast out demons,'* [3] Matthew says, as if by way of explanation, *'by the Spirit of God'.* [4] And so a golden crown four

---

1 Exod. 31:18; *digitus,* which literally means 'finger', is also the word for 'inch'.
2 John 8:6-7
3 Luke 11:20
4 Matt. 7:28

inches high is set upon the golden lip of the table because the most pure words of the holy preachers anticipate the hope of celestial blessedness, which is contained and described in the four books of the holy gospel by the ministry of the Holy Spirit. Not only do the preachers themselves receive in heaven the reward of their labour, but with the certain authority of evangelical truth they also promise the same crown of life to all those who attend to them.

Now that same crown is properly commanded to be made embossed, doubtless because the reward of the eternal kingdom is not given indiscriminately to everyone but is distributed to one and all in accordance with the character of the recipients, as distinguished by divine examination. For surely the golden crown on the Lord's table would be unadorned and not [24] embossed if the brightness of the future reward of the righteous were revealed equally to all, after the fashion of the sun in this present world, whose splendour God makes to rise indiscriminately upon the good and the bad;[1] but just as star differs from star in brightness, so will it be in the resurrection of the dead.[2] A crown was set upon the Lord's table, adorned with various carvings that were diverse but decorously arranged; for surely the future life has been promised to all the righteous but the glory in it is multiform, according to the diversity of individual merits. Wherefore after one crown has been described first, there is added:

25:25 **And over the same, another little golden crown.** This can be rightly understood as the reward of those who surpass the general commandments of Holy Scripture by willingly choosing the more perfect life, and can therefore expect a special reward beyond that of the rest of the faithful in return for their voluntary offering. A golden crown four inches high is set upon the golden lip of the table because through the gospel eternal life is promised to those who keep the commandments of the divine law, as the Lord says to the rich man: *'If you want to enter into life, keep the commandments. You shall not commit murder. You shall not commit adultery. You shall not steal. You shall not bear false witness. Honour father and mother, and love your neighbour as yourself.*[3] Over that crown is set another little golden crown, because farther on there is added: *'If you would be perfect, go, sell what you have and give to the poor, and you will have treasure in heaven; and come, follow me.'* To this crown pertains that new song which the virgins are reported to sing so much before the Lamb—those *who have been purchased from among humankind as first fruits for God*

---

1 Matt. 5:45
2 1 Cor. 15:41-2
3 Matt. 19:17-21

and the Lamb; to this it pertains that they *follow the Lamb wherever he goes.*[1]

Or perhaps a golden crown is set upon the lip of the Lord's table because we learn in the words of Sacred Scripture that when souls go forth from the flesh they will be admitted to eternal rewards in heaven, and over that [crown] another little golden crown is added because in the same Scripture it is discovered that a glory even more sublime is laid up for them in the reception of immortal bodies also, at the end of the age.

25:26 **You shall prepare also four golden rings, and you shall put them in the four corners of the same table at each foot.** These things here are also to be taken as we set forth above in relation to the ark.[2] For surely the four golden rings are the four books of the gospels, through faith in which it has come to pass that all Sacred Scripture is read and understood throughout the whole world.[3]

Now the table has four feet because the whole succession of the Divine Eloquences is distinguished by a fourfold system, for *in all the holy books* [25] *it is necessary to consider what eternal things are announced, what deeds are narrated, what future things are foretold, and what things are enjoined or admonished to be done.*[4] Likewise, the table of the tabernacle has four feet because the words of the celestial oracle are customarily taken in either a historical, or an allegorical, or a tropological (that is, moral), or even an anagogical sense.[5] For it is history when something is reported as having been done or said in plain discourse according to the letter; for example,

---

1 Rev. 14:3-4

2 Bede, *De tab.* 1, 4 (*CCSL* 119A: 15, 419-24)

3 Gregory the Great, *Reg. past.* 2, 11 (*SC* 381: 254, 25-8)

4 Augustine, *Gen. ad litt.* 1, 1, 1 (*CSEL* 28, 1: 1, 7-10)

5 Note that Bede does not say here that every verse in Scripture contains each of the four senses; in fact, he selects a different verse to illustrate each sense. Cf. *De sch. et trop.* 2, 2 (*CCSL* 123A: 169, 273-9), where Bede did suggest that a single verse can be interpreted in multiple senses. Here he quotes the words of Augustine in support of the fourfold scheme, but immediately thereafter names the senses in an entirely different order, which is similar to that of John Cassian in *Coll.* 14, 8 (*SC* 54: 190), except that Cassian put anagogy third and tropology fourth while Bede has it the other way around. By making no effort to harmonize the two schemes, Bede implied that he did not understand the four senses to be arranged in a definite hierarchical pattern. Note also that each of the four senses is divided into two: history and allegory may appear in either words or events [cf. the discussion of *allegoria in factis* and *allegoria in verbis* in *De sch. et trop.* 2, 2 (*CCSL* 123A: 164, 218 - 166, 235)], whereas tropology and anagogy may be indicated either openly or figuratively. In *De sch. et trop.* Bede spoke of all three non-literal senses as 'allegorical', which seems to imply that they are necessarily expressed in symbolic language, but this passage shows that he, like Augustine, could consider a straightforward ethical injunction as 'tropology' and a direct promise of future reward as 'anagogy'; see Barrows (1963), 69.

the people of Israel, after they had been delivered from Egypt, are said to have made a tabernacle for the Lord in the wilderness. It is allegory when the presence of Christ and the sacraments of the Church are designated by mystical words or things; by words, certainly, as when Isaiah says: *'A shoot* [virga] *shall come forth from the root of Jesse, and a flower shall rise up from his root,'*[1] which is to say openly, 'The Virgin Mary will be born from the stock of David and Christ will proceed from his lineage;' and by things, as when the people delivered from Egyptian slavery through the blood of the lamb signifies the Church freed from the devil's domination by the passion of Christ. Tropology (that is, a moral manner of speech) has regard to the establishment and correction of manners, pronounced in words that are either plain or figurative; in plain words, as when John admonishes, saying, *'My little children, let us love not in word or speech but in deed and in truth,'*[2] or in figurative words, as when Solomon said: *'Let your garments be always white and let not oil be lacking on your head,'*[3] which is to say openly, 'At all times let your works be pure and let not charity be lacking from your heart.' Anagogy (that is, speech leading to higher things) is that which discusses, in words either mystical or plain, future rewards and what the future life in heaven consists of; in plain [words], such as *'Blessed are the pure in heart, for they shall see God,'*[4] and in mystical [words], such as *'Blessed are those who wash their robes, that they may have a right to the tree of life and that they may enter the city by its gates,'*[5] which is to say openly, 'Blessed are those who cleanse their thoughts and deeds so that they may be able to see the Lord Jesus who says, *"I am the way and the truth and the life,"*[6] and that they may come into the kingdom of heaven through the teaching and by the example of the fathers who went before.'

25:27-8 The golden rings shall be under the crown, so that the poles may be put through them and the table may be carried. The poles themselves, which are used to bear the table, you shall also make out of acacia wood, and you shall overlay them with gold. The rings are aptly *[26]* under the crown because we enjoy the books of the holy gospels in this life, but we hope for the future crown of celestial life in heaven. The poles used to bear the table are put through these rings because it is necessary for the holy teachers to keep their minds entirely fixed on the text of the gospels,

1 Isa. 11:1; Bede's interpretation depends upon the similarity in sound between *virga* (='shoot') and *virgo* (='Virgin').
2 1 John 3:18
3 Eccles. 9:8
4 Matt. 5:8
5 Rev. 22:14
6 John 14:6

so that they can renew the hearts of their hearers with the words of Sacred Eloquence.[1] They must direct every sense of their interpretation of the text in accordance with faith and the intention of its own doctrine, and in all the Scriptures they must diligently take care lest they should teach that anything is to be done, hoped, or loved other than what is to be found in the four books of the gospels. As long as they relate all the eloquence of the Scriptures to that faith and love which are written in the gospels, it is as if on four rings they carry the whole table of the Lord with its loaves and vessels.

7.   THE VESSELS FOR [THE TABLE], AND THE LOAVES OF PROPOSITION, AND THE INCENSE

25:29 **Out of purest gold you shall prepare also dishes and bowls, censers, and cups, in which the libations are to be offered.** The various vessels that were made for the offering of the libations are the various aspects of Divine Eloquence which correspond to the disparate capacities of those who hear it. For it is not possible for one and the same doctrine to be suitable for everyone. Surely the wise are to be taught in one way, the foolish in another; the rich in one way, the poor in another; the healthy in one way, the sick in another; the old in one way, the young in another; men in one way, women in another; celibates in one way, married persons in another; prelates in one way, subjects in another.[2]

Nevertheless, every one of the vessels is suitable for all of the libations to be offered on the table of the tabernacle. For whatever different things the skilled teacher exounds to different hearers, all are found in the rule of Sacred Scripture, and they stir up the hearts of the hearers to offer vows of good works to the Lord. This opportune diversity of holy preaching was commended by the mouth of the Lord himself when he said: *'Who do you think is the faithful and wise steward whom the master will set over his household, to give them their measure of wheat at the proper time?* [3] Surely the faithful and wise steward gives the measure of wheat to those fellow servants at the proper time when the discerning minister of the word not only observes the opportune time in speaking, but also diligently inquires into the condition and capacity of the hearers and tempers the manner of his speech according to their differences in that regard.

---

1 Gregory the Great, *Reg. past.* 2, 11 (*SC* 381: 254, 38 - 256, 55)
2 Ibid. 3, 1 (*SC* 382: 262-6)
3 Luke 12:42

25:30 **And upon the table you shall set loaves of proposition, in my sight always.** The loaves of proposition set always upon the table are the spiritual teachers who meditate upon the law of the Lord day and night[1] and offer the refreshment of the heavenly word to all who enter the Church. Rightly are they called 'loaves of proposition', because the word of salvation ought to be always in plain view before all the faithful, and devout hearers in the Church must never lack the comforting word. For the Lord has willed it to be always manifest in the world through the heralds of truth who set it before his face, and to abound constantly for those who hunger and thirst for righteousness, until the end of the age.[2]

[27]

In Leviticus it is explained more fully how many of these loaves are to be made, of what sort they should be, and how they are to be presented. For the Lord says to Moses: *'And you shall take the finest wheat flour and bake twelve loaves of it, each of which shall have two tenths. You shall place them in two rows of six on the most pure table before the Lord, and you shall put the clearest frankincense upon them, that the bread may be a memorial of the oblation of the Lord. Every sabbath day they shall be changed before the Lord, being taken up by the children of Israel as an everlasting covenant; and they shall be for Aaron and his sons, that they may eat them in the holy place.*[3] In the first place, the figure of the twelve apostles is clearly foretold here in the very number of the loaves, for when the Lord appeared in flesh he chose them to be the first of those by whose ministry he gave the food of life to all nations. And then to these same disciples of his (that is, to our apostles), he says in reference to the multitudes hungering in the wilderness, *'You give them something to eat;*[4] and when five thousand men had been satisfied from the five loaves, they *gathered twelve baskets of fragments,*[5] doubtless because those sacraments of the Scriptures which the multitudes are not able to receive belong to the apostles and the apostolic men.

The twelve loaves on the table of the tabernacle, then, are the twelve apostles and all those in the Church who follow their teaching; since until the end of time they do not cease to renew the people of God with the nourishment of the word, they are the twelve loaves of proposition which never depart from the table of the Lord. And those same loaves are properly ordered to be made not from just any flour but from the finest wheat,

---

1 Ps. 1:2
2 Matt. 5:6
3 Lev. 24:5-9
4 Matt. 14:16-21
5 John 6:13

doubtless because all those who minister the word of life to others must first devote themselves to the fruits of virtue, so that they may commend by their actions those things that they counsel in their preaching, being conformed to the example of him who says concerning himself: *'Unless a grain of wheat falls into the ground and dies, it remains alone.* '[1] Those same loaves are also properly commanded to be set on the table in two rows of six for the sake of concord (that is to say, charity and fellowship); for the Lord is also said to have sent his disciples out to preach two by two,[2] suggesting figuratively that the holy teachers never disagree with one another in either their ardour for love or their defense of truth.

Now that clearest frankincense which is put upon the loaves designates the power of prayer, because the same teachers commit both their ministry of preaching and their labour of devotion unto the Lord; for prayer is designated by frankincense, as the psalmist testifies when he says: *'Let my prayer be set forth in your sight as incense.* '[3] The clearest frankincense is put upon the loaves as a memorial of the oblation of the Lord when the pure prayer of the saints is added to their pious action and teaching, so that when each is duly joined to the other, the remembrance of the sacred oblation will always appear in the sight of the Supreme Judge.

[28]

The loaves are properly commanded to be changed before the Lord every sabbath day; for surely the loaves that were set out on the table of the Lord through the six days of work are exchanged for new loaves on the sabbath when all the teachers in the Holy Church, once the time of their holy labour is completed, are rewarded in heaven with eternal peace and leave others behind them in the same work, labouring in the word with the hope of the same reward. And in this way it is brought to pass that the table of the Lord is never left destitute of bread, but as soon as one loaf is taken away another is put in its place, as long as the churches never lack ministers of the word who follow one another in succession. In their words and in their deeds, they always manifest the faith of apostolic piety and the purity of apostolic action, continuing as in that most beautiful verse in which it is said in praise of that same Holy Church: *'Instead of your fathers, sons are born to you; you will make them princes over all the earth.* '[4] In other words, that is as if it were being said to the tabernacle of the Lord: 'Instead of your old loaves, new ones are prepared for you; you will designate them for the refreshment of the spiritual hearts of the faithful in all the world.'

---

1 John 12:24
2 Mark 6:7
3 Ps. 141:2 (140:2)
4 Ps. 45:16 (44:17)

Therefore loaves were exchanged for loaves, but the table itself always stood in the tabernacle; for the teachers of the word come and go, and others follow in the succession of those who pass away, but the Sacred Scripture remains for all time without ever being abolished, until the time when the Lord shall appear at the end of the world. Then we shall have no further need for Scriptures or for those who interpret them, since there will be a long-awaited fulfilment of that promise of the Lord which says: *'And they shall not teach their neighbour and brother saying, "Know the Lord," for they shall all know me, from the least of them to the greatest.*'[1]

The loaves were baked before the sabbath, as Josephus writes: *Before the sabbath they were divided two by two, and on the sabbath morning when they were to be offered upon the holy table they were set out in two rows of six, and two golden bowls full of frankincense were put upon them; these remained until another sabbath, and then others were brought in place of those, and they were given to the priests; and the frankincense was burned in the sacred fire in which all the sacrifices were made, and other frankincense was added upon the other loaves.*[2] And what is written in the Book of Kings, that David went into the tabernacle and received the holy loaves from the priests,[3] happened on a sabbath morning; for he came to the tabernacle at the hour when the loaves from the preceding week were being removed from the table of the Lord so that new loaves which had been baked the day before might be set out, and thus he received the holy loaves in such a way that the table of the Lord did not remain without bread for even a fraction of an hour.

Perhaps we should now consider more closely how the loaves were ordered to be changed each sabbath, for they were changed in such a way that each of them were placed on the table on the sabbath and could then be taken away on the following sabbath to serve as food for the priests. On the six days of work they were to be found laid out on the table, but on the sabbath day (that is, the day of rest) they were being put out upon the table, and on the next sabbath day they were being taken off the table again. Mystically, what are we to understand in the sequence of this arrangement except that the holy teachers (or, indeed, all of the righteous) attain rest after the good works with which they shone brightly in the Church, and are

[29]

---

1 Jer. 31:34

2 Josephus, *Ant. Jud.* 3, 10, 7 (ed. Blatt, 251, 11-16); Bede has changed the tenses of the verbs from present to imperfect. He quoted the same passage in his commentaries *In Luc.* 2 (*CCSL* 120: 128, 1132 - 129, 1139) and *In Sam.* 3 (*CCSL* 119: 197, 2590 - 198, 2596).

3 1 Sam. 21:6. The book commonly known as 1 Samuel in modern versions of the Bible is called 1 Kings in the Vulgate, and Bede uses that terminology here, even though he had earlier (*c.*716) entitled his commentary on that book *In primam partem Samuhelis.*

kindled by the hope of future rest and blessedness so that they may take pleasure in doing good works?

On the sabbath, therefore, the loaves were set upon the table of the Lord, and those who placed them there intended that when the sabbath was ended they might remain in the same place through the six days of working, and when the next sabbath came they might be consumed for the refreshment of the high priest and his sons. Doubtless this was because in the beginning those of us who lead lives devoted to God are promised that we shall receive the rest of life eternal, but only on condition that we attain to it through the labours and good works of this transitory life. Now the eating of the loaves of proposition by the high priest and his sons pertains to the entry into heavenly life, but it will be more appropriate to relate the explanation of this in its own place, in the exposition of the following verse.

The same loaves were taken up from the children of Israel because those who succeed to a position of priesthood or of teaching ought to be chosen and ordained from among the company of the spiritual servants of God. And that which is added in conclusion, *And they shall be for Aaron and his sons,*[1] contains a mystery which can be understood in two ways. For surely Aaron in company with his sons eats the holy loaves that are taken from the table of the tabernacle when our High Priest takes his elect out of this life and leads them into the increase of his body which is in heaven (that is, the whole multitude of his elect). Or perhaps the holy loaves belong to Aaron and his sons when all the leaders and the peoples who are subject to them in the Lord are nourished unto life eternal by the examples of the fathers who have gone before.   *[30]*

8.   THE LAMPSTAND

25:31 You shall also make a lampstand of beaten work of the purest gold. Like the table, the lampstand in the tabernacle also designates the Church universal of the present time. For surely they are in front of the veil within which the ark of the covenant was placed because the Church does not yet deserve to be admitted to the vision of its Redeemer in heaven. [The Church] is a table, because every day it provides celestial nourishment to those who hunger and thirst for righteousness,[2] lest they should fail in the midst of temptations; it is a lampstand, because it has shown the path of light to those who have gone astray; it is both table and lampstand together, because it has been taught by the Holy Writings and has learned to fill the

---

1 Lev. 24:9
2 Matt. 5:6

hungry soul with good things[1] and to supply the light of the word to those who sit in darkness and the shadow of death.[2] Surely it is made as a lampstand for this light, as it were, when by restraining itself from its own pleasures it humbly submits itself to do what the word of God commands, and when it agrees to hope and love what the word promises by raising itself above visible joys. In humbling itself, it is setting heavenly authority before its own desires in every way and showing forth to all the brightness of the word of God, both by preaching and by doing.

25:31 **Its shaft, and the branches, the cups, and the bowls and the lilies proceeding from it.** The shaft of the lampstand ought to be understood as *the one who is the head of the Church, the Mediator between God and humankind, the man Christ Jesus.*[3] It is as though the Apostle were speaking of branches proceeding from a shaft when he says of [Christ's] body (which we are) that *from him the whole body, nourished and knit together by its joints and ligaments, grows in the increase of God.*[4] Doubtless this is because Almighty God our Redeemer, who in himself does not make progress in anything, still has increase daily through his members. Therefore the branches proceeding from the shaft are the preachers established by the Lord who have brought forth a sweet sound (that is, a new song) into the world. The branches are all the children of the Church to whom the prophet says, *'Sing to the Lord a new song, his praise from the ends of the earth;'*[5] they willingly comply, resounding with praise to the Lord and saying, *'He directed my steps and put a new song in my mouth, a hymn to our God.'*[6]

Because cups are accustomed to be filled with wine, it is not unseemly for them to designate the minds of the hearers, which are filled with the wine of knowledge by the voices of those who are preaching. And because [31] the hearts of the faithful strive toward God with indefatigable desire when they are inebriated with that same wine of love within, rightly are the spherical bowls on the lampstand made after the cups. For a sphere rolls along in every direction, and the minds of the elect can neither be held back by any of the adversities of the world nor corrupted by prosperities, but in everything that happens they make progress toward God through holy

---

1 Ps. 107:9 (106:9); Luke 1:53
2 Luke 1:79
3 Col. 1:18; 1 Tim. 2:5
4 Col. 2:19
5 Isa. 42:10
6 Ps. 40:2-3 (39:3-4)

desire. And lilies are properly fashioned after the branches, cups, and bowls on the lampstand, because after the grace of preaching, after the intoxication of spiritual drink, after the incessant activity of holy labour, there follows that verdant homeland which blooms with holy souls (that is, with eternal flowers).

25:32 **Six branches shall come out from the sides, three from one side and three from the other.** It is well known that six, the number [of days] in which the world was made,[1] designates the perfection of works. But since the description of the branches specified that they were to be divided into two sets of three, it is more important for us to speak about the number three. Surely three branches shall come out from one side of the shaft and three from the other because before the coming of the Lord in flesh there were teachers who described the faith of the Holy Trinity in mystical language and preached as much as the ignorant people at that time were able to grasp. Hence there is that saying of the psalmist: *By the Word of the Lord were the heavens made, and all their power by the Spirit of his mouth.*[2] The Father he calls by the name of 'Lord', the Son by the name of 'Word', and the Holy Spirit by its own name: 'the Spirit of his mouth'. He clearly indicates that the power, will, and operation of that Holy Trinity are one when he asserts that the heavens are made by the Word of the Lord and all their power by the Spirit of his mouth. In like manner, the teachers openly preach the same faith in the Holy Trinity in such a way that all who belong to Christ are bound to be consecrated in that same faith, as the Lord says to the apostles: *'Go, therefore, teach all nations, baptizing them in the name of the Father, and of the Son, and of the Holy Spirit.'*[3] Hence Paul also, when he prays for the faithful and desires that they may be strengthened in the faith that they have received, says: *'The grace of our Lord Jesus Christ, and the charity of God, and the fellowship of the Holy Spirit be with you all.'*[4]

Likewise, three branches come forth from one side of the lampstand and three from the other because both before and after the Lord's incarnation there were in the Church three states of those who served the Lord faithfully,

---

1 Gen. 1:31
2 Ps. 33:6 (32:6); 'spirit' = *spiritus*, which also means 'breath'.
3 Matt. 28:19
4 2 Cor. 13:13

namely: the married, the continent, and the rulers.[1] Ezekiel the prophet
mystically distinguishes them from one another when he foretells that there
[32] are only three men who will be delivered when the time of plagues comes,
namely: Noah, Daniel, and Job.[2] For surely in Noah, who steered the ark
over the waves, he shows those who are set over the Church; in Daniel, who
was zealous to live continently in the royal court, he shows the continent
or virgins; in Job, who while situated in married life exhibited a wonderful
example of patience to all, he shows the life of the virtuous married people.
Similarly, in the New Testament the Lord suggests the diversity of the same
[states of life] under the figure of those who on the day of judgement will
be found in bed, in the field, or at the mill, some of whom, he says, will be
taken and some of whom will be left.[3] For surely the quiet life of the
continent is portrayed in the bed; the industry of those who preach in the
cultivation of the field; and the labour of those who are married in the
turning of the millstone. And because in all of these states some will be
chosen, some reprobated, it is rightly said of each state that *one* out of two
will be taken and the other left.

   In the company of the elect, the merit of those who preach is more
sublime than that of those who are zealous to devote themselves to continence only, and not to the work of teaching as well; likewise, the life of the
continent is more sublime than that of the married. Rightly, then, do the
highest branches that were proceeding from the shaft on one side and on
the other designate those in both testaments who have, among other virtues,
applied themselves to the pursuit of teaching; rightly do the lower branches,
which likewise come forth from both sides of the shaft, represent the
continents' life devoted to God; rightly do the lowest branches, which are
themselves sprung from the same stem of the one lampstand, show forth by
means of a type the life that virtuous married persons in the time of both
testaments faithfully devoted to one and the same Lord.

   The branches, then, proceed from different places on the shaft; nevertheless, they all reach to the same height at the top, each one in its own place

---

1 Cf. Bede, *In Luc.* 5 (*CCSL* 120: 321, 1019-26; *In Sam.* 1; 2 (*CCSL* 119: 21, 403-12; 97,
1221-25). A somewhat different triad appears below in Bede's comment on Exod. 25:34-5
(*CCSL* 119A: 34, 1167 - 35, 1173) and in *De templo* 1 (*CCSL* 119A: 163, 642-68), where he
speaks of the married, the continent (who were formerly married but have put away their
spouses), and the virgins. On Bede's explanation in the latter passage that it was the continent
who established the primitive Christian community in Jerusalem along monastic lines, see
Olsen (1982), 527-9. For the various patristic exegetical traditions delineating three levels of
perfection in the Church, see de Lubac (1959-64), 1, 2: 571-4 and Quacquarelli (1953).
   2 Ezek. 14:14
   3 Luke 17:34-5

bending upward in succession so that the lights which are on them remain positioned at the same level. The elect are doubtless imbued with one true faith, even if their merits differ in rank; for they will come to one light of eternal truth in heaven, even though the ones who endeavour to cleave to Christ higher up in this life will enjoy a closer vision of him in that life. Accordingly, it is said of certain ones on account of the merit of their great virtue, *These are those who follow the Lamb wherever he goes;*[1] just before, it is said of others, as if of the nearby branches on the lampstand, *And they were singing a new song, as it were, before the throne and before the four living creatures and before the elders.*[2] By this it is shown that all the saints throughout the streets of that heavenly city sing a new song of gladness to God, but those who in this life transcended the common life of the faithful by the special privilege of sacred virginity are there raised up into a special position above the others in the joy of song.

    25:33 **Three cups shaped somewhat like nuts for every branch,** *[33]* **together with a bowl and a lily; and three cups, likewise in the form of nuts, on the other branch, together with a bowl and a lily. This shall be the workmanship of the six branches that are to extend out from the shaft.** Solomon bears witness that a nut is customarily employed as a figure of the present Church when in the Song of Songs he speaks in the character of the faithful teachers, saying: *'I went down to the nut garden, to see the fruits of the valley.*[3] For just as a nut has a sweet fruit on the inside but does not show it on the outside unless its hard shell can be broken, so in the same way do the righteous maintain the sweetness of spiritual grace in their inmost heart while they are in this present life, so that its magnitude cannot be perceived by their neighbours until the time when the bodily dwelling is dissolved and the souls freed from it can gaze upon one another in heavenly light, and they individually shine so much with the grace of the Holy Spirit, and they are loved so much by one another, that absolutely nothing remains hidden. The cups on the lampstand are shaped like nuts when any of the elect, desiring to be filled with the wine of knowledge, are busy to conform themselves to the example of the righteous who have gone before, whom they know to have been filled with the great sweetness and love of invisible blessings.

    That there were three cups, bowls, and lilies for every branch signifies the three divisions of time in which the elect lived devotedly for God, both before and after the Lord's incarnation. For there were righteous persons

---

1 Rev. 14:4
2 Rev. 14:3
3 S. of S. 6:10

before the law, as there were under the law, and as there were in the time
of the prophets; likewise, after the Lord's ascension the primitive Church
was gathered from Israel, now it is gathered from the Gentiles, and at the
end of the world it will be gathered from the remnants of Israel. The first
branch had three cups, bowls, and lilies on one side because in the company
of teachers before the incarnation of the Lord there were three orders of
those who like cups thirsted for the drink of heavenly grace, who like round
bowls ran quickly in the way of the Lord, and who waited joyfully for the
gift of supernal reward as for the radiance and scent of lilies; that is, there
were thŏse before the law, those under the law, and those under the prophets.
The second branch also had three cups, bowls, and lilies, because the
continent ones of that time similarly had three orders of saints [distin-
guished] according to the previously-mentioned distinction of times, desiring the spiritual drink, running in the way of the Lord's commandments,
and expecting heavenly rewards. Similarly, the third branch had three cups,
three bowls, and three lilies, because there were many married persons
[34]   before the law, many under the law, and many in the days of the prophets
who rejoiced to hear the word of the Lord, and to run in his way, and to
expect from him the rewards of good works. Likewise, on the other side of
the shaft the first branch, and the second, and the third, each had three cups
and bowls and three lilies also, because in the New Testament there were
among the teachers, and among the continent, and among the married
persons devoted to God, three groupings at different times, that is: in the
primitive Church, from Israel; in [the time of] our election, from the
Gentiles; and in the final collecting, from the remnants of Israel. Each group
in its own time, they all desired to be intoxicated with the word of life, to
hasten in the way of peace, and to see the radiance of perpetual light.

25:34-5 **And on the lampstand itself there shall be four cups shaped
like nuts, and for every one there shall be bowls and lilies—the bowls
under two branches in three places, which together make six proceeding out of the one shaft.** We have said that the lampstand (that is, the middle
stem of the lampstand from which the branches were proceeding), designates the Lord Saviour, by whose grace the righteous have received whatever good things they possess. Hence in the gospel, after he himself had
said to the disciples, *'I am the vine, you are the branches,'*[1] he immediately
added: *'As the branch cannot bear fruit by itself, unless it abides in the vine,
so neither you, unless you abide in me.'* It is as if he were saying in other
words: 'I am the lampstand and you are my branches. As the branch is not
able to set itself up to bring light unless it abides steadfast in the stem of the

---

1 John 15:4-5

lampstand, *so neither are you, unless you abide in me,* able to bear the light
of truth and faith in yourselves.'

Four cups were made on this lampstand, doubtless because in the four
books of the holy gospel which were written about the Lord we find the
taste of new wine (that is, of heavenly doctrine) that old wineskins (that is,
minds still clinging to earthly desires) cannot receive, but only the hearts
of the faithful renewed by the Spirit of grace.[1] Bowls and lilies are fashioned
together for every cup because the same Lord who brought us the goblet of
spiritual wisdom has also shown us that we should take the smooth and easy
path of pious labour, and he has given us the power to take it, and lest we
should run in vain he has promised us the brightness of the heavenly
homeland to which we have been directing our course, and by his grace he
has disclosed to us the entranceway into it. Or, since the cups, bowls, and
lilies are commanded to be made under two branches in three places,
perhaps we can interpret these things mystically to mean that to the three
grades of the faithful of which we have spoken more than once (namely,   [35]
the married, the continent, and the virgins), he has revealed the doctrine of
truth, enjoined the path of good work, and both promised and delivered the
blessing of an inheritance that is always unfading and uncorrupted.[2]

The cups, bowls, and lilies of the lampstand are aptly ordered to be not
over the branches but under the branches, because the hearts of those who
preach (or perhaps we should say of all the elect) are upheld by the Lord's
gifts, commandments, and promises, and lifted up to love and to seek
heavenly things, lest they should be liable to fall to the depths below. For
here indeed the Holy Church (that is, the bride of Christ) boasts about him,
saying: *'His left hand is under my head, and his right hand shall embrace
me.*[3] Surely the left hand of the bridegroom is placed under the head of the
bride because the Lord raises up the minds of the faithful with temporal
benefits, separating them from earthly pleasures and longings so that they
may desire and hope for eternal blessings. And he shall embrace her with
his right hand because by revealing the vision of his majesty he glorifies
her without end.

Aptly are the cups, bowls, and lilies under two branches, because in each
of the two testaments the same devotion in serving the Lord is commanded
of the faithful (albeit in different religious ceremonies), and the same glory
of the heavenly kingdom is maintained. But the fourth cup, bowl, and lily
which were over the branches, all near the highest point of the lampstand

1 Matt. 9:17
2 1 Pet. 1:4
3 S. of S. 2:6

itself, properly pertain to the Lord Saviour. Not only did he impart the knowledge, labour, and reward of virtues to his elect, but the same human Christ also exhibited the figure of a cup in his own person when he declared himself full of the Holy Spirit. He held out the form of a round bowl when he appeared in the world and *rejoiced like a giant to run the way*[1] without any hindrance from the things that were clamoring round about. And he showed the semblance of a lily when in rising from the dead and ascending to heaven he was glorified with the glory that he had with the Father before the world existed.[2]

And rightly did this cup, this bowl, and this lily protrude higher than the branches, doubtless because the gifts that God the Father conferred upon the Mediator between God and humankind, the man Jesus Christ,[3] transcend every manner of human comprehension. For *to every one of us grace was given, according to the measure of Christ's gift*,[4] but in Christ himself, as the Apostle says, *all the fullness of Divinity dwells corporeally.*[5] And there properly follows:

25:36 **Then both the bowls and the branches shall all be of the same beaten work of the purest gold.** Every piece of work on the lampstand (that is, both the middle stem and the branches proceeding from it, with each of their ornaments) is made from gold. For the Lord himself appeared in the world especially free from sin and splendid in all the works of righteousness, and his members imitate the same innocence and righteousness in this transient life as far as they are able, but in the future they will make true progress by cleaving to him. And because something is made of beaten work by being smitten, aptly was the same [lampstand] made of beaten gold. For our Redeemer, who from his conception and birth existed as perfect God and perfect man, endured the pains of suffering and thus came to the glory of the resurrection. *All who want to live godly in* him *suffer persecution;*[6] it is through the blows of suffering that they make progress toward the grace of immortality, just as metal is stretched out by being smitten. Hence also in the fourth psalm, which is entitled *In verses,*[7] the Church in the guise of the mystical branches of faith says to her Redeemer, *'In distress, you have enlarged me,*[8] as if beaten gold should

[36]

---

1 Ps. 19:5 (18:6)
2 John 17:5
3 1 Tim. 2:5
4 Eph. 4:7
5 Col. 2:9
6 2 Tim. 3:12
7 Ps. 4:1 (Vulg.)
8 Ps. 4:1 (4:2)

say to its maker, 'With a metalsmith's pummelling you have stretched me out, and by pounding me you have afforded me greater progress.'

9. THE LAMPS FOR THE LAMPSTAND, AND THE SNUFFERS

25:37 **You shall also make seven lamps, and you shall set them upon the lampstand, to give light on the opposite side.** The seven lamps are the seven gifts of the Holy Spirit, all of which remain in our Lord and Redeemer forever and are distributed in his members (that is, in all the elect) according to his will. Therefore the seven lamps are set upon the lampstand because upon our Redeemer, the firstborn *from the root of Jesse,* rested *the Spirit of wisdom and of understanding, the Spirit of counsel and of fortitude, the Spirit of knowledge and of godliness, and he* was filled *with the Spirit of the fear of the Lord.*[1] As he himself also says through the same prophet: *'The Spirit of the Lord is upon me because the Lord has anointed me.'*[2]

But what is [then] said, *to give light on the opposite side,* is what the prophet immediately adds: *'He has sent me to bring good news to the meek, to heal the contrite of heart, and to preach release to the captives, and deliverance to those who are imprisoned, to proclaim the acceptable year of the Lord, and the day of vengeance of our God.'*[3] For surely the lamps of the lampstand gave light on the opposite side and illuminated the tabernacle of the Lord when the Lord who was full of grace and truth gave to us all from his fullness, and *grace for grace,*[4] when he committed the word of the gospel to the meek and the poor in spirit, and when he conferred the healing of remission upon sinners. For he declared that now is the time for pleasing the Lord, but the day of universal judgement is coming.

What John says in the Apocalypse accords with the number and position *[37]* of these lamps: *And I looked, and behold, in the midst of the throne and of the four living creatures, and in the midst of the elders, there was a Lamb standing as if it had been slain, having seven horns and seven eyes, which are the seven spirits of God sent out into all the earth.*[5] For if in that place the seven horns and seven eyes of the Lamb can suggest the seven gifts of the Holy Spirit, why should the seven lamps of the lampstand not also deserve to be believed to designate the same? More precisely, just as the same sevenfold Spirit is rightly signified by horns and eyes on account of

---

1 Isa. 11:1-3
2 Isa. 61:1; Luke 4:18
3 Isa. 61:1-2
4 John 1:14, 16
5 Rev. 5:6

the omnipotence of power with which it rules all things and the plenitude
of knowledge with which it perceives all things, so also is it aptly expressed
through the figure of lamps on account of the light of grace with which it
illuminates the shadows of our blindness in the night of this world. Here it
is also aptly added:

25:38 **The snuffers also, and [the trays] in which the snuffings shall
be extinguished, shall be made of the purest gold.** There are some
commands in the Divine Scriptures which must always be observed, both
in this life and in that which is to come, such as that [command]: *'You shall
not have strange gods before me,* '[1] and *'You shall love the Lord your God
with all your heart, and with all your soul, and with all your strength,* '[2] and
'You shall love your neighbour as yourself. [3] Other things are ordered to
be observed throughout the entire duration of this life but the eternal reward
of their observance is received only in the life to come. Such is that
[command] of the gospel: *'Make for yourselves friends of the mammon of
iniquity, so that* they too *may receive you into everlasting dwellings;* [4] for
the time for giving alms is now, but only then will the fruit of almsgiving
be perpetually received. Still other things, however, were diligently kept in
the time of the Old Testament in accordance with the Lord's command, but,
now that the gospel gleams throughout the world, they are ordered to be
observed in the Church not according to the letter but according to the
mystical sense. These are such things as the keeping of the sabbath, the rite
of the bloody sacrifices of the paschal lamb, and other things of this sort.
In their own time, when these things were being kept scrupulously by the
people of God, it was as if wicks were burning in the lamps of the lampstand,
filled with the oil of pious devotion and lit with the fire of the celestial word.
But when the apostles and apostolic men proclaimed that the Lord had
imposed an end to these and other such observances and that all these things
were to be kept in the Church spiritually rather than according to the letter,
it was as if the wicks of the lampstand were being snuffed, so that after
being repaired they might give better light. For they supplied the Holy
[38] Church with the light of saving doctrine more sublimely once they began
to be understood through the Spirit.

The Lord makes a promise to his people concerning this reparation of
the lamps of the tabernacle (that is, the more sublime understanding of the
Divine Scriptures) when he says in Leviticus: *'You shall be multiplied, and*

---

1 Exod. 20:3
2 Deut. 6:5; Mark 12:30
3 Matt. 22:39
4 Luke 16:9

*I will establish my covenant with you; you shall eat the oldest of the old
[grain], and you shall cast away the old [to make room] for the new that
is coming on.*[1] The children of Israel being so multiplied, the covenant of
God was confirmed with them, and with the Gentiles called to faith, by the
grace of the New Testament planted with a firm root in the hearts of the
elect. And we eat the oldest of the old [grain] when we retain in our hearts
the sweet memory of the old commandment which was given to the human
race from the beginning, by loving the Lord our God with all our heart, all
our soul, and all our strength, and by loving our neighbour as ourselves.[2]
And we cast away the old [to make room] for the new that is coming on
when we cease to keep the typic statutes of the Mosaic law according to the
letter, but keep these same statutes quite gladly as they are understood
through the Spirit, our hearts being renewed in the hope of the heavenly
kingdom in accordance with that [saying] of the Apostle: *If then anyone is
in Christ a new creature, the old things have passed away; behold, things
have been made new;*[3] and [with that saying] in the Apocalypse: *And he
that sat upon the throne said, 'Behold, I make all things new.*[4]

Now the snuffers with which these things were accomplished are the
very words of Sacred Eloquence, in which it is clearly indicated in many
places that the letter of the law is to be annulled, and that it is to kept only
in a spiritual sense. Among those [passages] is that [account] in the Acts of
the Apostles in which believers from among the Gentiles were forbidden
to be circumcised and were enjoined to be obedient to the grace of the
gospel, without the ceremonial sacrifices of the law,[5] as well as what the
Apostle says to the Hebrews in expounding a verse from one of the psalms:
*When he said above 'You did not want sacrifices, and oblations, and
holocausts for sin, neither are those things pleasing to you' which are
offered according to the law, 'then I said, "Behold, I come to do your will,
O God,"' he takes away the first, that he may establish that which follows.
In that will, we have been sanctified through the oblation of Christ Jesus.*[6]
Therefore the snuffers and the trays in which the snuffings are extinguished
are made of the purest gold, because they are the divine words with which
the cessation of the ceremonies of the law is proclaimed and the hearts of
those in whom the same figurative shadow of the law receives an end, which
are illuminated by the grace of God so that the truth of the gospel that

1 Lev. 26:9-10
2 Deut. 6:5; Mark 12:30-1
3 2 Cor. 5:17
4 Rev. 21:5
5 Acts 25:28-9
6 Heb. 10:8-10, with reference to Ps. 40:6, 8 (39:7, 9)

follows may shine more clearly in the world. For it is well known that in the gospel the first apostles broke the sabbath before the Lord's passion, and after the ascension of the Lord and the coming of the Holy Spirit they completely put an end to the legal sacrifices, and many things that were decreed by the letter of the law were changed by the grace of the liberty of the gospel. Therefore in these [trays] were extinguished the wicks that were put out, in which the literal observance, being completed, displayed the beginning of grace shining clearly in the world. In the same way, when the mortal life is ended and the immortal follows, the works (or gifts of light) that we now enjoy will for the most part cease, so that the reward of eternal light may follow in the presence of the Divine Vision.

[39]

The gold snuffers are doubtless those scriptural testimonies which bear witness that things will come to pass in this way, because [they are] distinguished by the hope of future brightness. And surely the trays in which the snuffings are extinguished are the immortal bodies and souls[1] of all the righteous. Quite rightly are they made to be like gold, for they will undergo a most highly desired alteration, so that after the temporal benefits of God they may come to the ones that are eternal. Accordingly, the Apostle shows us that the snuffers of the lamps of God and the places where the snuffings are extinguished are made of gold when he speaks of the difference between present and future blessings, saying, *Prophecies shall be made void, and tongues shall cease, and knowledge shall be destroyed, for we know in part, and we prophesy in part, but when that which is perfect comes, that which is in part shall be made void.*[2] And a little after: *We see now in a mirror, dimly; but then face to face. Now I know in part; but then I shall know just as I am also known.*[3]

25:39 **The whole weight of the lampstand with all its vessels shall be a talent of the purest gold.** The whole weight of the lampstand with all its vessels is the whole body of Christ, with himself as our Head, the Mediator

---

1 *corda*, literally 'hearts'
2 1 Cor. 13:8-10
3 1 Cor. 13:12

between God and humankind,[1] and all his elect from the highest to the lowest, from those of whom he says, *'Among those born of women, there is no one greater,'*[2] down to those of whom he says, *'See that you despise not one of these little ones who believe in me.*[3] Although they are diverse in their ranks, ages, sexes, conditions, abilities, and times, all of these, in their own times and places, cleave by the fixed root of their minds to one and the same Author and Giver of perpetual light, as if to a golden lampstand in which they are able to become partakers of his own light.

It is rightly said of this lampstand that it ought to weigh a talent of purest gold. A talent is a full and perfect weight, because *the Lord is righteous in all his ways,*[4] and he who imparts his grace to the faithful in this life so that they may work well is the very same one who in that life will render the crown of righteousness in return for their good deeds. On the other hand, Zechariah the prophet describes Wickedness as sitting [before the Lord] upon a talent of lead,[5] because in the same just weighing he will also recompense the reprobate according to their deeds. *'For you will render,'* it says, *'to all according to their works.*[6] But it makes a difference whether one brings gold or lead to the divine weighing. For those who shine like gold with good works advance to the lampstand of the Lord, because they are partakers of their Maker's glory; but those who appear at the strict weighing heavy with sins are plunged into the raging[7] water like lead, because by reason of their sins they fall into the abyss of grave punishment. But both the lead and the gold measure one talent, because it is certain that the decision of our Maker is just, both in damning the impious and in saving and crowning the elect.

[40]

---

1 1 Tim. 2:5. Jones (1969-70), 146, suggested that in this section Bede had in mind the seven exegetical rules of the fourth-century Donatist author Tyconius as reported by Augustine in *De doct. chr.* 3, 30-56 (*CCSL* 32: 102-16). The first rule of Tyconius explains that Scripture often speaks of Christ and the Church as the head and the body of a single person, which is clearly the case in Bede's interpretation here. The second rule warns that biblical passages referring to the present Church must sometimes be understood as referring to a mixed body containing both the elect and the reprobate, as Bede does in his comments on the lampstand which follow. Whether or not he was consciously thinking of Tyconius when he composed this section, Bede was certainly well familiar with Augustine's exposition of the Tyconian rules, which he discussed in the preface to his *In Apocalypsin* (*PL* 93: 131B-133B); see Bonner (1966) and Mackay (1979).

2 Luke 7:28

3 Matt. 18:6, 10

4 Ps. 145:17 (144:17)

5 Zech. 5:7-8; *talentum* (Vulg.) translates the Hebrew אֵיפָה ('ephah'), a unit of measure here referring to the capacity of a basket.

6 Ps. 62:13 (61:13)

7 *validissima*, literally 'strongest'

25:40 **Look, and make [these things] according to the pattern that
was shown you on the mountain.** The mystery of this commandment is
quite readily apparent from the things that have been set forth above. For
surely the pattern of the lampstand that he was to make was shown to Moses
on a mountain because it was on the height of most secret contemplation
that he openly learned the manifold sacraments of Christ and the Church.
Nevertheless, he was not able to bring them forth openly to the people whom
he was instructing; instead, he signified them by means of a type through
the form and the workmanship of the lampstand and its vessels, until such
time as our Lord and Redeemer himself might come in flesh and disclose
the inner meaning of that same form to his Church by conferring the grace
of the Holy Spirit. Hence, when he died on the cross he tore asunder the
veil of the temple and opened those secret places of the saints that had been
covered up,[1] and after the resurrection when he appeared to his disciples he
opened the meaning to them,[2] so that they might be able to understand these
things and the other secrets of the Scriptures spiritually, with their minds'
eyes unveiled.

But when *every scribe instructed in the kingdom of heaven*[3] is enjoined
both to follow diligently those things that he has learned in the Sacred
Writings concerning the catholic faith or pious action, and to teach them to
others, is that scribe not being commanded to look, and to make [things]
according to the pattern that was shown to him on the mountain? The scribe
looks diligently at the pattern that is shown to him on the mountain and
makes things according to it when he returns to the regions below, for those
things which by the sublimity of the divine word he inwardly understands
[41]   are to be believed or done he considers earnestly in his heart, and shows
their perpetual exemplar to his hearers both by the performance of right
action and by the word of saving doctrine.

---

1 Matt. 27:51-2
2 Luke 24:45
3 Matt. 13:52

BOOK TWO

1.   THE TABERNACLE AND THE TEMPLE

The tabernacle that Moses made for the Lord in the wilderness, like the   *[42]*
temple that Solomon made in Jerusalem, designates the state of the Holy
Church universal, part of which already reigns with the Lord in heaven,
while part is still journeying in this present life away from the Lord, until
its members die and follow after one another. The principal difference
between the figures in the construction of the two houses is that the
tabernacle designates the building of the present Church, which is daily
employed in its labours, while the temple designates the repose of the future
Church, which is daily being perfected as it receives souls departing from
this [world] after their labours. For Moses built the tabernacle while he was
still set on the road by which he was proceeding to the promised land along
with the people of God, but Solomon constructed the temple after he had
already taken possession of the same promised land and the kingship in it.
Moses built the tabernacle in the wilderness, but Solomon constructed the
temple in Jerusalem, which is interpreted as 'vision of peace':[1] here the
Church is built amidst the labour and toil of this transient life, thirsting and
hungering for the everlasting kingdom, but there it is completed in the vision
and possession of true peace.

It is properly said that in the construction of the temple *there was neither*
hammer nor axe nor any tool of iron heard in it *when it was being built,*[2]
because all the stones and wood were prepared outside Jerusalem in such a
way that when they were properly fitted into position in their courses there
it would be easy to put them back together with confidence, each one in its
own place and fastened with cement or nails. For in the peace of heavenly
blessedness our faith will certainly not need to be tried with tribulations,
nor our life put to the test, but what is being chastened now in the present
age will there be fitted together with the glue and bands of mutual charity
so that they can never be dissolved, to form heavenly dwellings according
to the pattern, bound together in the sight of their Maker and King. For when
the multitude of believers is made *of one heart and soul* in this life, and *all*
things are *common to them,*[3] is it not as if living stones are being squared
to form the building of the future house of the Lord, and are then transported
from this place to be set into their courses without any tedious labour, and

1 Jerome, *Nom.* (*CCSL* 72: 121, 9-10)
2 1 Kgs. 6:7
3 Acts 4:32

are joined to one another with the bond of a love that is divine, and at the same time properly their own?

It is also possible to distinguish the figures of the two sanctuaries generally in this way: the workmanship of the tabernacle is the time of the synagogue (that is, of the ancient people of God), but the workmanship of the temple signifies the Church (that is, that multitude of the elect which *[43]* has come to faith after the Lord's incarnation). For Moses completed the tabernacle with the people of the Hebrews alone, but Solomon finished [building] the temple with a multitude of proselytes gathered together, and also with the help of the king of Tyre and his artisans, who were Jews neither by birth nor by profession.[1] For it is well known that the teachers of the earlier people of God presided over no one except those from their own nation, but although the first rulers of the Church were from the Hebrews, even so, soon afterwards, as it grew and spread throughout the world, its builders came forth from the Gentiles as well, so that even Luke the evangelist himself, and the apostolic men Timothy and Titus, attained to their jurisdiction[2] from the calling of the Gentiles.

But if we consider each of them more carefully, the building of both houses mystically represents the state of the whole present Church, which never ceases to be built from the beginning of the world's creation up until the last elect person who is to be born at the end of the world. In the wondrous truth of their figures, they also depict the glory of the life to come, which the Church enjoys now in part but will enjoy forever in all its members after the end of this age. Hence as we embark on saying some things with the Lord's help concerning the tabernacle, we first invoke him with humble prayer to unveil the eyes of our hearts so that we may be able to consider the wonders of his law,[3] and so that we may understand that in the beauty of precious metals and vestments we have been advised to make our character illustrious with the ornamentation of faith and devotion. Otherwise, unless we imitate the material ornamentation of the tabernacle or temple by the devout and pure adornment of heart and body, there cannot apply to us that word of the Apostle in which he says, *For you are the temple of the living God; as God says, 'I will dwell in them, and walk among them,* [4] and what John heard, *a great voice from the throne, saying, 'Behold the*

---

1 1 Kgs. 5:1-18; 7:13-44
2 *praesulatum*
3 Ps. 119:18 (118:18)
4 2 Cor. 6:16

tabernacle of God is with humankind, and he has made his dwelling with them.[1]

But first we must reflect for a little while upon the text of the material letter itself, so that we shall be able to discuss the spiritual sense with greater certainty. The tabernacle was a house sacred to the Lord, thirty cubits in length, ten in width, and ten also in height,[2] having a roof that was level throughout, in a manner of house construction that is customary in Egypt and Palestine.[3] Three of its walls—namely, the southern, the northern, and the western—were put together from wooden boards that were gilded on both sides. But in front of the eastern wall, where the entrance was, there *[44]* was a rod that came through the middle boards from corner to corner (that is, from the very top of this wall to the top of the opposite wall), so that it was possible for the curtains of the tabernacle and the roof to rest on this rod while the tent was suspended on five posts.

Now the house was covered on the top and also on all sides with curtains woven in a wonderful variety [of colours]; this is the tabernacle properly so called. And it was covered on all sides with curtains of goats' hair reaching to the ground. But on the roof there was also another covering made from rams' skins dyed red, and on top of this yet another covering of blue-coloured skins. And there was also a variegated veil of embroidery work which was hung from four posts, by which the sanctuary and the holy of holies were divided. The ark of the covenant was placed within this veil, and opposite the ark, outside the veil, there was the altar of incense. In addition, in the middle of the sanctuary itself there stood a lampstand on the south side, and a table on the north, with the altar of holocaust outdoors before the entrance to the sanctuary, and a bronze basin between this altar and the tabernacle. The court of the tabernacle round about all these things was a hundred cubits long and fifty wide. For the sake of greater clarity with respect to these things which have been briefly examined, let us look at the words of the history themselves, so that through them we may be able to come to a more profound and more lucid understanding of the meaning of the allegory.

---

1 Rev. 21:3
2 Josephus, *Ant. Jud.* 3, 6, 3 (ed. Blatt, 233, 6-7)
3 Jerome, *Ep.* 106, 63 (*CSEL* 55: 278, 20-4)

2.   THE TEN CURTAINS

When the Lord delivered the ceremonies of the law and the code of behavior to Moses, who was with him on Mount Sinai for forty days and nights, among other things he said:

26:1 **And you shall make the tabernacle in this manner: you shall make ten curtains of fine twisted linen, and blue and purple and scarlet twice dyed, variegated with embroidery work.** The tabernacle of the Lord is made from curtains variegated with diverse sorts of colours because the Holy Church universal is built from many elect persons, from many churches throughout the world, and from the flowers of diverse virtues. All its perfection is contained in the number ten because in whatever direction the Church has been spread throughout the world, among diverse nations and tribes and peoples and tongues,[1] it stands completely firm in the single love of God and neighbour which was contained in the Decalogue of the law. And there is no other way for persons truly to attain to membership in the Church, unless with a whole heart they will learn to love both him through whom the Church is built and those in whom it is built (that is, God and his elect).

[45]   Now the diverse beauty of the colours with which these same curtains were distinguished is the grace of the various virtues with which the Holy Church shines in the sight of its Maker, being composed with wonderful and quite heavenly skill. Surely blessed Peter was eager to build the tabernacle of God with such variety and with embroidery, as it were, since he says: *As every one of you has received grace, administer the same to one another, as good stewards of the manifold grace of God.*[2] Paul saw that this appertains to the curtains of the tabernacle (that is, to the minds of the faithful), since he says: *To one, indeed, is given through the Spirit the utterance of wisdom, and to another the utterance of knowledge according to the same Spirit, to another faith by the same Spirit, to another the grace of healing by the one Spirit, to another the working of miracles, to another prophecy,* and the other things in that passage.[3]

Surely John also bears witness that the fine linen, which is mentioned first, represents the beauty of virtues, since he says in the Apocalypse: *For the marriage of the Lamb has come, and his spouse has prepared herself, and to her it has been granted that she should clothe herself with fine linen,*

---

1 Rev. 5:9
2 1 Pet. 4:10
3 1 Cor. 12:8-10; 'other things', namely: the discernment of spirits, various kinds of tongues, and the interpretation of tongues

glittering and white—for the fine linen is the righteous deeds of the saints. [1] Solomon says of the same spouse of the Lamb (that is, the Church of Christ) that *her clothing is fine linen and purple,* [2] but when John expounds the figure of one colour he implies that the others are to be interpreted figuratively as well.

Fine linen does indeed spring up from the ground, [3] but it is then dug out of the ground [and subjected to] a long process of drying, pounding, cleaning, baking, and spinning, so that it is accustomed to lose its grassy colour and take on the colour of white. Therefore, it designates bodies that are gleaming with the beauty of chastity, for although they are indeed begotten in the enticements of the flesh, by the great labour of continence they sweat out (as it were) their natural moisture and come to the beauty of a purity that is worthy of God, diligent in fasts and vigils, in prayers and reading, and in the practice of patience and humility. Of these [bodies] can rightly be said that apostolic [word]: *Or do you not know that your members are the temple of the Holy Spirit which is in you?* [4] And this fine linen is twisted into the curtains of the tabernacle because we do not gird only the loins of the flesh but also, as Peter admonishes, the loins of our mind in sobriety, [5] so that we may restrain both the flesh from lascivious impulses and the heart from enticing thoughts.

Blue, because it resembles the appearance of air and heaven, designates the minds of the same elect, who are seeking heavenly things with every hope and desire. Commending the sacrament of this colour to us, the *[46]* Apostle says: *If you have risen with Christ, seek the things that are above, where Christ is, sitting at the right hand of God.* [6]

Purple, because it displays the colour of blood [7] and is also dyed with the actual purple blood of shellfish, designates the devout hearts of those who are able to say with the Apostle, *I am ready not only to be bound but even to die in Jerusalem for the name of the Lord Jesus,* [8] and to the Lord with the prophet, *'Because for your sake we are being killed all the day long; we are counted as sheep for the slaughter.* [9]

---

1 Rev. 19:7-8
2 Prov. 31:22
3 Isidore, *Etymol.* 19, 27, 1, 4 (ed. Lindsay, vol. 2); Pliny *Nat. hist.* 19, 1, 5 (*LCL* 5: 422)
4 1 Cor. 6:19
5 1 Pet. 1:13
6 Col. 3:1
7 Isidore, *Etymol.* 12, 6, 50 (ed. Lindsay, vol. 2)
8 Acts 21:13
9 Ps. 44:22 (43:22)

Scarlet, because it has the appearance of fire,[1] is rightly compared to the most ardent love of the saints. For this same reason, some of those who had been smitten with this [love] while the Lord was present and keeping company with them were saying: *'Was not our heart burning within us while he was speaking on the road and opening the Scriptures to us?'*[2] On the other hand, with reference to this love it is said concerning the reprobate: *And because iniquity has abounded, the charity of many will grow cold.*[3] This is dyed twice, as it were, when it is inflamed with the love of God and neighbour, when we love the former with all our heart, all our soul, and all our strength, and the latter as ourselves.[4]

And so, the four just characteristics of the elect are expressed in these four colours of the curtains: in fine linen, the purified flesh that is shining with chastity; in blue, the mind that is desiring things above; in purple, the flesh that is subject to afflictions; in scarlet twice dyed, the mind that in the midst of afflictions is shining with the love of God and neighbour.

26:2 **The length of one curtain shall be twenty-eight cubits, and the width shall be four cubits.** The length of the curtains expresses the long-suffering patience of the Holy Church, and their width expresses the breadth of that love, which is accustomed not only to return love to those who love us (God and the neighbour), but also to receive the adversary who hates us into our bosom spread wide with sweetness, and with knees bent in prayer to commend our persecutors to the Lord, saying: *'Lord, do not hold this sin against them.'*[5]

This width is aptly four cubits because there are four books of the gospels in which we are taught by the exemplary deeds and words of our Lord and Redeemer how that same charity is to be maintained. There are also four virtues through the performance of which this same charity is to be exercised, namely: temperance, fortitude, justice, and prudence. Thus, charity should be kept incorrupt and whole in God; that pertains to temperance. It should not be crushed by misfortunes; that pertains to fortitude. It should serve no one else; that pertains to justice. And it should be vigilant in matters of discernment, lest deceit and guile steal it away little by little; that pertains to prudence.

[47]   Now the length of the curtains was twenty-eight cubits, which is the number produced by multiplying seven times four; on account of the

---

1 Isidore, *Etymol.* 19, 28, 1 (ed. Lindsay, vol. 2)
2 Luke 24:32
3 Matt. 24:12
4 Mark 12:30-1
5 Acts 7:60

sabbath day, the eternal rest of the saints is accustomed to be represented by the number seven. Therefore the length of the curtains extends to four times seven cubits because by believing and keeping evangelical doctrine, and through exercising the spiritual virtues of which we have spoken, the long-suffering patience of the Holy Church stretches out toward eternal rest.

There is also another sacrament in the number twenty-eight which likewise pertains to the number seven. If you will count the whole succession of numbers between one and seven, you will reach the sum of twenty-eight, for one plus two plus three plus four plus five plus six plus seven make twenty-eight. Therefore, the length of the curtains is rightly contained in the number twenty-eight because the parts of the number seven are found in it. For in everything that they do or suffer, the saints whose faith and patience are adorned with a variety of virtues are not expecting the glory of human favour but the blessedness of heavenly rest. That explains why the psalm of this number is entitled *At the finishing of the tabernacle,* for the whole of this song concerns the perfection of the Holy Church, as is particularly apparent from those [verses] which say, *Adore the Lord in his holy court,*[1] and again, *And in his temple all shall say 'Glory!'*[2] The twenty-eighth psalm is aptly inscribed *At the finishing of the tabernacle,* since it contains the perfection of the Holy Church's pilgrimage in this world, so that through faith and through good works it may proceed to its rest in the world to come. And there properly follows:

26:2 **All the curtains shall be of one measure.** Although the curtains differed from one another in having different colours of embroidery, they were nevertheless all proportioned with lengths and widths of the same measure. For although the elect have gifts that differ according to the grace that is given them,[3] there is nevertheless *one Lord, one faith, one baptism, one God and Father of all.*[4]

26:3 **Five curtains shall be joined to one another; and the other five shall be attached in the same way.** Josephus relates that the tables of the covenant were composed in such a way that each table in the Decalogue of the law contained five words.[5] For this reason it was fitting that the ten curtains that were joined together to complete the beauty of the tabernacle were also divided at a suitable interval so that five on each side might remain together. When those who ministered the holy things, with the people of   *[48]*

---

1 Ps. 29:2 (28:2)
2 Ps. 29:9 (28:9)
3 Rom. 12:6
4 Eph. 4:5-6
5 Josephus, *Ant. Jud.* 3, 6, 5 (ed. Blatt, 235, 26-7)

God, saw this, they would have been reminded of the law that is always to be observed, which was comprised of ten words in two tables, divided so as to number five in each table.

Furthermore, on account of this verse we are also able to speak of the number of the curtains as two times five, so that they represent those in each testament who follow the divine law. Surely the first five, which covered or formed the front and foremost part of the tabernacle, bore a type of the ancient people of God, who fulfilled the decrees of the law according to the letter in the sacrament of circumcision and the observance of the various sacrificial rites. But the five curtains that follow, which covered the rear sides of the tabernacle or actually formed them by covering them, designated those of us born after the coming of the Lord in flesh, who keep the books and sacraments of the law spiritually, as he himself has revealed and provided.

All the curtains were embroidered with one and the same handiwork and colours but they were joined together in [groups of] five, because all the worshipers in both testaments believed in one and the same God and served him with works of one and the same piety and charity, but in the celebration of the sacraments each people played its own separate part. For they celebrated the sacrament of the Lord's passion (through which each of the two peoples has been redeemed) in the flesh and blood of sacrifices, but we celebrate it in the oblation of bread and wine. They believed in and confessed as things to come the Lord's nativity in flesh, his preaching, his working of miracles, his temptation, his passion, his burial, his resurrection and ascension, as well as the coming of the Holy Spirit and the faith of the Gentiles, but we believe and confess that all these things have already happened and that there is nothing more left to be accomplished. Nevertheless, at the time when the tabernacle was being erected all the curtains were fastened to one another, because when the beauty of the whole Catholic Church from the beginning unto the end of the world is considered, it is assuredly as if ten curtains joined together into one adorn the tabernacle of the Lord.

26:4 **You shall make loops of blue on the sides and tops of the curtains, so that they may be joined to one another.** We have said that blue, because it is the colour of the air, is appropriate as a sign of heavenly blessings.[1] Therefore the curtains are joined to one another with blue loops when a single hope of supernal blessedness joins the hearts of all the elect throughout the world together in one and the same devotion. These loops [*ansulae*] are aptly named, because they were to be made not only on the

[49]

1 Bede, *De tab.* 2, 2 (*CCSL* 119A: 45, 149-51)

sides of the curtains but also on the tops, that is, at the extreme ends of the corners [*angulorum*].[1] For not only do the life and the work of the saints hasten to perfection along the common road of right intention, but even the first stage of the good life, which we obtain by confession of the faith and the reception of the heavenly sacraments, is not alien or different, but all are linked by an equal and similar grace of truth. Likewise, at the end of temporal life we all have the common assurance of one and the same hope when we close our eyes in death, so that having first received the viaticum of the heavenly mystery,[2] we may be confident of finding ourselves very quickly in the true life and of remaining in it forever.

This agrees with that passage in the Book of Numbers in which the children of Israel are instructed *that they should make for themselves fringes on the corners of their garments, putting in them blue cords.*[3] Surely the children of Israel have fringes and blue cords on the corners of their garments when the elect and all those who wish to see God so labour to clothe themselves with works of righteousness that they do not esteem these mortal things as a praiseworthy goal, lest by chance it could be said of them that *they have their reward,*[4] but amidst those things they look rather to the eyes of the inner Judge, and to eternal rewards. For this reason, in that place it is also immediately added by way of explanation: *When they shall see these things, let them remember all the commandments of the Lord, lest they should follow their own thoughts, and their eyes that have gone whoring after diverse things.*[5]

We should also make use of these words in our explanation of the blue loops. For we may say that the reason that the curtains were joined together with loops of that sort was in order that the children of Israel who then had them in their sight might be reminded of the heavenly commandments, and that we who read about them now might be mindful that as long as we continue in this life as children of the eternal promise we are separated from one another in time and space, but in heaven there is a homeland in which its citizens, being gathered from the four winds of heaven, are forever joined together in an indivisible fellowship.

26:5 Every curtain shall have fifty loops on both sides, inserted in such a way that one loop may be set against another, and one may be

---

1 Bede's point is that it is appropriate for the *ansulae* ('loops') to be so called, because they are located in the similar-sounding *angulae* ('corners').

2 On Bede's emphasis on the importance of receiving communion from the reserved sacrament as viaticum ('food for the journey') at the time of death, see Carroll (1946), 109-10.

3 Num. 15:38

4 Matt. 6:5

5 Num. 15:39

fitted to the other. We read in the law that the fiftieth year was ordered to be designated as a jubilee (that is, a [year for] releasing or exchanging[1]), in which the whole people should rest from all cultivation of the land and everyone's debts should be cancelled,[2] and we know that in the New Testament the grace of the Holy Spirit came upon the apostles on the day
[50] of Pentecost (that is, the fiftieth day of the Lord's resurrection) and hallowed the beginnings of the Church that was being brought into existence by its coming.[3] It is agreed, then, that by this number can rightly be figured either the grace of the Holy Spirit or the joy of future blessedness, to which one is brought through the gift of the same Spirit and in the perception of which alone is true rest and joy.

Aptly did the curtains have fifty loops by which they were fastened to one another, because only by the gift of the Holy Spirit does it happen that the elect are joined to one another in the fellowship of peace *which is the bond of perfection,*[4] and nothing but the hope and remembrance of future fellowship and peace makes those who are in this life still separated in time and space into servants of Christ united in a common piety. And it is properly said that the curtains had loops on both sides so that every single curtain embraced the curtains near to it on either side as if with arms extending in both directions, because it is doubtless necessary that we should with the open arms of pure piety embrace all the faithful, both those who preceded us in Christ and those who have followed us, and that all of us who are in Christ should revere with one affection both those who taught us in Christ and those whom we have taught with the help of Christ himself.

We ought to hasten to see the face of our Creator by living well, so that we by no means forsake the neighbours who are running with us, but are eager to come into the presence of the Divine Glory together with them. For all the curtains were supported by the boards in such a way that they extended to the ceiling and shone up above with the varied luster of their own embroidery on the inside, so that they by no means fell short of those curtains that together with them were either borne aloft or shone from their position on high. After the fashion of those curtains, we should assist the faithful by admonition and by example as they advance with us in the service of God. And in whatever virtue we have been able to make progress, in the same way we should treat all our companions in that virtue in a manner appropriate to these virtues. Therefore, loop is set against loop so

---

1 Jerome, *Nom.* (*CCSL* 72: 67, 10)
2 Lev. 25:10-11
3 Acts 2:1-2
4 Col. 3:14

that one can be fitted to another when the righteous are allied with one another in the harmonious and equal disposition of their virtues. **26:6 You shall make also fifty rings of gold with which the veils of the curtains are to be joined, so that the tabernacle may be made one whole.** This passage is explained more fully later on, when it is said: *And he cast fifty rings of gold, that they might grip the loops of the curtains, and the tabernacle might be made one whole.* [1] Since the number fifty designates true rest in the Holy Spirit, and a ring seems to have neither beginning nor end, and gold is the most precious of metals, excelling all others in its brightness, what is expressed in the fifty golden rings except the perpetual brightness and bright perpetuity of the highest repose? And the rings grip the loops of the curtains in such a way that one tabernacle might be made out of them all when the glory of the heavenly kingdom graciously pours itself into the pure minds of the faithful, so that with the glue of such healing inspiration the Church is made perfect out of the two peoples, or perhaps we should say out of all Christ's elect.

[51]

3.   THE ELEVEN COVERINGS [OF HAIRCLOTH]

26:7 You shall also make eleven coverings of haircloth to cover the roof of the tabernacle. This passage recurs later on in this way: *He also made eleven coverings of goats' hair to cover the roof of the tabernacle.* [2] Accordingly, the coverings with which the tabernacle is covered are the rulers of the Holy Church, by whose industriousness and labour the dignity of the same Church is protected and defended with unceasing care, lest the life and faith of the elect should be liable to be corrupted by the seduction of heretics, or defiled by the depravity of false catholics, or contaminated by the filth of tempting vices, or brought down into despondency by a lack of material resources. The more carefully they prepare themselves to endure and repel the savageries of attacking temptations, the greater freedom to serve the Lord do they give to those who are subject to them. It is as if they provide the curtains with an abundance of splendour on the inside, while

---

1 Exod. 36:13
2 Exod. 36:14

on the outside they themselves bear the tempests of affliction, after the fashion of coverings.[1]

Now it is rightly said that those same coverings were made of haircloth or from goats' hair, and were eleven [in number], doubtless because the holy preachers who are higher in merit ought to be that much the more humble in spirit, in accordance with that saying of the wise man: *The greater you are, the more you must humble yourself in all things.*[2] Surely [the number] eleven, which goes beyond ten but does not come to the apostolic number twelve, signifies the transgression of the Decalogue of the law.[3] For this same reason, in the eleventh psalm the prophet complains that holy people are in short supply and that human beings have exchanged truths for vanities and deceits, saying, *'Save me, Lord, for there is no one who is holy,*[4] implicitly indicating by this number [eleven] that people of this sort, who are duplicitous in tongue and heart, neither keep the legal precepts of the Decalogue nor understand the apostolic grace of the gospel.

Haircloth is also the clothing of penitents, as the psalmist bears witness, saying, *'But as for me, when they were troublesome to me, I clothed myself with haircloth,'*[5] that is, 'I put on the clothing of penitence and humility, with which I endured the rage of persecutors with calm equanimity, or even [52] mitigated it.' For if goats and the hair or skins of goats always signified the foulness of sinners and never the humility of penitents, that animal would by no means have been reckoned among the clean [animals], nor would it have been said in praise of the bride: *'Your hair is like a flock of goats.'*[6] Therefore the coverings that represent the holy preachers are made of haircloth and are eleven [in number] because the more zealously they purify their hearts in faith, the more things do they find in them for which to reproach themselves. Hence they also humbly confess that *we all offend in many things,*[7] and *If we say that we have no sin, we deceive ourselves, and*

1 Gregory the Great, *Moral.* 25, 16, 39 (*CCSL* 143B: 1263, 137 - 1264, 167). A similar interpretation appears in Isidore, *Quaest. in Exod.* 54 (*PL* 83: 314C-315A), but Bede shows no direct dependence on him. As Laistner wrote in Thompson (1935), 237: 'Mere similarity in thought between Bede and Isidore is therefore not enough to prove borrowing of the one from the other, seeing that many of Bede's ideas will have been formed or influenced by direct study of the same Fathers whom Isidore followed.'

2 Sir. 3:20
3 Augustine, *De civ. Dei* 15, 20 (*CSEL* 40, 2: 104, 21-7)
4 Ps. 12:1 (11:2)
5 Ps. 35:13 (34:13)
6 S. of S. 4:1
7 Jas. 3:2

the truth is not in us.[1] Nevertheless, the degree to which their hearts are perfect is mystically declared in the words that follow, in which it is said: **26:8 The length of one covering shall be thirty cubits, and the width four.** Behold, here you have a length that is not a number containing eleven, but one containing ten, and that [number is] multiplied by three. By this is openly suggested the virtue of those who fulfill the Decalogue of the law in the faith of the Holy Trinity *that works by love;*[2] there can be nothing higher than this perfection, at least in this life. You also have a width of four cubits, by which (as we have said before) is signified the expansiveness of genuine charity, that is, of that charity which is both commended and given to us in the gospel through Jesus Christ. Therefore there are eleven coverings covering the roof of the tabernacle, and these are made of the hair of goats but are thirty cubits long and four cubits wide. For surely those most eminent preachers who protect the life of the faithful with their exhortations, intercessions, constant solicitude, vigils, fasts, and nakedness[3] humbly acknowledge themselves to be sinners when they contemplate the excellence of heavenly purity; nevertheless, among humans and those who are above they appear to be pure, within the limits of human perfection.

    26:8-9 All of the coverings shall be equal in measure. Five of them you shall join by themselves, and the six others you shall connect to one another, so as to double the sixth covering at the front of the roof. There was one measure for all the coverings, doubtless because there is one faith in which the whole Church is saved, and one eternal life to which it hastens. For the same reason, those who entered into the vineyard of the Lord to work at different times are all rewarded with one denarius.[4] Surely the division of the coverings into [groups of] five and six can be understood in accordance with what we explained previously concerning the curtains divided into [groups of] five and five, because they evidently designate the teachers of both testaments.[5] The five coverings are aptly compared to the ancient teachers of the people of God, either because they preached only the sacraments of the Mosaic law (however much they preached the secrets of evangelical truth also), or because they lived in the [first] five ages of

[53]

---

1 1 John 1:8
2 Gal. 5:6
3 2 Cor. 11:27-8
4 Matt. 20:8-10
5 Bede, *De tab.* 2, 2 (*CCSL* 119A: 48, 234-43)

this world.[1] And it is not inappropriate to take the six curtains as the teachers of the New Testament, because they accepted all the things that Divine Scripture reports to have been done or said in the six ages of the world as things to be understood spiritually, for aids and examples in their preaching. For they openly proclaim to their hearers that they should believe and confess the Lord's passion, through which the world was redeemed on the sixth day before the sabbath, and they are called to bear witness [to them] that they can only be saved through the sacrament of this passion.

For this reason the sixth covering is rightly commanded to be doubled at the front of the roof, evidently on account of the confession and the imitation of the same passion of the Lord. For it is not enough for believers if they are only baptized and consecrated in the confession of the Lord's death and resurrection, if once baptized they are not also eager to be conformed to the likeness of the Lord's death as far as they are able, by living continently and by suffering for his sake, so that they may also merit to become partakers in his resurrection. According to the letter it speaks of 'the front of the roof', which is the entrance of the tabernacle where there were no boards but rather (as we said just above[2]) it was commanded that columns and a rod should be stretched from [one] corner of the boards to [another] corner, and therefore as far as the design of the handiwork itself is concerned, the handiwork was to be greater in that place in which the protection of the coverings was doubled, where the solid firmness of the wall was lacking. But mystically the sixth curtain is doubled at the front of the roof when all those who enter the Holy Church are initiated in the faith and

---

1 The doctrine of the six ages of the world is found in Augustine, *De civ. Dei* 22, 30 (*CSEL* 40, 2: 669, 17 - 670, 16) and Isidore, *Etymol.* 5, 38-9 (ed. Lindsay, vol. 1). It appears in many of Bede's works, especially *De tempor.* 16-22 (*CCSL* 123C: 600-11), *De temp. rat.* 66-71 (*CCSL* 123B: 463- 544), *Ep. Pleg.* (*CCSL* 123C: 617-26), and the hymn *Primo Deus caeli globum* (*CCSL* 122: 407-11); the later works include discussions of the transhistorical seventh and eighth ages. For detailed treatments of this theme in Bede's writings, see Jones (1969-70), 191-8, Siniscalco (1978), and Hunter Blair (1970), 265-8. For its later development in medieval literature, see Burrows (1988). A concise explanation is given by Plummer (1896), 1: xlii-xlii: 'The first age is from the Creation to the Flood; the second from the Flood to Abraham; the third from Abraham to David; the fourth from David to the Captivity of Judah; the fifth from the Captivity to the birth of Christ; the sixth age lasts until the day of Judgement, and its duration is known to God alone. These six ages, during which the faithful labour for God in this world, correspond with the six days of God's labour in the works of Creation. The seventh age, answering to His sabbath rest, is that in which the souls of the faithful, separated from their bodies, rest from their labours in the unseen world, and is therefore contemporary with all the other six, beginning when God's first martyr Abel was slain, and lasting till the general resurrection, when the souls of the faithful being united to their glorious bodies, the eighth age begins, which lasts for ever.'

2 Bede, *De. tab.* 2, 1 (*CCSL* 119A: 44, 77-9)

sacraments of the Lord's passion in such a way that they understand that they must always live in imitation of it as well. For it is as if the sixth covering is doubled for us at the entrance of the sanctuary when we are both consecrated by the sacraments of the Lord's passion and instructed by examples of it. Concerning the reception of the sacraments, surely Peter says: *According to his great mercy he has given us a new birth into a lively hope, through the resurrection of Jesus Christ from the dead;*[1] concerning the imitation of the passion, he says: *Christ therefore having suffered in the flesh, arm yourselves also with the same thought.*[2]

26:10-11 You shall make also fifty hooks on the border of one covering, so that it can be joined with another, and fifty loops on the border of the other covering, so that it can be joined with the other. [And you shall make] fifty clasps of bronze with which the hooks can be joined, so that from all there may be made one tent. These things here can also be understood in the same way as we explained above in the case of the curtains,[3] because it is evident that the recollection of heavenly rest (which is accustomed to be expressed by the number fifty) unites the hearts   *[54]* of the saints in the bond of peace.[4] Or, if it pleases you to hear something new, let the coverings designate the humility of those sublime persons who desire to remember their own transgressions rather than to proclaim their own virtues, and are more eager to feel compunction about those virtues that they are not yet able to acquire than they are to boast about those that they have already acquired, inasmuch as the humility of their compunction can be designated by fifty, which is the number of the hooks and of the clasps. For the fiftieth is a psalm of penitence, and rightly so, because the gift of penitence is not granted unless the Holy Spirit imparts it, and the gift of pardon is not bestowed upon penitents unless it is administered by the grace of the same Holy Spirit.[5]

The coverings are properly connected to one another with fifty hooks or clasps, because there is no virtue that binds the faithful together in one bond of charity more than humility. For the weaker they consider themselves to be, the more eagerly they seek to be strengthened by their neighbour's aid. And the clasps are properly made of bronze, which is well known as a metal [that makes] a loud sound, doubtless because the humble conscience of the

---

1 1 Pet. 1:3

2 1 Pet. 4:1

3 Bede, *De tab.* 2, 2 (*CCSL* 119A: 50, 344-9)

4 Eph. 4:3

5 Ps. 51 (50). The number fifty symbolizes the Holy Spirit which descended upon the disciples on Pentecost, the fiftieth day of the Easter season; cf. Bede's comment above on Exod. 26:5 at *De tab.* 2, 2 (*CCSL* 119A: 49, 305 - 50, 308)

righteous speaks before God with a great voice. For this same reason, when that poor man in the Psalms of David[1] was anxious, he did not cry out before human ears but poured out his prayer in the presence of the Lord, saying, '*Lord, hear my prayer, and let my cry come to you.* '[2]

26:12-13 And with what remains of the coverings that are prepared for the roof, that is, with half of the one covering that is longer, you shall cover the back of the tabernacle. The cubit that remains on one side, and the other [cubit] on the other side, which are over and above in the length of the coverings, shall hang down, covering both sides of the tabernacle. In order that these things might be understood more clearly, it is necessary for us to conduct a somewhat more extensive investigation of the position of the tabernacle itself as a whole. We have said that the walls of the tabernacle, which were composed of boards and columns, were thirty cubits long, ten cubits wide, and also ten cubits high. [Let us imagine], then, that someone wanted to encircle the breadth of the building with a little cord, say from the base of one board on the south side unto the base of the board that was directly opposite on the north side. Surely it is evident that the same little cord would have to be thirty cubits long, that is, ten cubits going up on the south wall, ten more again running horizontally between the walls, and a third ten going down on the north side. Likewise, if you *[55]* wanted to stretch the little cord through the length of the building (that is, from the bases of the columns and up through the length of the whole building all the way to the west wall and then all the way down to its bases), that little cord would be fifty cubits long. There would be ten going up beside the columns, thirty running horizontally along the length of the building, and ten more going down beside the boards on the west wall.

Bearing these things in mind, then, consider also how the measurements of the curtains with which the building was covered might be consistent with the aforementioned measurements. There were ten curtains, each being twenty-eight cubits long and four wide, which when joined together and constructed into one tabernacle made up a breadth of forty cubits. Therefore, if you hang the curtains, which are each twenty-eight cubits long, and set them up in the building which measures thirty cubits across, you will see that the curtains will be ten cubits horizontally between the walls, and nine cubits up and down beside the walls. Thus, they are made in such a way that the lowest part of the curtains is unable to touch the ground but is left above the ground by the measure of one cubit. Likewise, you will see that the curtains are thirty cubits horizontally through the length of the building,

---

1 literally, 'that Davidic poor man'
2 Ps. 102:1 (101:2)

and five cubits going up and down (that is, on the east side of the building
and on the west). Once again, therefore, the lowest part of the curtains which
are on the side cannot possibly reach all the way to the ground, but is left
five cubits higher than the ground. Thus it becomes necessary that those
five cubits of the curtains remaining above the bare walls should be spread
over one another on the east side and on the west as well, and joined to one
another. And it should be done in such a manner that the curtains cover the
building all over, except for one cubit next to the ground. So much for the
curtains.

The coverings, however, are thirty cubits long and four wide, and because
eleven [of them] were joined to one another at the sides they amounted to
forty-four cubits. Therefore, if you set these [coverings] up in the building
also, because the length of the coverings is the same as that of the little cord
with which you measured the building crosswise, it happens that their
lowest part extends all the way to the ground. For they will be ten cubits
horizontally between the walls, and ten up and down on each side as well.
That explains why Scripture says that a cubit hangs down on the one side,
and another on the other side, which was over and above in the length of
the coverings, covering both sides of the tabernacle. For what it calls the
'tabernacle' in the proper sense is the actual conjunction of the curtains.   *[56]*
The coverings certainly extended beyond the curtains by one cubit on the
south side of the building and by another [cubit] on the north, and for this
reason they reached to the ground, because the coverings are thirty cubits
in length, the curtains two less. Likewise, the measure of the coverings
extended through the length of the building for forty-four cubits, being
thirty cubits horizontally from the front of the building all the way to the
highest point of the boards on the west side, seven cubits hanging down at
the front of the building, and seven more hanging down on the west side.
Thus, it was made in such a manner that the measure of the coverings on
the west side exceeded the measure of the curtains by two cubits. This is
evident, since the curtains that came down from above (as we have also
related previously[1]) covered five cubits of the wall and left the other five
bare, but the coverings covered seven cubits of the same western wall and
left three bare.

And that is what is said now: **And with what remains of the coverings
that are prepared for the roof, that is, with half of the one covering that
is longer, you shall cover the back of the tabernacle.** Surely the half of
the covering was two cubits in width, and this half completely covered the
back of the tabernacle (that is, the curtains which were the tabernacle

1 Bede, *De tab.* 2, 3 (*CCSL* 119A: 55, 523-8)

properly so called), for the last covering extended beyond the curtains by two cubits, stretching to the bottom, as we have said. And so the coverings coming down from above completely covered only seven cubits of the western wall, while the other three [cubits], which were left bare all the way to the ground, were exposed to the rigours of the weather. However, when the seven cubits of coverings that extended beyond the limits of the walls on both sides were added together, they protected the back parts of the building quite securely, all the way to the ground. Now these [coverings] were not only able to reach one another and, after the fashion of the curtains, to meet each other in the middle of the wall, but because they were seven cubits [long] they extended beyond the middle of the wall by two cubits on both sides and overlapped one another when they were joined together. We believe this should also be understood in the same way in every respect with reference to the eastern side of the building; it was for this reason that the sixth covering in the front of the roof was previously enjoined to be doubled.[1] In so far as we have been able to understand them, we have taken care briefly to explain these things concerning this most difficult subject, but we are ready to learn more accurate information about these matters if anyone wishes to instruct us.

Regardless, in all of these things the meaning of the allegory is openly transparent. For surely the coverings protected the curtains up above and below and on every side, and in order that the comely appearance of those on the inside might shine freely, those on the outside rendered them immune [57] from every rigour of storms, rains, and heats.[2] Doubtless this was because the perfect ones who preside over the Holy Church are in a similar manner accustomed with expert care to look out for the lives of the faithful who are entrusted to them, so that they lack neither assistance in the carnal life or aid in the spiritual life. [The faithful] must be kept safe from both the teachings of heretics and the examples of false catholics; they must be aided by the salutary doctrine which will strengthen them so that they will be able both wisely to refute the words of those who teach erroneously, and patiently to endure the actions of those who inflict evil upon them; they

---

1 Bede is referring back to Exod. 26:9, where Moses is commanded to double the sixth covering at the front of the roof. By explaining that doubling as an overlapping similar to that of the coverings at the back of the tabernacle in 26:12, Bede is here silently differing with Josephus, who in the Cassiodorian translation of *Ant. Jud.* 3, 6, 4 (ed. Blatt, 235, 5-9) had explained the doubling at the front as creating something like a gable for the sanctuary within.

2 Gregory the Great, *Moral.* 25, 16, 39 (*CCSL* 143B: 1263, 137 - 1264, 167). As noted in reference to Bede's comment on Exod. 26:7, the fact that a similar interpretation is found in Isidore, *Quaest. in Exod.* 54 (*PL* 83: 314C-315A) does not necessarily imply that Bede is dependent upon him here.

must be aided by the heavenly life of [their teachers], which will enable them to make use of a silent text just as if it were a tongue that is always alive. For the coverings repel rains, resist storms, hold off the heat of the sun, and boldly drive away all adversities on the outside so that the beauty of the curtains on the inside might remain undefiled when Augustine removes all the poisons of the heretics which have been able to disturb faith,[1] when Gregory unravels those temptations of the ancient enemy that assail good morals,[2] when Cyprian strengthens the weak with pious exhortations lest they should waver in the face of martyrdom,[3] and when other venerable bishops and teachers ward off every temptation that has been disturbing the Church for a long time and with skillful scrutiny look out for everything that may be conducive to its salvation. In this way, the faithful are made utterly secure in their religious life, so that they can devote themselves to virtue with a free heart, that their deeds may shine brightly in the sight of their Creator, even while they direct their mind's eye to the contemplation of him.

4.   THE THIRD AND FOURTH COVERINGS OF RAMS' SKINS

Because those who are worthy of the highest honour among the holy preachers are those who also shed their blood for Christ as a result of their service in the office of preaching and guiding the people, it is rightly added: 26:14 **You shall also make for the roof another covering of rams' skins dyed red.** Surely the holy teachers are often understood by the word 'rams', since they are the leaders of the flocks that follow the Lord. Hence the psalmist says in a pleasing manner: *Bring to the Lord, O children of God, bring to the Lord the offspring of rams,*[4] which is clearly to say, 'Bring to the Lord, O angels of God (to whom the responsibilty for this task has been delegated[5]), bring to the Lord in heaven the spirits of the faithful who, through the imitation of the blessed apostles' life and faith, have proved worthy to become their offspring.' For this reason, when the people of God

1 The writings of Augustine of Hippo (354-430) contain refutations of a variety of heretics and schismatics, including Manichaeans, Donatists, and Pelagians.

2 Gregory the Great (*c.*540-604) wrote a massive commentary on the Book of Job known as the *Moralia* (*CCSL* 143, 143A, 143B).

3 Cyprian of Carthage (*c.*200-258) wrote a letter *Ad Fortunatum* (*CCSL* 3: 183-216) which is an exhortation to martyrdom.

4 Ps. 29:1 (28:1)

5 On the early Christian belief that angels serve as escorts who convey faithful souls to heaven after death, see Daniélou (1957), 95-105; cf. Luke 16:22. The same idea appears in Bede's historical writings: *Hist. eccl.* 5, 12-3 (ed. Colgrave and Mynors, 488-502) and *Vit. Cuth. pros.* 34 (ed. Colgrave, 262).

went out from Egypt their sixth resting place, in which *there were twelve*
[58]   *fountains of water and seventy palm trees,*[1] was called 'Elim' (that is, 'of
rams'),[2] so that both by its name and by its appearance it might contain the
figure of the apostles and the apostolic men.

Now the rams' skins for the covering of the roof of the tabernacle are
dyed red when the apostles and the apostolic men do not cease to pursue
the teaching of the word all the way to the suffering of martyrdom, so that
they might protect those in their care more securely from the dangerous
onslaughts of temptation, while they themselves do not refuse to suffer
persecution unto death for righteousness' sake. And rams' skins dyed red
cover the tabernacle of the Lord and defend it from the rigours of the
weather just as through the example of their suffering and patience the holy
preachers guard the hearts of the weak lest they should give way to the
afflictions of tribulations.

And because sacred virginity holds a special place among the pre-
eminent members of Christ and the Church, after the variegated decoration
of the curtains, after the protective shelter of the hair-cloth coverings, after
the rams' skins dyed red, there is then aptly added:

26:14 **And over that again another covering of blue-coloured skins.**
Surely blue is the colour of heaven, and skin is the characteristic mark of a
dead animal. And what is signified by blue-coloured skins, except the virtue
of those who in a certain manner live a pure heavenly life on earth by putting
to death all the allures of carnal concupiscence?[3] Although situated among
humans, do they not imitate rather the purity of angels, and is this not what
is promised to all the elect in the time of immortality which is to come? For
they neither marry nor take wives, but are equal to the angels of God;[4] even
while still detained in mortal flesh, are they not eager to anticipate their
future state?

Hence there is a great reward that deservedly awaits those of such great
virtue, as the prophet bears witness: *For thus says the Lord: 'To the eunuchs
who will keep my sabbaths, and will choose the things that please me, and
will hold fast my covenant, I will give a place in my house and within my
walls, and a name better than sons and daughters; I will give them an
everlasting name that shall not be taken away.'*[5] Concerning this place and
this name, John the evangelist, who was himself one of those [virtuous

---

1 Exod. 15:27
2 Jerome, *Nom.* (*CCSL* 72: 75, 4)
3 Gregory the Great, *Hom. in evang.* 7,3 (*PL* 76: 1101C)
4 Luke 20:35-6
5 Isa. 56:4-5

persons], also reports that he had heard them singing before the throne of God a new song, which no one else could [sing], and immediately he added: *These are they who have not been defiled with women, for they are virgins; these are they who follow the Lamb wherever he goes.*[1] Therefore the blue-coloured skins deservedly hold the highest place in the house of God, and the heavenly colour is assigned the position near to heaven, so as to indicate that the choirs of those who are virgins in both soul and body will follow the Lamb especially closely and will sing hymns of praise to him.   [59]

Now it is properly said of the veils of the curtains and the coverings that although they were placed on high, nevertheless they fell so that they hung to the ground—even though the curtains were never allowed to extend all the way to the ground. And although the columns and boards of the tabernacle also stood erect on high, nevertheless they had bases on which they stood, and these were set in the ground. Concerning the skins dyed red and the blue-coloured skins, however, it is said that they covered the roof on high, but it is not added that they hung down to the ground, because the other kinds of virtues doubtless appear to be related to those who are still being rewarded upon earth, but it is evident that the prize of martyrdom and the dignity of virginity which is consecrated to God are in a sense elevated above the lowly things of earth and associated in a special way with the citizens of heaven. For the martyr enduring torture has a mind intent on nothing else but leaving everything in this world behind as soon as possible, and the world itself as well, so as to be set free from all afflictions, and thus to come to see the Creator of the world and to possess those joys that are beyond the world. And as for those who are celibate, although in consideration of a greater reward they rightfully go beyond the universal law of the human race in which it is said, *'Increase and multiply and fill the earth, '*[2] while they are in this world they never choose for themselves a seat that is higher than the rest of the faithful; thus they live in common with the Church so that they might surpass the Church's common manner of life by meriting a higher honour. For this reason, it is appropriate for John to write concerning such persons that *they have been redeemed from humankind as first fruits for God and the Lamb;* rightly are such persons called in the Latin language either 'virgins' (as if they were outstanding in virtue) or 'celibates' (as if they were blessed in the celestial realm, that is, as if they were imitating on earth the life of the citizens of heaven).[3]

---

1 Rev. 14:2-4

2 Gen. 1:28

3 Bede is playing on the similarity in sound between *virgines* ('virgins') and *virtute* ('in virtue') and between *caelibes* ('celibates') and *caelo* ('in the celestial realm').

5.   THE BOARDS OF THE TABERNACLE

26:15-16 You shall also make the upright boards of the tabernacle of acacia wood. Let each of them be ten cubits in length, and a cubit and a half in width. The acacia wood from which the tabernacle was made is naturally incorruptible, exceptionally white and lightweight, and not much different from whitethorn, except of greater size.[1] Hence in the *Book of Hebrew Names*, and in his other works as well, Jerome often translated 'acacia'[2] as simply 'thorns', on account of the word 'Abelsetim', [which means] 'grief of thorns'.[3] Now this kind of wood is not easily found except in the deserts of Arabia, where the tabernacle was built. Hence the Greek and Latin translaters were unable to give it any name other than the Hebrew one, since there was no knowledge of it in their lands. Some of them, however, wishing to indicate its characteristic nature, translated it as 'incorruptible wood'.

[60]

The boards of the tabernacle, then, designate the apostles and their successors, through whose word the Church has been expanded throughout the world. For the width of the boards is the expansion of the faith and the sacraments, which formerly lay hidden among the one Israelite people but through their ministry came [to fill] the wideness of the whole world. However, the width of the boards can also be rightly understood as the expansion of the hearts of the saints, through which they are accustomed to despise the world and are enkindled eagerly to desire the lofty things of heaven, and through which they rejoice to love not only their friends in God but also their enemies for God's sake.[4] Accordingly, let us consider that one of the boards of the tabernacle might suggest how the apostle Paul expanded himself in two ways. Concerning [his] inward parts (that is, the wideness of [his] heart), he says: *Our mouth is open to you, O Corinthians; our heart is expanded. You are not being restricted in us, but you are restricted in your own inmost parts. I speak as to children— be yourselves*

---

1 Jerome, *In Es.* 12 (*CCSL* 73A: 474, 51-7); *In Ioel.* 3, 18 (*CCSL* 76: 207, 349-52)

2 *sethim*

3 Jerome, *Nom.* (*CCSL* 72: 77, 2; 79, 12); see Num. 33:49

4 In his critical apparatus, the editor Hurst suggested a parallel between Bede's comments here (*CCSL* 119A: 60, 709-10) and those of Origen in *Hom. in Exod.* 9, 4 (*GCS* 29: 240, 29 - 241, 5). Origen also recalled 2 Cor. 6:13 when reflecting on the spiritual meaning of Exod. 26 and used the phrase 'enlargement of heart' from 2 Cor. 6:11 to refer to the attitude one should have toward one's enemies, but Bede need not have been directly dependent on Origen. There may have been an intermediate source such as a florilegium, or simply a coincidental similarity of ideas. The six other parallels to Origen's work suggested by Hurst are even less persuasive. For a full discussion, see Holder (1989b), 45-8.

expanded also;[1] and concerning the [wideness] that he was accustomed to employ for the enlargement of the tabernacle (that is, of the Holy Church), he says: *So that from Jerusalem round about as far as to Illyricum, I have filled up the gospel of Christ.*[2]

Now the boards were made out of acacia wood, that is, a thorny sort [of wood], and according to the Saviour's pronouncement thorns are the cares of this world, its pleasures, riches, and false delights.[3] But the pricks of sins may also not incongruously be compared to thorns, for it is written here that thorns grow in the hands of a drunkard,[4] that is, sins in the works of a fool. Because the holy preachers are eager both to expurgate themselves from the pricks of vices and to strip away all the cares and delights of the world so that with a free mind they might be able to be expanded in the love of God and neighbour and to run far and wide to preach the word, it is therefore rightly said that the boards of the tabernacle were made out of acacia wood (that is, out of thorny [wood]), for they were indeed made of thorns, but thorns from which all the thorny barbs had been completely stripped away, so that they shone with a pure whiteness. For that universal condemnation in which it was said to Adam when he sinned, 'Your ground *shall bring forth to you thorns and thistles,*'[5] applies to all alike. Even the saints and all of those who shine with virtues were conceived and born with the sin of the first transgression, but by the grace of God through Jesus Christ they have been stripped of the sharp points of all their sins and fitted for the building of his house by the appropriate exercise of virtues. *[61]*

Now all the boards were ten cubits long and a cubit and a half wide. The length of the boards is the height, which is ten cubits because the holy teachers stretch out toward perfection through the observance of the Decalogue of the law, and because they labour in Christ's vineyard to receive a daily denarius.[6] That is, they continue in the teaching of the word with the aim of restoring in themselves, with the help of their Creator and King, that image of him which they had lost by Adam's sin, so that by living rightly they may receive his name which they had lost by sinning; for surely a king's name and image is customarily contained on a denarius.[7]

But because the name of a denarius is derived from the fact that it is made up of ten [smaller] coins, it also aptly corresponds to the condition of our

---

1 2 Cor. 6:11-13
2 Rom. 15:19
3 Matt. 13:22; Luke 8:14
4 Prov. 26:9
5 Gen. 3:18
6 Matt. 20:8-10
7 Jerome, *In Matth.* 3 (*CCSL* 77: 204, 1775-6)

future blessedness, which is perfected in the true love of God and neighbour. God, because he is a Trinity, is often accustomed to be represented by the number three. The human being is represented by [the number] seven, since the body is taken from the four well-known elements, but in the Scriptures the substance of the soul (that is, of the inner person) is customarily understood as having three different aspects; for it is there that we are commanded to love God with all our heart, all our soul, and all our strength.[1] Therefore it is appropriate that each of the boards which comprise the tabernacle is built to stand ten cubits high, because the teachers and rulers of the Holy Church are devoted to God with the aim of deserving to see him in soul and body at the end of this life, being immortal and blessed forever; they always strive to rouse their hearers and to support them (as it were) both by word and by deed.

The same boards were a cubit and a half wide because that full cubit indicates the perfection of good work, while the half of a cubit which is added over and above indicates the beginning of divine knowledge. For in this life the righteous are doubtless perfectly able to persevere in alms, to devote themselves to prayer, to chastise themselves with fasts and other such pious acts, and to do [good] works. In the meanwhile we know God by faith, but we hope to know him fully in the future, as our God and Lord Jesus Christ himself says, *'If you will continue in my word, you will truly be my disciples, and you will know the truth.'*[2] Returning to the Father, he said, *'And this is eternal life, that they may know you, the only true God, and Jesus Christ whom you have sent.'*[3] And when the Apostle also says, *For we know in part, and we prophesy in part,*[4] is he not saying, 'We labour for Christ in part, we pursue the preaching of the word in part, we are devoted to good works in part'? Therefore, in this life the elect have a full cubit of good works, but they have a cubit of blessed reward [only] in part, to the extent that they are able to have a foretaste of the presence of their Maker and the joys of the eternal kingdom with its heavenly pleasures. But they are then blessed with the completion of this cubit, when at the last there will come to pass the word that he promised to the whole people of the elect, saying, *'I will deliver them, and I will glorify them; I will fill them with length of days, and I will show them my salvation.'*[5]

[62]

---

1 Mark 12:30
2 John 8:31
3 John 17:3
4 1 Cor. 13:9
5 Ps. 91:15-16 (90:15-16)

26:17 On the sides of a board there shall be two mortises, with which one board may be joined to another board, and all the boards shall be prepared in this way. The mortises on the sides of the boards designate the virtue of humility which is in the minds of the righteous, through which they are closely joined together in fraternal charity. For while they all prepare receptacles in themselves by loving their neighbours with a contrite and humble heart, they also hold out the worthiness of their piety and devotion by loving the brethren, just as all the boards of the tabernacle are joined to one another by connecting mortises.

When the tabernacle is built and the boards are joined together in accordance with the pattern prescribed above, the form of the mortises is not perceived at all; nevertheless, the firm stability of the unwavering wall itself shows with what great strength[1] it is joined together through the boards. For it is true that people on the outside cannot see the saints' humility of heart, by which they are united to one another; however, the most tranquil condition of the Holy Church itself makes what is being done on the inside plainly apparent to all. By the marvelous grace of the divine dispensation, it has come to pass through this [humility] that we *upon whom the ends of the ages have come*[2] can love with sincere affection those faithful who were in the beginning of the world, and receive them into the bosom of our love no less than those who live with us in the present, and believe that we are also being received by them with a charitable embrace.

Now there are two ways to understand figuratively why it is ordered that two mortises are to be made on each board, that is, on both of its sides: [it means] that we should keep the law of charity toward the brethren inviolate in prosperity and likewise in adversity, advancing (in accordance with the Apostle's analogy) *with the armor of righteousness on the right hand and on the left,*[3] and [it means] that we should stretch out toward the heights of perfection by clasping everyone into our arms with one and the same love, both those who are greater and those who are lesser (that is, those who have preceded us in Christ and those who have come after).

6.   THE ARRANGEMENT OF [THE BOARDS]

There follows: *[63]*
26:18-19 Twenty of them shall be on the south side, facing southward. You shall set forty silver bases beneath them, so that there are two bases

---

1 *virtute*, referring back to the 'virtue of humility' mentioned above.
2 1 Cor. 10:11
3 2 Cor. 6:7

placed underneath at the two corners of each board. It is not explicitly stated how long the length of the tabernacle will be, but it is implied by the fact that its sides were made from twenty boards and each of these is said to have been a cubit and a half wide; for surely twenty cubits and twenty times a half cubit will make up a height of thirty cubits, which Josephus also writes was the length of the tabernacle.[1] And the length of the tabernacle is appropriately comprehended in this number, because the entire perfection of the Holy Church principally consists in three virtues (namely, faith, hope, and charity), which are multiplied by ten to make up the number thirty when the good works which are contained in the Decalogue of the law are joined to the virtues of the mind, lest anyone should suppose that faith, hope, and love for God can be sufficient in themselves apart from the performance of works.

The fact that twenty is the number of the boards also contains a mystery of the great perfection of the saints, for the Mosaic law is comprehended in five books and the grace and truth of the New Testament in the four volumes of the holy gospels, and four times five makes twenty. Therefore the holy teachers are rightly designated by the number twenty, because by the marvelous concordance of truth they disclose the secrets of the law to be revealed and completed in the gospels, and they declare that the sacraments of the gospel were prefigured in the law. When they teach that the Old Testament has been made clear in the New and its wider meaning made manifest, and when they suggest that the New has been foreshadowed in the Old and signified beforehand by the revelation of various types,[2] it is as if in the breadth of their speech they show the number of the boards to have been both four multiplied by five and five by four.

Now the bases by which the boards were supported are the words and the books of the law and the prophets, by which the apostles and evangelists proved that the things they wrote and preached were divine and true. For this reason is it so often repeated in the gospel: *Then was fulfilled what was spoken by the prophet;*[3] and *Now all this happened so that the writings of the prophets might be fulfilled.*[4] The apostle Peter also added a testimony concerning the Lord, saying: *And we have a surer prophetic word, to which you do well to pay attention.*[5]

---

1 Josephus, *Ant. Jud.* 3, 6, 3 (ed. Blatt, 233, 6-7)

2 This way of understanding the relationship between the two testaments is found in many of the writings of Augustine of Hippo; see, e.g., *Enarr. in ps.* 105, 36 (*CCSL* 40: 1567, 9-10): 'The Old Testament you see revealed in the New, the New veiled in the Old.'

3 Matt. 2:17

4 Matt. 26:56

5 2 Pet. 1:19

Now it is appropriate that two bases are set under each board, so that the concordance of the prophetic testimony may be shown in everything that the apostles said. Or perhaps the reason that two bases are placed under each board at the two corners in such a way that the whole board, being well [64] supported at the corners, can stand upright without leaning is because the whole beginning and end of the apostolic and evangelical word is found signified beforehand in the prophetic writings, and it is well known that the whole life of the apostles and their successors, from the beginning of the faith unto the end of this present life, was included in the same mystical pages of the Old Testament. It is certainly appropriate that the same bases were made of silver, on account of the splendour of the heavenly word. *For the words of the Lord are pure words, silver from the earth tried by fire.*[1]

26:20-1 And on the second side of the tabernacle, which faces northward, there shall be twenty boards with forty bases of silver; two bases shall be set under each board. The south side of the tabernacle, which faces southward, designates that ancient people of God who, having received the light of knowledge of the law a long time ago, were accustomed to burn with the love of their Creator, but the second side, which faces northward, depicts that multitude of the Gentiles which did not cease to languish in the darkness and cold of unbelief right up to the time of the Lord's incarnation. Concerning their noble calling the Lord says through the prophet: *'I will say to the north, "Give [them] up," and to the south, "Do not hinder [them],"*[2] which is to say openly, 'I will say to the people of the Gentiles who have been freezing for a long time without faith, "Give up your children that they may come together in faith to the confession and love of me," and I will say to the people of the Israelites who have already enjoyed the light that comes from knowing me, "Do not hinder the Gentiles from being admitted into a share of election." I will say to Cornelius and his house, "Receive the faith and the baptism of Christ."*[3] I will say to the Jews, "Do not compel the believers from among the Gentiles to be circumcised, for to those who are consecrated in the font of baptism, faith and a true confession are sufficient for salvation."'*[4]

Now each of the two sides had boards of the same measurements and design, doubtless because one and the same faith, hope, and charity are preached to both peoples by the apostles; both are invited into the same

---

1 Ps. 12:6 (11:7)
2 Isa. 43:6
3 Acts 10:44-8
4 Acts 15:1-21

promises of a heavenly kingdom; both receive the Saviour's precept concerning them both: *'Go into the whole world and preach the gospel to every
creature,* '[1] that is, to the circumcised and to the uncircumcised. In the same
place it is also added without any distinction: *'The one who believes and is
baptized will be saved.* '[2]

[65]   **26:22-3 But on the west side of the tabernacle you shall make six
boards, and another two again which shall be erected in the corners at
the rear of the tabernacle.** Josephus writes concerning the tabernacle that
it was ten cubits wide; he also writes that the boards that raised it up from
the ground measured four inches.[3] From this it appears that he wishes it to
be understood that the bases of the boards themselves were made to be
precisely that high. He goes on to speak in this way concerning this section
[of Scripture] which we have just set forth, and concerning the rods for the
boards:

Now *the six boards on the back walls made up nine cubits; to them were
joined two other boards cut in half cubits, which they placed at the corners
after the fashion of the larger boards. And all the boards had golden rings
projecting through their outer surfaces, fixed to them by roots, as it were,
and facing one another [to form] a row of circles. Through them passed
gilded rods, each of them being the size of five cubits, which served to join
the boards together, the head of each rod entering into the head of another
rod in the form of a spiral, as it were. And at the rear of the long walls there
was one row extending across all the boards, by means of which the sides
of the two walls were held together with hooks, as pegs were made to be
inserted into each of them. For this reason was it so carefully [made], in
order that the tabernacle might not be shaken by the winds nor disturbed
for any other reason, but might be kept unmoved in untroubled tranquility.*[4]

Josephus [writes] these things concerning the letter of the text. According
to the allegorical sense, however, the western side, which finishes the
building of the tabernacle by receiving both walls into itself, rightly
designates the completion of the entire Holy Church universal which is
perfected at the end of this world, until which [time] faith and just works
will continue among both peoples, just as the length of the two walls extends
[to the west]. For it is not plausible either that at any time before the Lord's
incarnation there were lacking those from among the Gentiles who believed, or that now, however grievously the people of the Jews may be

---

1 Mark 16:15
2 Mark 16:16
3 Josephus, *Ant. Jud.* 3, 6, 3 (ed. Blatt, 233, 7-11)
4 Ibid. (ed. Blatt, 233, 18 - 234, 4)

damned on account of faithlessness, there are not some among them, even
if only a very few, who live in exile among Christians and come to salvation
every day by believing. If anyone will presume to deny this, let us say what
can by no means be denied, namely, that the spiritual teachers and inter-
preters of both testaments, who in accordance with the word of the Lord
bring forth *out of their treasure new things and old,*[1] are to remain in the
Holy Church until the end of the world.

Aptly is the tabernacle completed on the western side, in which it is
customary for the sun to end the day and all the stars to fall, either on account
of the death of every elect individual or on account of the collective end of
the entire world. For just as the sun falls for anyone who migrates from this
temporal light through the transitory shadows of death to the joys of eternal
light and life, and just as the sun falls in the west for the whole Church so
that it may surely rise in the east as the shadows pass away, so in the same
way, when the Lord comes [again] and the life of this present world is over,
will the morning and the true day of eternity then appear for the righteous
in the world to come.

[66]

And since the reprobate perish in eternity while the righteous are reigning
with the Lord, rightly is it said further on that this side of the tabernacle
looks to the sea.[2] Now this signifies the Red Sea, in which Pharaoh with
his host was drowned and from which Israel, having been saved by the Lord,
went up to Mount Sinai where they made the tabernacle. Therefore, the
western side of the tabernacle looks to the sea when after the perfection of
good works the Holy Church is crowned in Christ and gazes freely upon
the failings or the punishments of the impious, which [Christ] has decreed
by his own command. Isaiah bears witness to this when he says: *'For as
the new heavens and the new earth, which I make to stand before me,' says
the Lord, 'so shall your seed and your name stand;*[3] and a little after: *'And
they shall go out and see the dead bodies of the men who have transgressed
against me; their worm shall not die, and their fire shall not be quenched.*[4]
For surely the waves of the deep, brackish, and turbulent sea can signify
both the sins among which the reprobate are lost in this life when they
delight in evil, and also the pit of future perdition, when at the last judgement
they will be sent with the devil into eternal fire.

We should not forget that when the tabernacle was built on Mount Sinai
it had the Red Sea to its west, and when it was brought into the land of

---

1 Matt. 13:52
2 Exod. 36:27 (Vulg.)
3 Isa. 66:22
4 Isa. 66:24

promise and set up at Shiloh by Joshua it had the Great Sea in the same direction.[1] Mystically, therefore, we can understand by this that the saints who serve the Lord in this life and make a tabernacle for him in their hearts despise the proud boasting of the impious, confidently mindful that it is soon to pass away: when they are established with the Lord in the future homeland they shall look at the perpetual punishment of the impious without any interruption of their own felicity. Consequently, the elders give thanks to the Lord because they not only enjoy the good things which he has given them, but they also contemplate the evil things from which he has delivered them.

Now it is appropriate that the same western side of the tabernacle (or that which was said to have looked to the sea) was composed of six boards. This is either because the perfection of a good work is customarily expressed by the number six, since on that day the Lord completed the preparation of the world,[2] on that day he created humankind in the beginning,[3] and on that day he restored the human race by his own passion,[4] or because there are six ages of this world, in which it behooves us to be perfected in good works so that in the future we may be able to enter into eternal rest and the glory of the resurrection.

[67]   Another two boards again, besides the first six, are commanded to be erected in the corners at the rear of the tabernacle, coming from the eastern side to meet the wall and join it to the wall of the western side. This pertains to the reward of the life to come, which after labours will follow the time of this world, because it is divided into a twofold keeping of the sabbath, namely: the rest of holy souls after release from their bodies, and the glory of resurrection with the reception of incorruptible bodies. Both parts of this common reward are appointed for both peoples forever without end. For when the time of resurrection comes the souls' rest is not diminished at all but rather enhanced, and our spirits' union with immortal flesh continues inviolable forever in heaven. Now concerning the same boards it is properly added:

26:24 **And they shall be joined together from the bottom to the top, and one binding shall hold them all.** Doubtless this is because the entire life of the elect stretches out toward heaven with one and the same faith and charity and comes to one and the same end in the Divine Vision, and because

---

1 Josh. 18:1
2 Gen. 1:31 - 2:1
3 Gen. 1:26-31
4 All four gospels relate that Jesus was crucified on Friday, the sixth day of the week, which was also known as the day of Preparation (for the sabbath); see Matt. 27:62, Mark 15:42, Luke 23:54, and John 19:31.

every utterance of the holy preachers harmonizes in one and the same voice of right teaching. For surely there would be a gap in the binding of the boards if one prophet or apostle should deny what another has said. But the harmonious speech of the Divine Eloquences builds up the fabric of the Church; indeed, it binds all the boards of the tabernacle together into one juncture and does not allow them to be separated from one another.

26:24-5 **A similar juncture shall also be maintained for the two boards that are to be put in the corners, and there shall be eight boards with their sixteen silver bases, reckoning two bases for each board.** The boards in the corners are united with the boards of the walls in every way, because the glory of future rest and immortality is very closely connected with our present manner of life through faith, hope, and charity. Or, more precisely, the reason that our present manner of life remains stable and unshaken is because it believes in, hopes for, and loves the gifts of recompense to come, and because with the continual help of the citizens of heaven it is held together lest it should fall down amidst the stormy blasts of unclean spirits.

These boards designate either the perfection of our good action or the future rewards for good deeds. Each of them is supported by two bases because with a harmonious voice the holy prophets have predicted all these things that are to come, so that they may be confirmed by the preaching of the evangelists and apostles.

7.   THE BARS FOR [THE BOARDS] AND THE RINGS

26:26-8 **You shall also make five bars of acacia wood, to hold together**   *[68]*
the boards on one side of the tabernacle, and five others on the other side, and the same number on the west side, and they shall be stretched across the middle of the boards from one end to the other. The five bars that hold the boards of the tabernacle together are the five books of the Mosaic law, which are like a rampart wonderfully protecting the Holy Church from the pressure of every wicked temptation and every evil spirit. This [arrangement is to be] on both sides, because not only did the letter of the law educate the former people of God in faith and good works, but when it is spiritually understood with a sweeter grace by those of us who serve God in the time of the new covenant, the same letter instructs us in faith and works of virtue also in the present and incites us to the hope of eternal reward in the future.

There are the same number of bars on the west side because when it is properly understood by us the law also foretells the fulfillment of good works, when we leave the flesh for the rewards that are to come. For this reason, to the rich man who questions him and says, *'Good Teacher, what must I do to possess eternal life?'*[1] the Good Teacher himself responds, *'If you wish to enter into life, keep the commandments,'*[2] and he did not lay anything else upon him, other than the commandments of the law.

26:29 **The boards themselves you shall also overlay with gold, and shall cast for them rings of gold through which the bars [may be set] to hold the boards together.** The boards of the tabernacle shine with gold overlay when the entire life and every utterance of the holy preachers show forth the light of heavenly wisdom, and nothing is seen in them except the splendour of virtues.

Now the rings of gold through which the bars [are set] to hold the boards together designate the blessedness of life in heaven, which is rightly compared to gold on account of the splendour of its brightness, and to a circle on account of its eternity. For this same reason the Apostle says concerning it, *There is laid up for me a crown of righteousness.*[3]

Each of the boards had five rings, not because there is a fivefold division of the heavenly homeland, but because the same perpetual brightness and bright perpetuity of that kingdom is contained written in Genesis, the same in Exodus, the same in Leviticus, the same in the Book of Numbers, the same in Deuteronomy. And five rings of gold were fastened to each of the boards of the tabernacle because the hearts of the righteous, which are greatly extended through love, read in all the books of the Mosaic law not only the reproach[4] of works but also the perpetual light of heavenly reward.

And, it says, **you shall cast for them rings of gold through which the bars [may be set] to hold the boards together,** for the bars hold the boards together through gold rings when the words of Sacred Eloquence strengthen the position of the Holy Church through the promise of a heavenly kingdom, so that it is less fearful of the agitations of the world in so far as it has learned about the steadfastness of the eternal reward with greater certainty. Now concerning the same bars it is properly added:

[69]

26:29 **These [bars] you shall cover with plates of gold.** The bars are covered with five plates of gold when the words of the divine law, which according to the literal sense are seen to be powerful and most suitable for strengthening the life of the faithful, are shown to contain a higher meaning which is very bright with evangelical brilliance. For (if I may cite one

---

1 Luke 18:18
2 Matt. 19:17
3 2 Tim. 4:8
4 'reproach' = *correptionem*; var.: *correctionem* = 'amendment'

testimony by way of example), when we read in the story of holy Noah how he miraculously escaped the flood which destroyed the impious by being preserved with his household in the ark,[1] from this it is evident to everyone that the Lord who loves righteousness and hates iniquity[2] knows how to deliver the pious from temptation and to punish the impious with the punishment they deserve. Therefore a text of this sort holds the tabernacle of the Lord together after the fashion of incorruptible bars, because with words of unfeigned truth it protects the minds of the faithful from the assault of temptations.

But the wooden bars are covered with plates of gold, as it were, when through spiritual understanding this same text is shown to be full of more sacred mysteries, when the ark is discerned to signify the Catholic Church;[3] the water of the flood, baptism; the clean and unclean animals,[4] those in the Church both spiritual and carnal; the wood of the ark which was smooth and covered with pitch,[5] the teachers who are stalwart[6] as a result of their faith; the raven that went out of the ark and did not return,[7] those who after baptism fall away into apostasy; the branch of the olive tree brought into the ark by the dove,[8] those who were indeed baptized outside (that is, among the heretics) but because they have the rich oil of charity are worthy to be brought into catholic unity by the grace of the Holy Spirit; the dove that went forth from the ark and did not return again,[9] those who fly to the clear light of the heavenly homeland when they are set free from the flesh, never to return again to the labours of the earthly pilgrimage. And so the bars of acacia wood are enveloped with gold when through mystical interpretation the most powerful testimonies of Sacred Scripture are proved to be transparent to these and other such heavenly and spiritual senses.

26:30 **And you shall erect the tabernacle according to the pattern that was shown to you on the mountain.** The pattern of the tabernacle was shown to Moses on the mountain, for while tarrying in secret with the Lord he saw the sublime life of angelic purity and immortality. He was com-   *[70]* manded to organize the affairs of human life on earth according to its likeness, in so far as it could be imitated by mortals, so that with [the angels]

---

1 Gen. 6:13-19
2 Ps. 45:7 (44:8)
3 1 Pet. 3:20-1
4 Gen. 7:2
5 Gen. 6:14
6 *roboratus*: derived from *robor* ('oak-tree').
7 Gen. 8:6-7
8 Gen. 8:11
9 Gen. 8:12

as our example we might devote ourselves to mutual love in God, to divine praise, to peace in one accord, to genuine chastity, and to other such virtues on earth, and might deserve to be their comrades also in heaven according to the promise of the Lord, who says: *'But those who shall be considered worthy of that world, and of the resurrection from the dead, shall neither marry, nor take wives, neither can they die any more; for they are equal to the angels, and are the children of God, being children of the resurrection.* '[1]

In the precepts of the law, then, Moses shows us the pattern of the angelic way of life which he saw on the mountain of contemplation; through the observance of these precepts we ourselves also can be raised up from the earth and enabled to attain to the fellowship of the angels in heaven. In the figure of the tabernacle and the priestly and levitical ministry which he describes, [Moses] exhibits for us this same pattern of a more perfect life and a blessed reward. And the tabernacle is erected according to the pattern that was shown to him on the mountain when all of the elect bring intention and deed together, in imitation of the angelic purity which he deserved to contemplate in secret.

Up to this point there has been set forth as much [information] as the Lord imparted concerning the southern, northern, and western parts of the temple; now, in what follows, it is shown how the eastern side also was to be constructed. But first Scripture decreed what was to be made known concerning the middle part, which divided the holy of holies from the first tabernacle.

8.   THE CURTAIN AND ITS PILLARS, AND THE PROPITIATORY ON THE ARK

There follows:

26:31-2 **You shall also make a curtain of blue and purple, and scarlet twice dyed, and fine twisted linen, woven with embroidery work in beautiful variegation, and you shall hang it from four pillars of acacia wood.** Josephus relates that this curtain with which the tabernacle was divided was placed in the middle in such a way that the first building was twenty cubits long, and the second ten.[2] This appears to be consistent in every respect with the measurements of the temple that was later made by Solomon, which, since it was sixty cubits long and twenty wide, had a third part of its length (that is, twenty cubits) set apart for the interior building [71] (that is, the holy of holies), so that the length and the width of that same

---

1 Luke 20:35-6
2 Josephus, *Ant. Jud.* 3, 6, 4 (ed. Blatt, 234, 5-9)

interior building might be equal.[1] In the same way, then, the interior part of the tabernacle also had a similar length and width (that is, ten cubits).

Figuratively, this represents the same curtain that the Apostle declares openly to the Hebrews, in the place where he also explains properly, according to the allegorical sense, the reason that *the priests indeed continually* entered *into the first tabernacle to carry out [their] sacrificial duties, but into the second, the high priest alone, once a year, not without the blood which he* offered *for his own and the people's ignorance.*[2] This curtain is interpreted as heaven. And the priests entered into the first tabernacle with sacrifices daily throughout the year, which further illustrates the circumstances of this life, in which the saints who serve the Lord as true priests of God and of his Christ ceaselessly atone for the daily errors of their frailty (without which they are by no means able to exist in this life) through the daily sacrifices of good works and the daily libations of their own tears. But [the Apostle] understands the high priest who went into the holy of holies with the blood of victims once a year to be the great High Priest himself, of whom it was said: *'You are a priest forever according to the order of Melchizedek.'*[3] He who as both priest and victim had offered himself through his own blood once for our sins entered *into heaven itself, that he might now appear in the presence of God on our behalf.*[4]

Now the same curtain was woven from blue, and purple, and scarlet twice dyed, and fine twisted linen with embroidery work. Who does not see that the literal meaning of this also corresponds with the beauty of the heavenly vision? For if you consider the blazing splendour of the stars, or the manifold beauties of the clouds, or the rainbow which trails a thousand different colours before the sun, will you not see for yourself that they delineate pictures set in a heavenly [tapestry] of colours, which are more numerous by far and more beautiful than those which are woven into the curtain of the tabernacle?

Now the four pillars before which this curtain was hung are the powers of the heavenly hosts, resplendent with the four most excellent virtues of which we have also spoken above,[5] that is: justice, prudence, fortitude, and temperance. Surely these virtues are exercised in one way by us who are among the labours and tribulations of this life, and in another way by the angels and holy souls who are in heaven. For here, justice (and this a wholly

1 1 Kgs. 6:2, 20
2 Heb. 9:6-7
3 Ps. 110:4 (109:4)
4 Heb. 9:24
5 Bede, *De tab.* 2, 2 (*CCSL* 119A: 46, 185-90)

immortal justice) pertains to those who are seen to be subject to God who
reigns, prudence to those who set no blessing above or equal to God,
fortitude to those who hold most firmly to God, temperance to those who
take no delight in disgraceful failure; but there, where there is nothing evil

[72] at all, justice does not come to the aid of the unfortunate, as it does here,
nor prudence guard against snares, nor fortitude endure discomfort, nor
temperance curb perverse pleasures.

Now it is appropriate that these pillars were made of acacia wood, either
because the angelic spirits were created incorruptible and immortal in
nature, or because being created free from sin they always preserve the
undefiled purity of their creation. Concerning this it is aptly added:

26:32 **These [pillars] shall also be overlaid with gold, and they shall
have heads of gold but bases of silver.** Surely the pillars from which the
curtain was hung were overlaid with gold because the angelic virtues, which
are situated within the curtain of heaven, are clothed with the grace of
utmost brilliance. They have heads of gold because they are ruled by a mind
illuminated by the presence of divine knowledge and vision, and they have
bases of silver because the very foundation, as it were, upon which their
whole nature stands is that they may sing hymns of praise to their Creator
and convey the will of that same Creator to us who are still sojourning upon
earth, as if to their fellow citizens who are situated outside the curtain. For
the same reason, we on earth who rejoice in company with their praises are
accustomed to call unceasingly as if with a cry of exhortation: *'Bless the
Lord, all his angels, you who are mighty in strength and do his will.* '[1] For
in the Scriptures the splendour of wisdom is often indicated by gold, and
the brightness of words by silver.

26:33 **Now the curtain shall be attached with rings; within it you shall
put the ark of the covenant, and by it the sanctuary and the holy of
holies shall be divided.** In Holy Scripture it is often customary to use rings
to express eternity, because they appear to have neither beginning nor end.
And aptly is the curtain by which heaven is figured said to have been hung
up with rings, either because it was in the eternal counsel of the Divinity at
the creation of the world, in which the nature of heaven has the first and
most distinguished place, or else because the firmament of heaven was
made in such a way that its fashioning could never be undone. For when
the Lord says, *'Heaven and earth shall pass away,* '[2] this is to be understood
as referring to that atmospheric heaven concerning which Jeremiah says,

---

1 Ps. 103:20 (102:20)
2 Matt. 24:35

The kite in heaven has known its time.[1] For that heaven which is to perish by fire at the [last] judgement is that which is known to have been destroyed by the waters of the flood, as Peter bears witness when he says: *By the word of God heavens existed in former times, and the earth was formed out of water and by means of water, through which the world of that time was deluged with water and perished, but by the same word the heavens which now exist have been reserved for fire, being kept until the day of judgement.*[2]   [73]

Now the ark of the covenant was placed within this curtain of the temple because after his passion and resurrection from the dead, *the Mediator between God and humankind, the man Christ Jesus,*[3] who alone is privy to the secrets of the Father, has ascended above the highest heaven and sits at the right hand of the Father. The sanctuary and the holy of holies are divided by this curtain because the Church, which consists of the holy angels as well as human beings, partly still sojourns below and partly reigns in the eternal homeland above, as its citizens are still separated from another by the dividing curtain of heaven.

26:34 **And you shall put the propitiatory on the ark of the covenant in the holy of holies.** Aptly is the propitiatory said to have been put on the ark, because it was given in particular to the Mediator between God and humankind himself by God the Father that he should be the *propitiation for our sins.*[4] For this reason Paul also says: *Jesus Christ who died, yes, who rose again, and who is at the right hand of God, who also intercedes for us.*[5]

26:35 **And the table outside the curtain and the lampstand on the south side of the tabernacle, opposite the table; for the table shall stand on the north side.** The table and the lampstand of the tabernacle designate the temporal benefits of God, with which we are refreshed and illumined in the present time, that the grace of our merits might increase as a result of being strengthened and sustained by these things for a while, so that we may be enabled to come to eat the bread of angels in heaven and to see the true Light of the world. Both of these are outside the curtain, for only in this life do we have need of the Holy Scriptures, or teachers, or the other sacraments of our redemption, but in the world to come, where the Lord will tell us plainly of the Father[6] (that is, he will show us the Father openly),

---

1 Jer. 8:7
2 2 Pet. 3:5-7
3 1 Tim. 2:5
4 1 John 2:2
5 Rom. 8:34
6 John 16:25

and where, as John says, *we shall see him as he is,*[1] there will then be no
need of the external props of salvation, because God Almighty, dwelling
internally in his elect, will shine upon them as the Light of life, satisfy them
as the Bread of life, and raise them up to perpetual blessedness, leading
them into the joy of his kingdom.

Now we have said above[2] that the south side of the tabernacle signifies
the ancient people of God who were the first to receive the light of divine
knowledge and the fire of divine love, but the northern part of the same
tabernacle indicates the Church gathered together from among the Gentiles,
which remained for a longer time *in darkness and in the shadow of death.*[3]
For this reason, it is also right to make a distinction between the lampstand
that was set up in the southern part, which can suggest the grace that was
given to the former people, and the table that stood in the northern part,
which designates those benefits of God that have been given to us.

Rightly is it said that the lampstand was put opposite the table, because
the Scripture of the law and the prophets doubtless looks to the grace of the
gospel in every respect by bearing witness to it, and through this grace
signifying its own meaning in a spiritual sense.

[74]

9.   THE SCREEN AT THE ENTRANCE OF THE TABERNACLE,
      AND ITS PILLARS

26:36 **You shall also make a screen at the entrance of the tabernacle,
of blue and purple, and scarlet twice dyed, and fine twisted linen with
embroidery work.** Having completed the account of the curtain that
divided the sanctuary and the holy of holies, [Moses] reverts to an explanation about the east side of the sanctuary, which he seems to have omitted
at the time when he was describing the rest of its sides, namely, the southern,
northern, and western. Thus the screen at the entrance of the tabernacle,
woven with a lovely variety of colours, is the beauty of the primitive Church
glorified with garlands of diverse virtues, of which Luke writes that *the
multitude of believers were of one heart and one soul; neither did any of
them say that anything they possessed was their own,*[4] and so on. For blue
was certainly present in the primitive Church, because it was accustomed
to think about celestial things and to lead a celestial life while on earth;
purple was present in it, because it was ready to die for Christ; scarlet twice

---

1 1 John 3:2
2 Bede, *De tab.* 2, 6 (*CCSL* 119A: 64, 867-73)
3 Ps. 107:10 (106:10)
4 Acts 4:32

dyed was certainly present in it, because it was on fire with the love of God and neighbour; and fine twisted linen was present in it, because it rejoiced in the continence of the flesh and in chastity.

26:37 **And you shall overlay with gold five pillars of acacia wood, before which the screen shall be drawn.** The pillars from which the screen was hung are the holy teachers, of whom Luke suitably added: *And with great power the apostles gave testimony to the resurrection of Jesus Christ our Lord.*[1] As stalwart[2] as their purpose was in being raised to supernal things, they were also just as firm in their capacity of lifting others up to the love of supernal things by their teaching. For just as the apostles and apostolic men can be rightly designated by boards, on account of the wideness of either the doctrine with which they *go into the whole world* and preach *the gospel to every creature,*[3] or of the charity which they show by loving not only their friends but their enemies as well, and by bestowing prayers and acts of kindness upon those who hate them, so also are they not unsuitably figured by the name and the form of pillars, on account of their indestructible strength[4] of heart and the attention which they are always lifting up to heavenly things, as the Apostle bears witness when he speaks of *James, Cephas, and John, who seemed to be pillars.*[5]

It is appropriate that five of these pillars were made, doubtless because that is the number of books of the law, with which it is necessary for holy *[75]* teachers to fortify the words of their preaching; this applied especially to those who instructed the primitive Church. Having been gathered together from among the people of the Hebrews, it acknowledged only what could be established by the authority of the Mosaic law, since the writings of the evangelists and apostles had not yet begun to shine throughout the world.

Surely these same pillars are properly commanded to be made of acacia wood but covered with gold, so that they might suggest that holy preachers ought to be distinguished on the inside by the steadfastness of a pure heart and also on the outside by the brightness of their works, since they are lacking in nothing. Or perhaps the pillars of acacia wood are overlaid with gold when the same teachers teach that the power of their deeds is always being shielded by divine assistance, and when in everything they do they seek the glory of the Father who is in heaven, and when in everything that they say they rejoice to proclaim Christ, saying: *For we preach not*

---

1 Acts 4:33
2 *robustius*: derived from *robur* ('oak-tree').
3 Mark 16:15
4 *robur*: literally, 'oak-tree'
5 Gal. 2:9

ourselves, but Jesus Christ our Lord.[1] Concerning these [pillars] it is aptly added:

26:37 **Their heads shall be of gold, and their bases of bronze.** Surely the golden heads designate him of whom the Apostle says: *And in him all things hold together, and he is the head of the body, the Church; he is the beginning, the firstborn from the dead.*[2] And it should not seem incongruous that Christ, the Church's one Head, is figured by the five heads of the pillars. For there were as many heads as there were pillars, doubtless because the same Lord Christ himself is the head of all the saints, in himself always remaining equal and indivisible, to be sure, but distributing the grace of his Spirit to each one of those who are elect, according to their capacity for receiving. For this reason, not only to the whole Church in general but also to each of its members in particular is it permissible to proclaim with confidence that prophetic [word]: *And now he has lifted up my head above my enemies.*[3]

It is aptly consistent with the significance of this head that the same heads of the pillars are not commanded to be overlaid with gold, as were the pillars and boards, but to be made of gold, for surely the saints have all been made partakers in the Holy Spirit and in heavenly grace. Moreover, [Jesus] himself was full of grace and truth,[4] and as his forerunner [John the Baptist] said concerning him: *'God does not give the Spirit by measure; for the Father loves the Son and has placed all things in his hand.'*[5]

[76] Now the bronze bases are the prophets, whose word is confirmed by the testimony of the apostles. And [they are] properly bronze, either on account of the unconquerable confidence in the mind of the prophets, or because their word can never be worn down by old age, though the world grows old or passes away; for surely the Lord comes not to abolish the law and the prophets, but to fulfill them.[6] The pillars of the tabernacle have bronze bases, and they have golden heads, because the apostles and the apostolic men were doubtless strengthened in faith by the words of the prophets and lifted up to see the face of their Creator by a desire for heavenly things. Likewise, they have heads of gold but bases of bronze because they received whatsoever was given to them by the Lord with heavenly authority, and

---

1 2 Cor. 4:5
2 Col. 1:17-18
3 Ps. 27:6 (26:6)
4 John 1:14
5 John 3:34-5; Bede treats vv. 31-6 as a continuation of John the Baptist's speech in vv. 27-30.
6 Matt. 5:17

they understood that all these things were sacraments that had been predicted in prophetic utterance a long time ago.

10. THE BAR THAT REACHED FROM CORNER TO CORNER

Since we are speaking of the eastern side, it certainly seems appropriate to relate some other things about the description of that particular bar which we have already referred to as having been extended from the corner of the boards all the way to the corner of the other wall, and as holding all the walls firmly together lest they should be liable to be shaken and bent to and fro by the force and pressure of violent winds. Further on in the sacred history, where Moses is related to have carried out everything that the Lord had commanded, it is written that *he also made another bar to pass through the middle of the boards from corner to corner.*[1] Here, therefore, we must assume that a bar was stretched across the ten cubits of the width of the tabernacle, from the top of the boards in front to the top on the other side, and firmly positioned with a head on the boards on each side in such a way that by means of it that side of the tabernacle which rested not on boards but on pillars might also remain immoveable, no less firmly fixed than the other [side], even when the wind was blowing against it.

If you should also wish to understand the sacrament of this bar, in a figurative manner it unambiguously signifies our Redeemer himself, who passed through from corner to corner, as it were, because he reached out from the Jewish people, which he had previously chosen for himself, to make atonement also for the sake of the salvation of the multitude of the Gentiles. Hence, just as in the prophets he can for good reason be called the 'corner-stone',[2] so also in the law can he be called the 'corner- bar'; 'corner-stone', evidently, in relation to the temple which is constructed for God out of living stones,[3] and 'corner-bar' in relation to the tabernacle which is built for him out of imperishable wood, that is, out of the souls of the elect, which are free from the stain of corruption.

11. THE ALTAR OF HOLOCAUST AND ITS VESSELS

27:1 **You shall also make an altar of acacia wood, which shall be five cubits long and as many wide (that is, a square), and three cubits high.**

---

1 Exod. 36:33
2 Isa. 28:16
3 1 Pet. 2:4-8

[77]   By this altar, which was properly called [the altar] of holocaust, he designates the hearts of the elect, which are consecrated as an offering for the
sake of presenting the sacrifices of their good works to God. Aptly is it
commanded to be made from acacia wood, because it is fitting for the hearts
and bodies in which the Spirit of God dwells to be pure and incorrupt. It is
five cubits long and as many wide when all the faithful are zealous to
exercise all the senses of their bodies in length of patience and in breadth
of charity, so that in their every act of seeing, hearing, tasting, smelling, and
touching they will always remember that it is to be handed over into God's
service,[1] in accordance with that [saying] of the Apostle: *Whether you eat
or drink, or whatever else you do, do everything to the glory of God.*[2] It is
three cubits high when the same hearts of the elect stretch out toward
heavenly things through faith, hope, and charity.

27:2 **And there shall be horns at the four corners of [the altar] itself,
and you shall cover it with bronze.** The altar of holocaust has four corners
because the Holy Church (which is rightly designated by the making of one
altar on account of the single heart and soul among the whole multitude of
believers[3]) has spread throughout the four regions of the world. Surely four
horns are made [to come forth] from this altar when the hearts of the
righteous are fortified with the four often- mentioned virtues, concerning
which it is said in praise of Wisdom: *She teaches sobriety, and prudence,
and justice, and valour; nothing in life is more profitable for humans than
these.*[4] The horns are brought forth from the altar itself when the faithful
do not exhibit the fortifications of virtues only in appearance and before
other people, but instead bring them forth from the innermost root of their
hearts, with God as their witness. The four horns are at the four corners of
the altar when through the spiritual power of its virtues the Church in all
ends of the world remains inviolable against all the snares of its enemies,
or is even made stronger by all those things that fight against it.

Surely this altar is covered with bronze when a virtue undertaken by the
faithful is persistently held firmly to the end; for since bronze is a metal that
is accustomed to remain incorruptible for a long time, it is rightly able to
designate the virtue of perseverance. And with respect to the literal sense,
if anyone is troubled about how the wood of the altar was able to remain

---

1 The image is that of a legal transaction in which a slave is handed over to become the
property of a new master.

2 1 Cor. 10:31

3 Acts 4:32

4 Wisd. 8:7: the terms for the virtues in Bede's quotation from the Vulgate are the accusative
singular forms of *sobrietas, prudentia, justitia,* and *virtus*; he equates the first and last of these
with *temperantia* and *fortitudo,* which are usually found in lists of the four cardinal virtues.

unburnt in the presence of so much fire, let that person hear blessed
Jerome's reply to this question: *The woods of the altar* he says, *which are
from the trees of Paradise, are not burned by contact with fire but are
rendered more pure; nor is it any wonder to imagine that this applies to the
sanctuary and the interior parts of the temple and the altar of incense, since
also with* ἀμίαντον *(which is a kind of wood that is somewhat similar to
flax), the hotter it is, the cleaner is it found to be.*[1]

27:3 **And for its use you shall make pots to receive the ashes, and
tongs and forks and firepans; you shall make all the vessels of bronze.**   *[78]*
We should understand the diverse vessels of the altar as the different
characters of the faithful, or perhaps as their various actions or thoughts
which are placed in the service of their Creator

First it is commanded that pots should be made to receive the ashes. Now
[Moses] declares that the ashes of the victims (which ought to be taken as
a great mystery) are *the sprinkled ashes of a* red *heifer,*[2] which (as the
Apostle also bears witness) sanctified *those who have been defiled, so that
[their] flesh is made clean.*[3] He also understands that the sacrament of the
Lord's passion, which saves us by purifying us forever, is prefigured in
these ashes. Thus, the burning of a red heifer designates the actual time and
event of Christ's passion, and the burnt ashes which were kept for the
cleansing of those who were unclean suggest the mystery of that same
passion which has already been completed, by which we are daily purged
from our sins.

Therefore, all the sacrifices and victims that were burnt on the altar
indicated figuratively either the passion of the Lord or the devotion of his
saints, which was burning with the flame of charity. Rightly, then, do the
ashes of the holocausts express either the consummation of the Lord's
passion, or else the perfection in virtue that will come to all the righteous
when, having been offered to God's service through the fire of the Holy
Spirit, they have now deserved to have done with the good works themselves and to be taken up to claim possession of the rewards for those works
in eternal life.

So that this might be even more evident, let us consider what Moses says
concerning the ashes of the holocaust: *This,* he says, *is the law of the
holocaust: it shall be burnt upon the altar all night until the morning, while
the fire shall be on the same altar; the priest shall be vested with the tunic
and the linen undergarments; and he shall take up the ashes of that which*

---

1 Jerome, *In Ezech.* 12, 41, 13-22 (*CCSL* 75: 601, 1554-9)
2 Num. 19:2
3 Heb. 9:13

the devouring fire has burnt, and putting them beside the altar, shall take off his former vestments, and being clothed with others, shall carry [the ashes] out to be consumed to dust in a very clean place outside the camp; and the fire on the altar shall always be burning.[1]

Consequently, a holocaust is burned on the altar when a good work is performed with the burning fire of charity in the heart of any elect person who is devoted to God completely (that is, with both body and soul[2]). This is done all night until the morning when one does not cease to persevere in good works throughout all the time of this life, until one is taken from the body and is merits seeing the morning of the world to come. The fire will be on the same altar, because we ought to be burning with that charity alone which the Lord gives to his Church through the Holy Spirit. Accordingly, when the sons of Aaron dared to offer an illicit fire before the Lord and not that which had once been given from heaven, they were immediately [79]   annihilated by heavenly fire;[3] for those who do heavenly works not with the aim of heavenly reward but with a view toward temporal favour or advantage are doubtless stricken with the judgement of heavenly wrath.

The priest shall be vested with the tunic and the linen undergarments.[4] The priest who offers the holocaust is the Lord who is himself accustomed to kindle in us the fire of his charity, and through it to make the sacrifices of our good actions acceptable to himself. And he is clothed in linen garments when he does these things because, in order that he may excite us to works of virtue, he sets before us the examples of his own incarnation, passion, and death, which can be signified by linen, as we have frequently said.

The same priest takes up the ashes of that which the devouring fire has burnt and puts them beside the altar when the Lord imposes an end to laborious works and orders that the righteous who are taken away from this life shall no longer strive for life eternal, but shall receive in life eternal the crown of righteousness. And putting the ashes beside the altar he shall indeed take off his former vestments when he displays the good deeds of the righteous for them to remember and brings back the aspects[5] of his passion which they need imitate no longer. But he puts on other vestments, namely, those of which he himself speaks in the gospel, *'Truly I tell you that he will gird himself and make them to sit down'*[6] (that is, he prepares

1 Lev. 6:9-12
2 *et carne . . . et corde*: literally, 'with both flesh and heart'
3 Lev. 10:1-2
4 Lev. 6: 10
5 'aspects' = *habitus*, which can mean both 'character' and 'attire'.
6 Luke 12:37

himself to bestow an eternal reward and makes them to be refreshed in eternal repose). And being clothed with other vestments he shall carry the ashes outside the camp when the Lord, being prepared to reward the labour of his elect, makes it appear that whatever good they have ever done is taken away from here into that other life.

Nor is it unrealistic that the entrance into life everlasting is figured by the place situated outside the camp. For the Lord says, *'Whoever enters by me shall be saved, and will go in and go out and find pasture,'*[1] and the psalmist says, *'May the Lord keep your coming in and your going out,'*[2]— coming in, evidently, to the Church in this life, and going out into that life where pastures of eternal plenty are to be found. It is not improper, then, for us to understand that the place outside the camp is situated in that life, especially since there [in Leviticus] it is said to be a 'very clean place', which is evidently impossible to find in this life. The very clean place outside the camp, then, is the souls of the righteous who have been carried away from this life and are rejoicing in the other life.

Surely the ashes of the holcaust are consumed to dust in this place when the reward for good works is rendered there in such a way that every labour is entirely consumed, in accordance with what [is said] in the Apocalypse of Saint John. For after he had spoken of the distribution of rewards, *Behold, the tabernacle of God is with humankind, and he will dwell with them, and they will be his people, and the Lord himself will be with them as their God,*[3] he immediately goes on to speak of the taking away of all labours: *And God will wipe away every tear from their eyes, and death will be no more, nor will mourning, or crying, or sorrow be any more, for the former things have passed away.*[4] [80]

Even when the labour of good works shall cease, however, that charity by which they were effected will by no means come to an end; instead, it will be inflamed all the more ardently when the one whom we love will himself be seen forever. Therefore it is rightly added: *And the fire on the altar shall always be burning;* and a little later: *This is the perpetual fire on the altar, which shall never go out.*[5] The fire on the altar will never go out even though the holocaust is consumed to ashes, because even when labouring of every kind is completely absent, charity alone will burn forever, never to be extinguished.

---

1 John 10:9
2 Ps. 121:8 (120:8)
3 Rev. 21:3
4 Rev. 21:4
5 Lev. 6:12-13

We have spoken rather expansively about these things concerning the law of the holocaust in relation to the pots of the altar, which were ordered to be made to receive the ashes of the sacrifices. Therefore the pots receive the holy ashes when all the faithful devoutly recollect and keep in mind the examples and the sacraments contained in the Lord's passion, or else when they diligently ponder the end of the righteous who have gone before, those who have striven for the Lord in great contests and have now completed their course, who rejoice without end for the sake of the prize that has now been obtained. By thus considering the virtues of those who are greater, [the faithful] are able to become great also, in accordance with the precept of the Apostle who says: *Remember your leaders who have spoken the word of God to you; contemplate the end of their way of life, and imitate their faith.*[1]

Now after the pots, there were tongs and forks and firepans that were ordered to be made. We must assume that the tongs were made to tend the fire of the altar; hence, they rightly designate the holy preachers, who by their exhortations are accustomed to kindle in us the fire of charity, as if on the altar of God. For just like the teeth of a pair of tongs they arrange firebrands on the altar for the kindling of this fire when they instruct us in the concordant pages of the two testaments and assemble in our hearts the eloquent words of truth, by which we are inflamed all the more with a desire for eternal things. Or perhaps the priests tend the fire on the altar with a pair of iron tongs when, in everything that they teach, the holy preachers instil in us the virtue of a twofold love [of God and neighbour] and command us both to burn and to shine for its sake.

The forks, which in Greek are called 'fleshhooks',[2] were employed for this purpose in the ministry of the altar, that by them the cooked flesh of the victims might be taken out of the pots and brought to be eaten by those who were to be refreshed by it. Their function likewise corresponds to the figure of the holy preachers, whose ministry it is to refresh the souls of the faithful with the word of faith. In accordance with the apostolic principle of discretion, to disciples who are still ignorant they supply elementary doctrine, which is the rational milk without guile,[3] but they provide the solid food of more sublime doctrine for those who are more nearly perfect.[4] For all those who have learned to investigate the greatest sacraments of Christ

[81]

---

1 Heb. 13:7
2 'fleshhooks' = *creagrae*; Bede gives the Greek word in Latin transliteration, as it appears in the Vulgate at 2 Chr. 4:11 and elsewhere.
3 1 Pet. 2:2
4 Heb. 5:14

and to accept them for imitation are content to be refreshed (as it were) with the flesh of a saving victim.

Since it belongs to spiritual teachers to discern most carefully which mysteries they should impart to be heard by each person, rightly is Moses ordered to make forks for the priests, with which they could arrange the flesh of the victims as would be necessary. Some of them indeed they offered up to be eaten by human beings, but only by those who were pure; others, however, they left to be consumed by the fires of the altar. This is because among the words of God there are some which he deemed right to reveal to our lowliness so that they might serve as food for our refreshment, but others are so profound that they are accessible to the understanding of the Holy Spirit alone and utterly exceed the capacity of our comprehension.

Next, the firepans are appointed for this purpose, that by means of them the holy fire may be brought from the altar of holocaust to the altar of incense, evening and morning, for the offering of incense. They, too, plainly contain in themselves the figure of the teachers who bring fire from the altar of holocaust to the altar of incense (as it were) when they teach their hearers to advance always from virtue to virtue, and to penetrate to the higher and inmost secrets of the Divine Vision by increasing in merits little by little. But all of those who hasten to imitate the hearts of the neighbours when they see them burning with piety also become like firepans, because they are eager to kindle in their own minds also the flame of heavenly sacrifice which they see in the brethren.

All of these vessels are doubtless made out of bronze when the faithful endeavour to obey the divine precepts with constant devotion, or else when the good they do for their neighbours also resounds as being done with the clear sound of zealous exhortation. For, as we have said more than once, bronze is frequently accustomed to designate both the perseverance in the minds of the faithful (on account of the durability of its incorruptible nature) and the voice of teachers (on account of the clarity of its sound).

12. THE GRATE OF [THE ALTAR] AND ITS RINGS AND POLES

27:4-5 **And a grate of bronze in the manner of a net, at the four corners of which shall be four bronze rings, which you shall set under the base of the altar; and the grate shall be level with the middle of the altar.** The altar was commanded to be made entirely hollow, as is clearly taught in what follows, but in the middle of it there was a grate perforated all over in the manner of a net, into which was put the flesh of the victims that was to be burned. And under [the grate] there was a base upon which

[82]

wood was laid and a fire was burning, so that it was always ready to consume the holocausts that were being placed upon it. For opposite the base, on the east side of the altar, there was an opening through which wood could be inserted as fuel for the fire or coals and ashes could be taken out. We have seen this depicted in the picture of Cassiodorus Senator, of which he himself makes mention in [his] *Exposition of the Psalms*; in this [picture] he also portrays four feet on each of the altars, that is, on both [the altar] of holocaust and [the altar] of incense.[1] We suppose that he learned both of these things from teachers among the Jews, in the same way that [he learned about] the layout of the tabernacle and the temple.

In the middle of the altar of God, then, there is a grate which is ready to bear the holocausts, because the elect prepare a place for the Lord in the inmost affections of their hearts, where they gather thoughts devoted to him.

---

1 Cassiodorus, *Exp. in ps.* 86, 1 (*CCSL* 98: 789, 40-3); Bailey (1983) has shown that Bede used a full text of this work, not just an epitome such as that in Durham Cathedral MS B.II.30. Here Bede is referring to a picture of the tabernacle that Cassiodorus had caused to be placed in the Codex Grandior. A picture of Solomon's temple in the Codex Grandior is also mentioned by Bede in *De templo* 2 (*CCSL* 119A: 192, 28 - 193, 52), where, as Meyvaert suggested in Bonner (1976), 61, it is implied that he made his own diagram based on the picture he had seen. Since the late nineteenth century, Cassiodorus' Codex Grandior has been identified as the Old Latin pandect which Ceolfrith brought from Rome to Wearmouth-Jarrow, where some of its illustrations served as exemplars for those in the still-extant Codex Amiatinus produced there in the last decade of the seventh century and later taken by Ceolfrith on his ill-fated trip to Rome in 716; *Vit. Ceol.* 20 (ed. Plummer, 1: 395) and Bede, *Hist. abb.* 2, 15 (ed. Plummer, 1: 379). See Fisher (1962), Halporn (1980), Bruce-Mitford (1967), and Alexander (1978), 32-5; the latter two contain plates of the bifolium tabernacle drawing, though both misidentify it as a picture of the temple of Solomon. A line drawing appears as the frontispiece to this volume.

Many have been tempted to imagine the drawing in Codex Amiatinus as a virtual reproduction of the Cassiodorian picture Bede had before him, but Corsano (1987), 9-11, has pointed out that the altar of holocaust in the Codex Amiatinus tabernacle is depicted as open on all four sides, not just on the east as Bede describes the one in the drawing he saw. In addition, note that the Codex Amiatinus picture locates the bronze basin in front of the altar of holocaust, contrary to Exod. 30:18 and Bede, *De tab.* 3, 14 (*CCSL* 119A: 137, 1729-31). Along with some distinctively Northumbrian features, these discrepancies indicate that the artist who produced the tabernacle picture in the Codex Amiatinus was not simply copying a model in every detail. In fact, Corsano, 23, suggests that Bede may not have been looking at the original pictures in the Codex Grandior at all, but at copies of them which had been inserted in a manuscript of one of Cassiodorus' other works. In her view, the illustrations in the Codex Amiatinus were inspired not by direct contact with the Codex Grandior but rather by the text of Cassiodorus' *Institutiones*; this assumes that a copy of that work, or at least a substantial excerpt from it, was available at Wearmouth-Jarrow. In this regard, however, it should be noted that when Bede supposed that Cassiodorus had learned about the layout of the tabernacle and the temple from Jewish scholars, he seems to have been unaware that in *Instit.* 1, 5, 2 (ed. Mynors, 22-3) Cassiodorus had explictly stated the memorable fact that his informant was a blind Novatian schismatic from Asia named Eusebius.

Under the grate [the altar] has a base upon which it bears the wood and the fire for the holocausts, because these same hearts of the elect prepare a receptacle in themselves by hearing the celestial words with which they are warmed (or perhaps I should say inflamed), so that through the gift of the Holy Spirit they might render pious thoughts as votive offerings acceptable to God. For surely the priest puts wood into the base of the altar when all the teachers convey to the yearning and eagerly-seeking minds of the faithful those testimonies of Holy Scripture with which they are strengthened all the more in faith and love, and they add fire to the wood when they teach that the understanding of the word and the efficacy of pious devotion[1] are to be sought from God. Wood burns on the altar when *the charity of God* is poured forth *into our hearts through the Holy Spirit that has been given to us,*[2] and this holocaust which is placed upon the fire is consumed when everything that we have managed to do well by the grace of the Holy Spirit is rendered acceptable to God through the power of love.

Hence the grate which bears the holocausts is properly commanded to be made in the form of a net, in such a way that the fire which is set under it may penetrate freely through its numerous openings to consume all parts of the sacrifices. For in the same way it is indeed necessary in all things that we should never harden our hearts or shut them up against the grace of God after the fashion of the Pelagians. Instead, we must open them diligently and pray earnestly, as if with many doors open wide at the same time, that in all the good things that we begin or that we desire to do, as if in every piece of his sacrificial victims, [God] will deign to enlighten us with mercy and to kindle us in his love. For surely the Pelagians, who presume that they are able to achieve something good apart from the grace of God, do not set a spotted grate in the form of a net over a holy fire in the altar of their heart, but instead they set a solid wall (as it were) between themselves and the fire of the Holy Spirit, so that they are never made warm in love. [83]

Now the four bronze rings which are ordered to be made at the four corners of the altar are the four books of gospels, which are aptly compared to rings because they promise to their hearers the eternal crown of life. Aptly are they bronze, because *their sound has gone out into all the earth;*[3] aptly are they placed at the four corners of the altar, so that with the word of faith and truth they may strengthen the Church of the faithful which is dispersed throughout all the regions of the world; aptly are they fastened under the

---

1 *piae operationis;* literally, 'of pious working'
2 Rom. 5:5
3 Ps. 19:4 (18:5)

base of the altar, so that they may lift up the souls of the humble with the bulwarks of their consolation.

27:6 You shall also make for the altar two poles of acacia wood, which you shall cover with plates of bronze. The poles with which the altar was carried are the teachers who are accustomed to carry the Holy Church (as it were) as long as they either bear the faith and the sacraments of truth by preaching to those who are ignorant of them, or strengthen[1] them by confirming them in those who have already come to know and accept them. Since they do not preach their own [interests] but *those of Jesus Christ,*[2] they are *not following clever myths*[3] but are rather making known to the world the power[4] of our Lord as it is ascertained from the heavenly oracle.

Aptly are the poles put into the rings[5] so that they may be able to carry the altar; for poles to carry the altar of the Lord through rings is surely for the holy teachers to lift up the hearts of the faithful by exhorting [them] through the words of the gospel, which will not pass away even though heaven and earth pass away.[6] And there are two poles so that the word may be preached to both peoples, that is, to both Jews and Gentiles. This is also amplified further in the words that follow, when it is added:

27:7 And they shall be on both sides of the altar to carry it. For there would be teachers who would call the Jews and those who would call the Gentiles into one and the same grace of faith by concordant speech and deed. Or perhaps there are poles on both sides of the altar to carry it when the holy preachers teach the minds of the faithful to hold virtue unshaken and constant both in prosperity and in adversity, lest the former should elevate them with its charms or the latter disturb them with its alarms.

[84]   **27:8 You shall not make it solid, but empty and hollow on the inside.** The reason that the altar was commanded to be made not solid but empty and hollow was so that it might have ample room to receive the most sacred fire and the wood for the fire as well as the holocausts which were to be consumed by the fire. After this example, you too, if you wish to be God's altar, must yourself be empty and devoid of every contagion of worldly things, so that there may be in you sufficient room for the wood of heavenly words and the sacrifices of virtues, and so that you may be able to hold the fire of the Holy Spirit, with which those same sacrifices are consecrated to

---

1 *roborant*: derived from *robur* ('oak-tree').
2 Phil. 2:21
3 2 Pet. 1:16
4 *virtutem*
5 This is a comment on Exod. 27:7 (*And you shall put them through the rings*), which Bede does not quote.
6 Matt. 24:35

the Lord and brought to the sure completion of perfection. Wherefore it is aptly added in conclusion:

27:8 **As it has been shown to you on the mountain.** In that celestial conversation in which Moses remained with the Lord for forty days, he had previously perceived that the citizens of heaven were doing with unwearied and unceasing attention all the things that he [later] signified mystically to us as having been done in the construction of the altar and of the whole tabernacle. For we should not doubt that he was able to see before the throne of God that most sacred altar which Isaiah merited to see filled with the living coals of charity within, and to see the holy tongs which that same prophet saw, one [pair] of which the angel used to carry from the altar a coal with which he cleansed [Isaiah's] lips.[1] For surely sins are forgiven and gifts of virtues are granted to human beings on earth by the grace of the same Spirit with which the angels in heaven are always on fire for the love of God.

Consequently, the altar is ordered to be made hollow and empty, as it was shown to Moses on the mountain, because just as the angels and the spirits of the righteous in heaven are devoid of sins and full of piety and righteousness, so in the same way, to the best of our ability, we who are on earth should turn away from evil and do good.[2] Just as we are taught by the open exhortations of the heavenly word that this is what we should always do, in the same way [we are instructed] also by the mystical figures of the tabernacle and its vessels and ceremonies.

13.   THE COURT AND THE VESSELS OF THE TABERNACLE

27:9 **You shall also make the court of the tabernacle on the south side; there shall be hangings of fine twisted linen.** Just as the holy of holies designates that part of the Holy Church which is in heaven, and the first tabernacle indicates by means of a type the perfect life of the faithful as long as they are sojourning in this world, so in the same way does the court of the tabernacle which was on the outside represent the first principles for beginners. For this reason were the hangings of that same court properly made from fine twisted linen, because beginners must be extremely careful to curb the allurements of both flesh and spirit, in accordance with that [saying] of the Apostle which he adds concerning the children

---

1 Isa. 6:6-7
2 Ps. 37:27 (36:27)

of adoption, saying: *Since we have these promises, dearly beloved, let us*
[85] *cleanse ourselves from every defilement of the flesh and of the spirit.*[1]
For fine linen, as we have quite often mentioned,[2] is green when it is
growing in the ground, but when uprooted from the ground it is dried,
crushed, baked, twisted, and by great and prolonged effort its colour is
changed from green to white. In the same way, it is also necessary for our
flesh to subdue itself by the practices of fasts, prayer, and vigils, and by
labours of complete continence, in order that it may come to the virtue and
beauty of charity.[3] By these means we are able to dry up its natural and
inborn pleasures, so to speak, and ascend to that excellence of virtue which
we desire. And fine linen is twisted so that it cannot easily be unraveled
when the rankness[4] of the flesh is not only bound fast, but even the memory
of it is completely torn out by the roots from the inmost heart.

27:9-10 **[The court] shall be a hundred cubits long on one side. Its**
twenty pillars shall have as many bases of bronze; their heads with their
engravings shall be made of silver. It is well known that in the Scriptures
the number one hundred, which in counting on the fingers is transferred
from the left hand to the right, often contains a figure of the heavenly life,
which is as rightly preferred to the present [life] as the right hand is to the
left.[5] Surely the mystery of this number is frequently found in the Divine
Writings. Noah completed the building of the ark in a hundredth year,[6]
because in the [life] to come the Lord perfects the Holy Church which he
builds during the time of this life. Isaac, the son of the promise, was born
in Abraham's hundredth [year],[7] because the blessing of the inheritance
which is promised to all the families of the earth through his seed will
doubtless be conferred in the heavenly homeland which is to come. [Abra-
ham] himself sojourned a hundred years in the land of promise,[8] because
all of us who are made children of Abraham through faith ought to live as

---

1 2 Cor. 7:1
2 Bede, *De tab.* 2, 2 (*CCSL* 119A: 45, 135-8)
3 'of charity' = *caritatis*; var.: *castitatis* = 'of chastity'
4 *luxoria*
5 In the system of finger-counting that Bede explains in *De temp. rat.* 1 (*CCSL* 123B:
268-73), the left hand was used to express the numbers one through ninety-nine, and the right
hand began to be used at one hundred. See Hunter Blair (1977), 166-8. This interpretation of
the number one hundred, along with those that follow, is also found in Bede, *In Gen.* 4, 21,
4-5 (*CCSL* 118A: 237, 1561-75).
6 According to Gen. 7:6, Noah was six hundred years old at the time when he built the ark.
7 Gen. 21:5
8 Gen. 12:4; 25:7. Abraham was seventy-five years old when he left Haran for the land of
Canaan, and one hundred seventy-five when he died.

sojourners in the present Church in hope[1] of a heavenly inheritance. In like manner, *Isaac sowed* in Gerar,[2] (which is interpreted as 'residence[3] [as an alien]'), *and in that same year he acquired a hundredfold,*[4] because as soon as we go forth from the body into the heavenly life, we receive back whatever good works we have done while sojourning in this life as children of the promise.

This figure also [represents] the seed of the evangelical word that fell on good soil and when it sprung up bore fruit a hundredfold,[5] as well as those who leave temporal goods for the sake of Christ and the gospel, who will receive in the present [world] a hundredfold, and in the world to come life everlasting[6] (that is, the joy of fraternal fellowship now, in the hope of heavenly life, and then, that very life itself when they are together in the kingdom of heaven). The side of the tabernacle, therefore, is a hundred cubits long because it is necessary for all those who belong among the members of the Church to take the labour of temporal patience and continence upon themselves, for the sake of eternal life in heaven.

Now the pillars upon which these hangings are suspended on high are *[86]* the holy teachers. When they have drawn the hearts of their hearers away from earthly contagions, they lift them up to the heavenly things which are to be desired, carefully stretching them out like a garment for the Lord so that there is no duplicity in them, in order that they may shine before the Lord with a taut intention[7] that is single and pure, like hangings of fine linen. These pillars were bronze but covered with silver, as is said more plainly further on;[8] bronze either on account of their perseverance in virtue or on account of the sound of their preaching, but covered with silver because they utter no sound other than the word of God (the clarity of which is often accustomed to be figured by silver), and because in their lives they show forth no deeds other than the observance of the Divine Eloquences. Not only were they overlaid with silver, but they also had heads made entirely of silver, because it is properly [said] of teachers that they submit themselves entirely to the words of Sacred Scripture and subject soul and body to them by meditating, preaching, and working. For just as our members are unable to exist or to live apart from the head, in the same way

---

1 *in spe*, a well-attested ms. variant for *ipsi*, 'ourselves'
2 Gen. 26:6, 12
3 *incolatus*; Jerome, *Nom.* (*CCSL* 72: 66, 26)
4 Gen. 26:12
5 Luke 8:8
6 Matt. 19:29; Mark 10:30
7 'taut intention' = *intentio*, which can mean both 'tautness' and 'intention'.
8 Exod. 38:17

those who value their life never cease to bear the Divine Eloquences by obeying them, and to raise them up by humbling themselves.

Now, how could we understand the bases of the pillars more aptly than to say that they are the beginning of wisdom, [which is] the fear of God?[1] Concerning it the son of Sirach also says, *The root of wisdom is to fear God*; whereupon he also adds pleasingly, *for its branches are longlived.*[2] Doubtless this is because the manifold sprouts of virtues which come forth from the fear of God (just as the handiwork and the engravings of the pillars come forth from the bases) never lack the fruit of their reward. Now, the reason why there were twenty pillars on one side of the court has already been explained above, [in reference to the verse] in which that same number of boards was commanded to be made on one side of the tabernacle.[3]

27:11 **In a similar manner on the north side there shall be hangings a hundred cubits long, twenty pillars, and the same number of bases of bronze, and their heads with their engravings made of silver.** The same things are repeated with respect to the north side which had already been set forth with respect to the south side, because the heralds of both testaments raise us up to heaven with a concordant voice, although they will have different sacramental rites on account of the [difference in] times. Or
[87] perhaps we should say that all those from both peoples who attain to salvation in the time of the New Testament have not only the same faith, confession, and working, but also the same sacraments for the cleansing of sins and the acquisition of heavenly life in the grace of God through our Lord Jesus Christ.

27:12 **But in the width of the court which faces westward, there shall be fifty cubits of hangings, and ten pillars, and as many bases.** The width of the court which faces the setting of the sun, where the sleep- bringing grace of night succeeds the labour of the day which is ended, rightly signifies that time after death when the active life is over and rest follows for the elect, with an eternal reward. Accordingly, those who were working in the vineyard of the Supreme Householder[4] when evening came have at last received the rewards of their labour,[5] because when all of the righteous come to the end of this life, each of them is then allotted entrance into true life. Hence John in the Apocalypse [writes]: *I heard a voice from heaven*

---

1 Ps. 111:10 (110:10)
2 Sir. 1:25
3 Bede, *De tab.* 2, 6 (*CCSL* 119A: 63, 821-3), commenting on Exod. 26:18.
4 *summi patrisfamilias*
5 Matt. 20:8

saying, 'Blessed are the dead who die in the Lord; from now on', says the Spirit, 'they may rest from their labours, for their works follow them.'[1]

On account of this rest, the western side of the court rightly had fifty cubits of hangings and ten pillars. For in the law the number fifty customarily signifies the fiftieth year, which had been entirely dedicated to liberty, rest, and remission.[2] For that reason it was commanded to be called the 'jubilee', for surely *iobel* is interpreted as 'releasing' or 'being exchanged'.[3] It is also well known that the number ten designates those same supernal rewards, in which human nature rejoices in the presence of the Divine Vision when it is raised up to immortality in both of its substances. For God is a trinity, our body is constituted out of four elements, and our inner person is comprehended in the number three when we are ordered to love God with all our heart, all our soul, and all our strength.[4] When our seven [parts] are eternally joined to the vision of the Holy Trinity in accordance with that [saying] of the psalmist, *'But for me it is good to be near to God,'*[5] that is surely the denarius which the cultivators of the Lord's vineyard receive as a reward on the day when their labours are complete.[6] Therefore, because the holy preachers promise us the presence of our Creator and eternal rest when this life is over, and because with these promises they lift up our desires from a longing for things below to the heavenly things which are to be sought, it is as if ten supporting pillars raise up hangings fifty cubits long on the west side of the court.

[88]

27:13 **In that width of the court which faces eastward there shall also be fifty cubits.** The width of the court which faces eastward signifies the origin of our good way of life, which begins with faith. This [width] is rightly said to face eastward on account of the first perception of heavenly grace, in accordance with that [saying] of blessed Zechariah: *'The dawn from on high has visited us, to enlighten those who sit in darkness and in the shadow of death.'*[7] There were fifty cubits on this side, doubtless because all those who are being catechized are taught, as soon as they enter upon the [Christian] way of life,[8] to hope for the remission of sins and for eternal rest; for the number fifty also pertains to the remission of sins. For

1 Rev. 14:13
2 Lev. 25:10-11
3 Jerome, *Nom.* (*CCSL* 72: 67, 10)
4 Mark 12:30
5 Ps. 73:28 (72:28)
6 Matt. 20:9-10
7 Luke 1:78-9; 'dawn' = *oriens*, which can also mean 'the east'.
8 'way of life' = *conversationis*; var.: *conversionis* = 'conversion'

the same reason, the psalm of that same number[1] described penitence and confession and remission of sins, so that those who had sinned against the Lord and done evil in his sight might be cleansed when they acknowledged their iniquity, and be washed whiter than snow by him against whom they had sinned, and might again possess the joy of God's Saviour (that is, of the Lord Jesus against whom they had sinned), and might be strengthened by his princely[2] Spirit, that they might not be liable to fall any more.

Thus the eastern width of the court has fifty cubits when the first confession of faith rejoices in the remission of sins and in the hope of future rest and peace in Christ. Accordingly, in the Apostles' Creed we confess that we believe in *the Holy Church, the remission of sins, [and] the resurrection of the flesh,* which the universal synod of the later fathers wished to express more fully, saying, *I confess one baptism for the remission of sins; I hope for the resurrection of the dead and the life of the world to come.*[3] Therefore, the fifty cubits on the eastern side generally designate the initiatory rites for believers,[4] which are celebrated for the remission of sins and the hope of future blessedness. Nevertheless, there is immediately added another specific division of these [fifty cubits] which, when carefully considered, is related to one and the same end. For there follows:

27:14-15 In these [fifty cubits] there shall be hangings of fifteen cubits allotted for one side, with three pillars and as many bases, and on the other side there shall be hangings of fifteen cubits, having three pillars and as many bases. Surely it is well known that fifteen, which is the sum of seven plus eight, rightly designates the joys of eternal life, which begin [89] with the sabbath-keeping of souls and are perfected in the resurrection of bodies. For the Lord rested in the tomb on the seventh [day], the sabbath, and rose again from the dead on the eighth day, that is, after the seventh [day] which was the sabbath.

Now, that there were three pillars on the side of the fifteen cubits, with as many bases, designates the holy preachers pre-eminent in faith, hope, and charity, who set their minds most firmly on the steadfastness of the fear of God. Therefore, when you enter into the court of the tabernacle you have on each side hangings of fifteen cubits suspended from three pillars, because

---

1 Ps. 51 (50)

2 *principali*

3 The Apostles' Creed was the baptismal creed used in the western churches. The Niceno-Constantinopolitan Creed was a more fully developed doctrinal statement that in Bede's time had not yet come to be recited in the Mass; the references to baptism, resurrection, and eternal life quoted here were added in 381 at the Second Council of Constantinople, which Bede refers to as the 'universal synod of the later fathers'.

4 'initiatory rites for believers' = *initia credentium*

anyone who is about to enter into the Holy Church, and who resolves to learn about the sacraments of faith by directing a mental gaze either to the synagogue or to the church of the Gentiles, will find that in both portions of the faithful there are teachers strong in faith, sublime in hope, fervent in charity, and grounded in the fear of the Lord, who promise to their hearers the rest of blessed souls and the resurrection of immortal bodies. They suspend hangings of fine twisted linen from themselves, as it were, when by their example they teach those same hearers to seek the things that are above, not the things that are on earth, and to keep their spirits, souls, and bodies blameless without complaining until the day of the Lord.[1]

27:16 **But at the entrance of the court there shall be made a hanging of twenty cubits, of blue, and purple, and scarlet twice dyed, and fine twisted linen, with embroidery work; it shall have four pillars with as many bases.** There are four pillars at the entrance of the court because no one is able to come into the unity of the Holy Church except through the faith and the sacraments of the gospel, which are contained in four books. For this reason, in that same Church the pleasing custom has developed from ancient times that the beginnings of the four gospels are recited to those who are about to be catechized and initiated into the Christian sacraments, and at the opening of their ears they are carefully instructed concerning the figures [of the evangelists] and their order,[2] so that from then on they may know and remember which books, and how many, [contain] the words by which they ought chiefly to be instructed in the true faith.

At this entrance there is also commmanded to be made a hanging of twenty cubits, which is a number the same as four times five. Now it is well known that we have five bodily senses, namely: vision, hearing, taste, smell,

---

1 1 Thess. 5:23

2 The liturgical rite known as the 'opening of the ears' was one of the so-called 'scrutinies' of those who were being prepared for baptism at Easter; see Dondeyne (1932), Chavasse (1948 and 1960), and Fisher (1965), 5-11. There are no surviving liturgical texts from early Anglo-Saxon England, but it is presumed that those used must have contained some mixture of Roman and Gallican elements; see Willis (1968), 189-242, and (on the baptismal rites) especially Foot (1992). The descriptions of the baptismal scrutinies in the Gelasian Sacramentary 34 (ed. Wilson, 50-2) and in *Ordo Romanus XI* 47-60 (ed. Andrieu, 2: 429-33) reflect the practice of the sixth-century church at Rome, although in their present forms the documents contain Gallican elements and date from the eighth and ninth centuries, respectively. They indicate that the opening of the ears took place on a weekday during Lent (in an earlier period it would have been on a Sunday) and involved the reading of the first few verses from each of the four gospels, with an explanation of the four symbolic figures in Ezek. 1:10 (man, lion, ox, and eagle) as representative of Matthew, Mark, Luke, and John. As noted above concerning Bede's comment on Exod. 25:12 at 1, 4, (*CCSL* 119A: 16, 436-40), this differed from the Augustinian order of the figures preferred by Bede.

and touch. Therefore a hanging of twenty cubits is properly suspended from four pillars at the entrance of the court, because all those who enter into the Holy Church should order both their faith and their action in accordance with the rule of the gospels, so that they may restrain all their bodily senses from carnal enticements by subjecting them to the divine commands. Not only is this hanging supported by four pillars, but in its length it also contains the number which is five multiplied by four when any of the humble and pious hearers who come to faith are not only imbued with the words of the gospel but also expend all their bodily senses in obedience to charity, since they desire to lead the evangelical life.

[90]

Now this hanging at the entrance of the court is rightly made not from fine twisted linen, as were [those] in the rest of the court, but from the four most noble colours, namely, blue and purple and scarlet twice dyed and the same fine twisted linen, with embroidery work. This is because the exterior face of the Church does indeed shine beautifully for those who are being catechized, but its dignity and virtue will appear much brighter to those who merit to enter it through the sacrament of baptism. *For no one attains to the highest place all of a sudden,* but it is necessary for us to move gradually from the lesser things to the more perfect.[1]

We have frequently said that blue signifies the hope for heavenly goods; purple, the endurance of temporal evils; scarlet twice dyed, the ardour of perfect love; and fine twisted linen, the curbing of carnal delight. Surely these colours are made to vary from one another with embroidery work when any one virtue of the faithful shines all the more when it is in the company of the virtues near it, in a kind of familial relationship[2] [with them], as it were.

However, the individual colours previously mentioned can also correspond to individual persons among the elect. For one, who merits to look upon heavenly things at a very great height, is blue; another, who suffers many things for righteousness' sake, is purple; this one, who is inflamed with a very fervent love for God and neighbour, is scarlet twice dyed; that one, who is especially white with the innocence of virginal flesh, is fine twisted linen. And when the righteous rejoice together on account of their virtues in one and the same evangelical faith and piety, it is as if the entrance of the court of the Lord is adorned with a beautiful hanging that is woven with a diversity of varying colours.

27:17 **All the pillars around the court shall be arrayed with plates of silver, heads of silver, and bases of bronze.** [Scripture] emphasizes even

---

1 Gregory the Great, *Hom. in Ezech.* 2, 3, 3 (*CCSL* 142: 238, 53-5)
2 'familial relationship' = *consanguinitate*

more diligently the things that had [already] been said, in order to remind the reader earnestly that no one can to be reckoned among the teachers of truth (that is, among the pillars of the heavenly court) who does not learn to be like bronze by having invincible patience in the midst of adversities; who is not careful to be fortified and equipped on all sides with the observance and announcement of the heavenly words, as if with plates of silver; who does not strive to submit to the divine precepts with complete subjection, as if to a silver head; who is not accustomed to stand fast in the fear of God, as if on a base of bronze.   [91]

27:18 **The court occupied a hundred cubits in length, fifty in width, and five cubits in height.** The Church is a hundred cubits long because it stretches out its arms in good works for the sake of eternal life.[1] It is fifty in width because it hopes for eternal rest in the grace of the Holy Spirit, which he willed to designate by the number fifty when by his coming he deigned to hallow Pentecost, which is the fiftieth day of the paschal feast.[2] [The Church's] height is five cubits, corresponding to the number of our bodily senses, because at that time we each shall receive the things appropriate to what we have done in our bodies, whether it be good or evil.

But the figure in the court of the Lord's house represents only those who have done good in the body, on which basis they merit to enter into the rest of eternal life. At present, they glisten like fine twisted linen in the works of righteousness which they perform with bodies and hearts that are chaste, but when they receive the rewards of righteousness forever, they will then rejoice in the same bodies, which will have been raised to the glory of immortality. Both of these aspects are mentioned together in the gospel parable in which the five virgins who had come to the bridegroom with works of light immediately entered with him into the wedding feast, but the other five, who had not performed works of chastity with a chaste soul, were cast out far from the doors of the kingdom, being driven away along with their darkness.[3] They numbered five and five, because both [groups] were judged according to what they had done in the flesh.

Consequently, the entire length and width of the court extended for one hundred and fifty cubits, and it had a height of five cubits, because we who have received the promise of a peaceful and heavenly homeland must

---

1 As in Bede's comment on Exod. 27:9-10 above, the number one hundred is here said to signify eternal life because in the system of finger-counting known to Bede this was the number at which one moved from the left hand to the right. See Bede, *De temp. rat.* 1 (*CCSL* 123B: 270, 50-1).

2 Acts 2:1-2

3 Matt. 25:1-12

cleanse ourselves from every defilement of the flesh and of the spirit.[1] Not only must we cleanse ourselves from defilement, but we must also make perfect our *sanctification in the fear of God,*[2] so that when the hour of the promised recompense appears we may merit to rejoice in the fear of God, not only in the spirit but also in the flesh. What was said previously with respect to this cleansing of both our substances (that is, both our soul and our flesh) in the fear of God, is now repeated once again, so that it might be even more diligently committed to memory:

27:18-19 **And it shall be made of fine twisted linen and have bases of bronze.** And then there is added: **All the vessels of the tabernacle for every use and for all its ceremonies, and its pegs and those of the court as well, you shall make of bronze.** The vessels of the tabernacle which are prepared for every use and for all its ceremonies are the people in the Church who serve the Lord, diverse in merit and in rank. As we have often said before, the fact that all of its vessels are ordered to be made of bronze doubtless holds the figure of a mystery. Either [it signifies] that whenever [the faithful] are assailed by adversities they should persevere to the end, and not lose through idleness the salvation which has been promised to *[92]* them, or else [it signifies] that they should not be afraid to confess openly, even to contentious enemies, the faith which they have learned, but should remember to use the gifts that they have received to make a constant sound before their friends as well. For it is the nature of bronze, and of the sounds that it makes, to last for a long while.

Now the pegs (which it says were of the tabernacle or of the court) were made in such a way that they protruded when they were affixed at the tops of the outside columns, so that when the cords were placed upon them [the pegs] were able to support the curtains or the hangings by lifting them up from the ground. It is not inappropriate for their making and position to be designated by the very speech of the teachers, which by preaching touches the hearts of the hearers, and by touching raises them up. For there are numerous instances in which Sacred Scripture is designated by cords. Hence it is written that *a threefold cord is not easily broken,*[3]

---

1 2 Cor. 7:1
2 Ibid.
3 Eccles. 4:12. Note that the number three in this quotation leads Bede to expound a threefold scheme for the interpretation of Scripture, just as the number four in Exod. 25:26 inspired him to set forth a fourfold scheme above in *De tab.* 1, 6 (*CCSL* 119A: 24, 773 - 25, 811). As noted by Barrows (1963), 70, the shape of Bede's statements of exegetical theory is often determined by number symbolism.

doubtless because Scripture, which is customarily interpreted in the historical, allegorical, and moral senses, cannot be corrupted by the perversity of
heretics or pagans.

Now in order for these hangings or curtains to be able to receive the cords,
it was necessary for them to have loops or rings on their upper [edges], into
which those same cords could be inserted. And if you wish to become God's
hanging, you must prepare in your heart a receptacle for his words, by which
you can be raised up to the things that are above. For the cords of the
hangings are put on the pegs of the pillars so that [the hangings] may be
spread out and lifted up in such a way that they fill out the beauty of the
tabernacle: let the holy preachers impart the Divine Eloquences to the hearts
of the faithful and remind them to be raised up from the depths by [taking]
these [words] for their example. When they are stretched out and raised up
by the cords, the curtains or hangings show forth the marvelous beauty of
their workmanship to everyone far and wide, which they could not do while
they were rolled up: let the faithful exhibit the amplitude of good works as
well as the beauty of the mind and of the inner grace which they have
received as a gift from the Lord, so that the neighbours who see their good
works *may glorify the Father who is in heaven*[1] and say, '*How lovely are
your tabernacles, O Lord of hosts; my soul longs and faints for the courts
of the Lord.*'[2]

---

1 Matt. 5:16
2 Ps. 84:1-2 (83:2-3)

BOOK THREE

1. THE OIL TO BE OFFERED FOR THE LAMP

[93]   **27:20-1 Command the children of Israel to offer you purest oil from olive trees beaten with a pestle, so that a lamp may always burn in the tabernacle of the testimony, outside the curtain that hangs in front of the testimony. And Aaron and his sons shall tend it.** The layout of the tabernacle is suitably furnished with every adornment, including the light of a lamp, so that just as its remarkable beauty is illuminated during the day by the light of the sun, so is it also at night by flaming lamps, lest any place in the house of God should be dark, or any hour be in shadow. In the gospel, the Lord declares what the light of the lamp signifies according to the mystical sense, for when he had spoken through a parable, *'No one lights a lamp and puts it under a bushel [basket], but on a lampstand, that it may give light to all who are in the house,'* immediately he aptly added, *'In the same way, let your light shine before others, that they may see your good works.'*[1] Consequently, the lamp shining in the house of God is the good works of the righteous; by their examples, they illuminate the minds of those who observe them.

But we should pay very close attention to the fact that it is the children of Israel who are ordered to offer oil so that the lamp may always be able to burn in the tabernacle of God, but it is Aaron and his sons who are ordered to tend the lamp itself. What, then, is [the significance of] this distinction, that to supply light in the Lord's house the people offer oil and the priests tend the lamp, unless figuratively it is being strongly enjoined that the faithful and religious hearers are to offer hearts made ready for obedience to the faith, and that by preaching to them the teachers are to administer the fire of the heavenly word, by which they will be both illumined to know God and inflamed to love him? For surely oil designates the fatness which is used both to revive limbs that are weary and frail, and to maintain the grace of light within—these are frequently [understood as referring to] the works of mercy and the love in one's mind. Hence the psalmist [says], *But I, like a fruitful olive tree in the house of the Lord, have trusted in God's mercy toward me forever and forever more,*[2] as if to say openly, 'Because I have provided the fruit of mercy to those in need, I have trusted that God will also render the grace of mercy to me forever.' Therefore, let the children of Israel offer oil, and let Aaron and his sons bring fire to tend the lamp that

---

1 Matt. 5:15-16
2 Ps. 52:8 (51:10)

burns in the tabernacle of God. [That is to say,] let the humble hearers offer the devotion of a pious mind, and let the ministers of the word teach them the secrets of heavenly knowledge. Regularly instructed in these [secrets], let them burn in the sight of their Creator with the fire of charity, and show *[94]* forth the light of good action to those who are outside.

Now we should note that the children of Israel are commanded to offer not just oil in general, but specifically oil from olive trees; moreover, it is to be the purest [oil from olives] beaten with a pestle. For oil is sometimes made from the myrtle, sometimes from the radish plant, and sometimes from linseed or nuts, and there are other types from different kinds of things,[1] but in the tabernacle of God no [oil] is to be offered except that which is prepared from [the fruit of] olive trees, just as no fire is to burn in the holy lamps or to be kindled on God's altar other than that which comes down from heaven. *For the Holy Spirit of discipline will flee from deceit.*[2] Consequently, let the children of Israel offer oil for God's lamp; not just any kind [of oil], but oil [from the fruit] of olive trees, and let it be the purest [oil from olives] beaten with a pestle. [That is to say,] let the honest hearers offer their spiritual teachers a pure conscience that is rich with the grace of charity and thoroughly cleansed from every admixture of vileness by the pestle of a meticulous examination, which is [a conscience] that delights to hear the words of the Lord with the sole intention of pleasing and serving him. Let Aaron and his sons offer not some illicit fire,[3] but rather the fire that was sent from above to kindle the lamp, and also to consume the holocausts and to diffuse the fragrance of the incense. [That is to say,] let the teachers preach not their own word but the Lord's, that they may declare with confidence, *For we do not adulterate the word of God as so many do, but in Christ we speak with sincerity, as from God and in the presence of God.*[4] This fire they use to enlighten the hearts of their hearers with the knowledge of faith, to complete the holocausts of their own good works and consecrate them to God, and to burn the incense of holy prayers.

Now it is properly said, **so that a lamp may burn always in the tabernacle of the testimony**, because the Holy Church should never lack either the light of preaching or the pure humility of hearers to receive it gladly, or, what is even better, eagerly to seek it out.

And there is properly added, **outside the curtain that hangs in front of the testimony.** Inside heaven's curtain we have no need of the lamp of the

---

1 Pliny, *Nat. hist.* 15, 7, 24-32 (*LCL* 4: 304-10).
2 Wisd. 1:5
3 Lev. 10:1-2
4 2 Cor. 2:17

Scriptures, for the ark of the Lord is there, and the cherubim overshadow
the propitiatory of glory, that is to say, the multitude of the heavenly hosts
preach with harmonious voice the glory of the incarnate Son of God, whom
God has appointed as *a propitiation for our sins.*[1]

There properly follows, **And Aaron and his sons shall tend it,** because
not everyone is intended to preach the sacraments of faith in the midst of
the people, but only those who have proved by the purity of their faith and
the performance of good works that they belong among the sons of the High
[95]   Priest, namely, our Lord and Saviour. But even though someone may seem
to be distinguished by the name or the status of a priest, if he either strays
from the purity of the faith by perverse teaching or defiles the integrity of
the acknowledged and preserved faith with the depravity of vile deeds, such
a one will surely hear from the Lord, *'Why do you declare my judgements,
and take my covenant in your mouth, when you hate discipline?'*[2] and so
forth. James also restrains such people from tending the lamp of God (that
is, from the word of preaching), when he gives some friendly advice, *Not
many of you should become teachers, my brothers, for you know that you
receive a stricter judgement;*[3] he means that judgement to which we have
just referred, the one pronounced long ago by the voice of the psalmist. Now
there is properly added:

27:21 **That it may give light before the Lord until the morning.** For
when the night of this world is over, the morning of the world to come will
begin to shine; concerning it the prophet says, *'In the morning I will stand
before you and watch.*[4] Then we shall no longer have any need of light
from books, for the true Light of the world will appear and enlighten us;
concerning him the prophet says, *'But for you who fear my name the Sun
of righteousness shall rise.*[5]

27:21 **It shall be a perpetual observance among the children of Israel
throughout their successive [generations].** This concluding injunction,
like those previously declared concerning the tabernacle and its vessels and
utensils, must be understood and expounded in a spiritual rather than a
carnal sense. For how can the observance of the sacerdotal duties be
perpetual according to the letter, when the priesthood itself, as well as the
tabernacle in which it conducted its duties and the people on whose behalf
they were conducted, have all long since ceased to be? Hence it is obvious

1 1 John 4:10
2 Ps. 50:16-17 (49:16)
3 Jas. 3:1
4 Ps. 5:3 (5:5)
5 Mal. 4:2

that this saying is meant to be fulfilled in the Holy Church, in which there are teachers and also hearers of the truth who succeed one another in turn. For [the Church] will never lack either spiritual children of Israel who offer gifts of piety in the house of the Lord, or sons of Aaron (that is, of our true Priest) who administer the light of the word to them, until such time as the order of this world will be finished and the entire tabernacle of God itself (that is, the whole multitude of the elect) will be transported to a heavenly kingdom where people will no longer be taught by other human beings, since *God will be all in all.*[1]

2. THE PRIESTHOOD OF AARON AND HIS SONS

28:1 **Bring to yourself also Aaron your brother and his sons with him, from among the children of Israel, that they may exercise the priestly office for me—Aaron, Nadab and Abihu, Eleazar and Ithamar.** After the making of the tabernacle has been described, the priests who minister in it are subsequently ordained. Surely their ordination and vesture rightly pertain to the priests of the Church, so that everything in the adornment of their vestments there which was shining brightly on the outside is here *[96]* understood spiritually as visible deep within, in the very thoughts of our priests, and as shining abroad gloriously in their deeds, which surpass those of the rest of the faithful in merit.[2]

For this reason, Moses is aptly commanded to bring to himself Aaron his brother and his sons with him, from among the children of Israel, to exercise the priestly office before the Lord. For all those who are to be advanced to a higher rank in the Holy Church must apply[3] their minds to the law of God with greater industriousness, that is, they should be attached to the observance of the divine commandments with a mind[4] that is more astute than the rest. This implies that those who are going to exercise the priestly office

---

1 1 Cor. 15:28

2 There was a widespread tendency in early Christianity to assimilate the threefold ministry of bishop, presbyter, and deacon to the Old Testament offices of high priest, priest, and Levite; see Dassmann (1970). Nevertheless, most early Christian writers followed Origen, *Hom. in Exod.* 9, 4 (*GCS* 29: 240-4) in understanding the vestments of Aaron and his sons as symbolic of virtues requisite not for the ordained alone, but for all members of the priestly body of Christ. Bede's interpretive emphasis on the clergy follows rather in the tradition of Gregory the Great, *Reg. past.* 2, 2-7 and 11 (*SC* 381: 176-230 and 252-56) and *Regist.* 1, 24 (*CCSL* 140: 22-32), on which see Judic (1985).

3 *applicent*; another form of the same verb is used in Exod. 28:1 above, where it is translated 'bring'.

4 *animo*, but apparently without any difference in meaning from *mens*, the word used earlier in the same sentence.

are brought to Moses from among the children of Israel and that the leaders and teachers of the Holy Church transcend the common life of the elect by the exceptional eminence of their minds. By habitual contemplation, they distinguish which law was spoken to all the elect in general, and which to the few who are more perfect, so that by the higher excellence of their merits they may be able to attain to higher rewards. For when Moses is commanded to ordain his brother and his sons with him to the priesthood, what else is he mystically recommending to us except that all who are appointed to the office of teacher must cleave to meditation on the divine law with so much zeal and love that they seem to be joined to it as though they were related to it as brothers?

Now Aaron's first [two] sons were destroyed by fire from heaven, when after their ordination they offered illicit fire before the Lord.[1] This is not far from being a sign of our unhappy time, in which some who have attained positions as priests and teachers—merely to mention it is both distressing and sad enough—are consumed by the fire of heavenly vengeance because they prefer the fire of cupidity to the fire of heavenly love; their eternal damnation was figured by the temporal death of Aaron's sons.[2] Yet this is the figure of a more excellent mystery. Just as the tabernacle with its decorations and vessels designates the Holy Church which is distinguished by the quite beautiful variety of virtues or characters [found] among the faithful, so also does the high priest of that same tabernacle contain a figure of the true High Priest,[3] Jesus Christ, who offered his very self for us as a sweet-smelling oblation and sacrifice to God.[4] He also can rightly be called Moses' brother, for who could be joined more closely to another in a fraternal covenant than Christ is to Moses, grace to the law, and the New Testament to the Old? Moses himself gives a testimony of this sort concerning [Christ], when he says to the people he has been teaching, *The Lord your God will raise up for you a prophet like me from your own people and from among your own brethren; you shall listen to him,*[5] and a little later on [he speaks] in the character of the Lord, *I will raise up for them a prophet*

---

1 Lev. 10:1-2

2 Bede's stringent criticisms of the Northumbrian clergy of his day are set forth in *Ep. Ecg.* (ed. Plummer, 1: 405-23), a letter written in 734 just a few months before his death. On correspondences between Bede's programmatic call for reform and the canons of the Council of Clofesho in 747 (ed. Haddan and Stubbs, 3: 360-76), see Plummer (1896), 378-88; Thacker (1983), 150-1; and Cubitt (1992).

3 *veri pontificis*; here and elsewhere in what follows, Bede does not seem to make any distinction between *pontifex* and *summus sacerdos*, both of which mean 'high priest'.

4 Eph. 5:2

5 Deut. 18:15

like you from the midst of their own brethren, and I will put my words in   [97]
his mouth. [1]
Those wonderful works of his, which no one else has done, are rightly
compared to Aaron's vesture, which is remarkable for the marvelous variety
[of its colours]. Or perhaps the assorted vestments of Aaron designate the
whole company of the elect, which clings to Christ in a variegated diversity
of persons and merits, as the Apostle bears witness when he says, *For as
many of you as have been baptized in Christ, have put on Christ.* [2] Now if
we take it that the Lord Saviour is figuratively suggested in the person of
Aaron, what are we to say is being signified by the sons of Aaron, who have
also been anointed with him into the priesthood, unless it is the apostles of
Christ and the successors of the apostles, and all those who instruct the
faithful? Certainly these things can be taken as referring in the first instance
to the Lord, but it is more fitting for us to contemplate in them the meanings
that pertain to our pious manner of life in the Lord and that have reference
to the correction of our character.

3.   THE VESTMENTS FOR [AARON AND HIS SONS]

There follows:
28:2-3 **And you shall make a sacred vesture for your brother, for
glory and for beauty, and you shall speak to all who are wise in heart,
whom I have filled with the spirit of prudence, that they may make
Aaron's vestments, in which he may minister to me when he is consecrated.** The sacred vestments of Aaron which Moses made for him are the
works of righteousness and holiness which the Scripture of the sacred law
recommends [the Church's] rulers to possess. In [the figures of] those who
have preceded them in Christ, it shows examples of these [works] for them
to imitate. The wise in heart, whom God has filled with the spirit of prudence
so that they may make these same vestments, are the prophets and apostles
and the other teachers of the truth who quite openly show us how priests
and ministers of the altar ought to live, and in what way they ought to teach.
This they do either by the example of their actions or by their words of
exhortation, among which there is that [saying] of the Apostle to Titus, *For
a bishop, as God's steward, must be without reproach, not proud, not
hot-tempered, not drunk with wine, not violent, not greedy for filthy lucre,*

---

1 Deut. 18:18
2 Gal. 3:27

but hospitable, kind, sober, just, holy, continent, embracing that faithful word which accords with doctrine.[1]

28:4-5 And these will be the vestments that they shall make: a rational and a superhumerale, a tunic and a close-fitting linen garment, a head-dress and a sash. They shall make the sacred vestments for your brother Aaron and his sons, that they may exercise the priestly office for me, and they shall take gold, and blue and purple, and scarlet twice dyed, and fine linen. Later on, it is explained more fully how each of these things is to be made. Now the rational is a garment for the chest, the superhumerale[2] for the shoulders; the tunic and the close-fitting linen garment (that is, the shirt[3]) cover the whole body; the head-dress adorns the head, and the sash holds both the tunic and also the superhumerale quite close to the body. Underneath these six articles of clothing there is added a seventh, namely, linen undergarments to cover the shamefulness of the flesh, and an eighth, which is a gold plate on the head-dress [bearing] an inscription of the Lord's name that stands out above all the rest.[4] Now the 'close-fitting linen garment' was so called because it clung to the body and was slender with tight sleeves, in such a way that there were no folds in it at all. Because it hung down to the feet, in Greek it is also called a *poderis*, that is, a long robe reaching to the ankles.[5] With these eight kinds of vestments was the high priest accustomed to be dressed at the time for the sacrifice. Among these there were four that were also granted to the lesser order of priests: the linen undergarments, the tunic, the sash, and the head-dress. For it was only fitting that someone distinguished by being in a higher rank should also be remarkable for shining that much more in many virtuous acts. And all of these are made of gold and costly dyes, because there should be nothing vile or sordid in a priest's speech or action, but each thing that he does, everything that he says, and all that he thinks should appear excellent before human eyes, and also glorious in the sight of the inner Judge.

[98]

---

1 Titus 1:7-9

2 *superumerale*; literally, 'that which is on the shoulder'. The Vulgate uses this term throughout Exod. 28 to designate the same garment that in Exod. 25:7 was called the *ephod*.

3 *camisia*

4 Exod. 28:36-8, 42

5 'a long robe reaching to the ankles' = *talaris*, a term the Vulgate uses in Gen. 37:23 to refer to the garment given to Joseph by his father Jacob. The Greek word ποδήρης literally means 'reaching to the feet'. Bede's source here is Jerome, *Ep.* 64, 11, 1 (*CSEL* 54: 598, 4-9), a long letter to Fabiola on the subject of the priestly vestments. Jerome's commentary is in three parts: a general description of the eight vestments of the priests and the high priest, giving their names in Hebrew, Greek, and Latin; an exposition 'in the manner of the Jews', for the most part following Josephus; and a Christian allegorical interpretation.

4. THE SUPERHUMERALE

28:6 And they shall make the superhumerale of gold, and blue, and purple, and scarlet twice dyed, and fine twisted linen, variegated with embroidery work. Since it is customary for us to carry burdens on our shoulders, what is being represented by the superhumerale of the high priest unless it is the labours of good works which he ought to bear continually before the Lord? And aptly does the commandment concerning the making of the superhumerale stand in the first place, because when anyone is to be promoted to the priesthood and to ministry for God's people, his works should first be examined, so that while what is on the outside and evident to human view is seen to be blameless, at the same time the integrity of his heart and the sincerity of his faith may also receive appropriate scrutiny. Consequently, let us take the superhumerale which the high priest bore on his shoulders as that burden of which the Lord speaks in the gospel, *'For my yoke is pleasant, and my burden is light;'*[1] elsewhere he commended this to us more plainly, saying, *'If any want to come after me, let them deny themselves and take up their cross and follow me.'*[2]

Now the same superhumerale is made of gold and blue and purple and scarlet twice dyed and fine twisted linen. [It is made] *of gold, so that in the vesture of the priest the understanding of wisdom might be conspicuous in the first place before everything else. To [gold] there is added blue, which is resplendent with the colour of air, so that in each thing that he penetrates with his understanding he will be motivated not by approbation from below* [99] *but by the love of heavenly things, lest while he is foolishly feeding on his own praises he should be emptied even of his understanding of the truth itself. And purple is mixed with the gold and the blue so that the priest, while he has hope in his own heart for the heavenly things that he is preaching, may also repress in himself even the intimations of vice and oppose them as if with royal power, inasmuch as he is always regarding the nobility of his inner regeneration and protecting it by clothing himself in the habits of a heavenly kingdom.*[3] However, as we have said above,[4] the colour purple can also be understood as the spilling of one's blood for Christ, or as the endurance of various afflictions; for it is the very cross that we who follow the Lord are ordered to bear daily. Hence rightly does the appearance of

---

1 Matt. 11:30
2 Matt. 16:24
3 Gregory the Great, *Reg. past.* 2, 3 (*SC* 381: 184, 43-53)
4 Bede, *De tab.* 1, 3; 2, 2; 2, 9 (*CCSL* 119A: 11, 247-8; 46, 154-60; 74, 1265-6)

such [a colour] shine among the others on the shoulder of the priest, that it may teach him to be always prepared to suffer adversities.

Now to gold and blue and purple there is added scarlet twice dyed, that all good [works] of virtue may be adorned with charity before the eyes of the inner Judge. As all [the vestments] appear before humans with a reddish hue, so does [charity] burn with the inner flame of love in the sight of the secret Judge. Surely this charity that loves both God and neighbour shines as if with a double dyeing.[1]

But when the mind has been directed toward the precepts of charity, doubtless it still remains for the flesh to be softened through abstinence. Hence fine twisted linen is also added to the scarlet twice dyed; since fine linen comes from the earth and its appearance is radiant, what could be designated by fine linen except chastity, which glows with the beauty of bodily purity? When it has been twisted, [fine linen] is joined to the beauty of the superhumerale, because chastity is then brought to the perfect brightness of purity when the flesh is made weary through abstinence.[2]

Perhaps it is not unsuitable to say of scarlet, which shines with the appearance of fire, that it was also commanded to be made twice dyed because it is characteristic of fire to possess a double power, namely, of burning and of giving light. Surely it is fitting for one who presides to imitate the nature [of fire] when [administering] the word of saving doctrine, taking care both to disclose the light of knowledge to those who desire [that word] and by reproving the rust of sins to burn it up in those who despise [that word]. For when he expounds to his hearers the sweetest secrets of the Scriptures, whether they be the miracles or the parables of the Lord in the gospels, it is as if he is showing the brightness of light in his vesture; and when he strikes out in order [to save] the life of those who are haughty by reminding them of eternal vengeance, it is as if he is showing the terror of the devouring flame to those who are looking at him. Anyone speaking a word to the people should not apply himself solely to rebuking the offenses of the wicked, for he may be listened to less willingly if he is only arguing about the reproof of sins. Nor should he apply himself solely to laying open the secrets of the Scriptures, for if he is only disclosing hidden mysteries he may be less helpful to those whom he ought to reprove. But when he tempers his speech with both, by explaining the sweetness of heavenly secrets to his hearers and by also urging the reproof of their behaviour, through which they are enabled to become partakers of those

[100]

---

1 Gregory the Great, *Reg. past.*, 2, 3 (*SC* 381: 186, 63-9)
2 Ibid. (*SC* 381: 186, 73-81)

[secrets], it is as if the high priest is displaying in his vesture the splendour of scarlet twice dyed.

28:7 It shall have two borders attached at the top on either side, so that they may be joined together. Here is what is said later on concerning this subject: *He made then a superhumerale of gold, blue, and purple,*[1] and a little further on: *And two borders were joined to one another at the top on either side.*[2] From this it appears to have been the case that the borders of two pieces were joined together from top to bottom on both sides into a doubled garment, in such a way that half of the garment would be visible to the eyes of those looking at it from the outside while the other half would be concealed on the inside, but the joined borders of the two would come all the way down to the lowest point below. What else are we to understand by means of this type, except that while we are displaying good works on the outside before our neighbours, we must keep them unblemished on the inside before the Lord? For we must never let the innocence of a pure thought be followed by a pious action that is less than perfect; nor should we let the apparent perfection of a work be left to some extent in the lurch, abandoned by a relatively imperfect intention in the mind. But it is as if the two borders of the superhumerale are joined together with one another, when all the good things that we show on the outside are being performed on the inside with the pure and simple intention of pleasing God. And this is to be on both sides of the superhumerale, so that we may serve our Creator in the midst of both adversity and prosperity, with our actions always in harmony with our thoughts. For surely the smaller border falls short of the wider one and they are unable to meet due to the difference in their measurements if, when externally we appear to be doing good for the sake of an eternal reward, in the inner recesses of our mind we are entangled with the intention of pleasing people, and seek the rewards of human favour rather than those of invisible life.

28:8 Its weaving also and all the variety of its workmanship shall be of gold, and blue, and purple, and scarlet twice dyed, and fine twisted linen. There was not supposed to be gold in one part of the superhumerale, blue in another, and various other colours in still other parts, but when they were woven together with the gold also, all the colours were doubtless meant to be throughout. For in the activity of a priest, none of the great virtues should ever be left off, even for an hour, but the priest or teacher of the faithful should always be luminous with the gold of wisdom; he should always be lifted up to higher things with the blue of hope; he should always

---

1 Exod. 39:2
2 Exod. 39:4

[101]   be courageous against the onslaughts of vices with the purple of a heavenly
kingdom; he should always be inflamed with the scarlet twice dyed of a
double love [of God and neighbour]; he should always be shining with the
fine twisted linen of flesh that has been kept under restraint.

**28:9-12 You shall take two onyx stones, and engrave on them the
names of the sons of Israel, six names on one stone, and the remaining
six on the other, in the order of their birth. With the workmanship of
an engraver and the carving of a jeweller, you shall engrave them with
the names of the sons of Israel, in gold and encircled, and you shall put
them on both sides of the superhumerale as a memorial for the sons of
Israel.** There were three reasons why Aaron always bore the names of the
patriarchs on his shoulders and also on his breast during the sacrifices: so
that he himself might remember to imitate the faith and life of the patriarchs; so that in his prayers and sacrifices he might retain the memory of
the twelve tribes that were descended from them; and so that the people
themselves, when they saw the names of the fathers written on the vesture
of the one who presided over them, might take painstaking care lest they
should depart from [the fathers'] merits and turn away to the filthiness of
error. For this is what it means when it says, **And you shall put them on
both sides of the superhumerale as a memorial for the sons of Israel.**
Even now, the high priest wears the names of the patriarchs on his superhumerale when, in everything that he does, anyone who teaches or
presides in the Church reflecting on the deeds of the fathers who went before
him is eager to conduct his life in imitation of them, and to bear the burden
of evangelical perfection.

Aptly were the names of these fathers commanded to be engraved on
precious stones, for the deeds of spiritual virtues are precious stones. The
priest has on his shoulders precious stones upon which the names of the
fathers have been inscribed when he is himself admired by everyone for the
radiance of his good works, and when he teaches them that this same
radiance is not a new discovery of his own but has rather been handed down
to him on the authority of the ancient fathers. And there are two reasons
why he carries them on his shoulders: so that he himself may make progress
by humbly subjecting himself to the precepts of the Lord, and so that he
may always be holding out heavenly models for his hearers to follow,
whether his own or those of the fathers.

Aptly also are the same stones commanded to be set in gold and encircled.
For gold suggests either the understanding, as we said above,[1] or else
charity, because just as gold is superior to other metals, so is charity superior

---
1 Bede, *De. tab.* 1 (*CCSL* 119A: 15, 420-1; 23, 710-13; 24, 774-6)

to the other virtues. The precious stones are set in gold and encircled when the exercise of virtues is surveyed[1] all around in every direction by an understanding of such great purity that there is no defect in them that shall escape detection, no foulness in them that shall remain, and when these same virtues are held together by the bond of charity in such a way that by no mutability of circumstances can those virtues fall from their place, or slip away from his character[2] because he has become sluggish about keeping guard over his mind. And there properly follows: [102]

28:12 And Aaron shall bear their names before the Lord on both of his shoulders for remembrance. Surely the priest bears the names of the fathers upon both of his shoulders for remembrance when at every hour, both in adversity and in prosperity, as he is diligently pondering the life of the saints who have gone before, *he is always protected by the ornament of virtues, striving only after those things that lie ahead and walking (in accordance with Paul's pronouncement) 'with the armour of righteousness on the right hand and on the left', that he may not be deflected on either side to base pleasure.*[3]

28:13-14 You shall also make hooks of gold, and two little chains of the purest gold, linked to one another; these you shall put into the hooks. It says that the craftsman was to affix the hooks on the top corners of the superhumerale, and it adds that the little chains were not on the superhumerale itself but rather on the rational, that is, on its uppermost edges. They seem to have been connected by golden rings, so that when the high priest got dressed the little chains that hung down from the rational could be connected with the hooks of the superhumerale; in this way, they were linked together with one another and held firmly in place. For it is written more clearly farther on: *They made on the rational little chains that were linked with one another, of the purest gold, and two hooks, and as many rings of gold. Then on either side of the rational they put the rings; from these hung the two golden chains, which they put into the hooks that protruded from the edges of the superhumerale.*[4] But it will be better to discuss the figure of these things in the exposition of the rational.

---

1 *circumspicitur*; Bede plays this off the word *circumdatos* ('encircled') used in his quotation of Exod. 28:11.

2 *de habitu*; *habitus* can mean 'attire' as well as 'character' or 'condition'.

3 Gregory the Great, *Reg. past.* 2, 3 (*SC* 381: 182, 30-3); quoting from 2 Cor. 6:7.

4 Exod. 39:15-17

5.   THE RATIONAL

**28:15-16 And you shall make the rational of judgement with embroi-
dery work of many colours; like the weaving of the superhumerale, it
shall be of gold, blue, and purple, and scarlet twice dyed, and fine
twisted linen. It shall be square and doubled; it shall be the measure of
a span in length and also in width.** By 'embroidery work of many colours'
it means 'embroidery work of various colours'. Now just as the perfection
of works is expressed in the superhumerale, so is the purity of the priest's
heart and thoughts expressed in the rational of judgement, with which his
breast was both protected and adorned.

The rational of judgement properly follows after the superhumerale, so
that whenever it appears to humans that one is innocent in the work of one's
hands, one will strive that much more to be pure in heart when one stands
in the sight of the Supreme Judge, resolving with all industriousness that
whatever one does or decides outwardly towards one's neighbours will
shine forth in complete accordance with the standard of inner reason, and
be pleasing to one's Maker. Moreover, the priest is commanded to bear the
rational of judgement upon his breast *because the ruler should always
discern good from evil with careful examination, and studiously consider
what is suitable, for whom, when, and in what manner.*[1]

[103]

Now the rational was made doubled so that it could bear the weight of
the stones more easily. But the doubling of this vestment on the breast of
the priest of the law admonishes us by means of a type that it is the invisible
Judge within who proves the reasonableness of our examination, and
external human estimation is never right to despise it. Or perhaps we bear
the rational of judgement twofold upon the breast when those things that
we say or think concerning the true faith and the invisible life are firmly
established upon reason, and those things that we do visibly, or decide that
we ought to do, are proved to have been weighed with the balanced
judgement of just discretion.

Now the fact that [the rational] was the measure of a span on all four
sides indicates the indefatigable and constant effort of pious intention. For
anyone who measures something by the span [of a palm] surely makes a
great effort to stretch out the hand with the fingers spread apart, so that it
will be possible to determine the desired measure properly and without any
trace of doubt. Hence, just as active work is expressed by the hand, so does

---

1 Gregory the Great, *Reg. past.* 2, 2 (*SC* 381: 178, 28-31). On Gregory's use of the term
rector ('ruler') to designate one who bears ecclesiastical authority (specifically, a bishop), see
Markus (1986).

the span [of a palm] rightly express the same unbending stretching out for good works, as long as one is eager to spread out one's right hand toward every possible adornment of virtue. And the same rational is properly commanded to be the measure of a span in length and also in width, because whether a priest is raising his mind's desire toward the length of eternal life or inclining his affection to the breadth of charity evident in concern for the neighbour, his priestly heart must never be sluggish or slothful in any way whatsoever, but must always stretch out with ardent zeal to grasp *the prize of the heavenly calling of God in Christ Jesus.*[1]

28:17-21 **And you shall set in [the rational] four rows of stones. In the first row there shall be a sardius stone, and a topaz, and an emerald; in the second a carbuncle, a sapphire, and a jasper; in the third a ligure, an agate, and an amethyst; in the fourth a chrysolite, an onyx, and a beryl. They shall be set in gold according to their rows, and they shall have the names of the sons of Israel; with twelve names shall they be engraved, each stone with the name of one of the twelve tribes.** This setting of the diverse gems in the rational designates the manifold grace of the various virtues which should always appear in the heart of a priest, arranged in harmonious succession.[2] Now each one of the stones is inscribed with the name of one of the fathers when the ruler searches out the life of the saints by careful investigation, considering how they are adorned with many works of virtues, and when he is eager to gather them all together in the hidden recesses of his breast by meditating on them, and to bring them forth by putting them into action.[3]

For not without a particular sacramental reason were these two vestments   *[104]* encircled with precious stones and marked with the names of the fathers in such a way that the names on the superhumerale were inscribed on two stones of exactly the same kind, but the twelve names on the rational were inscribed on stones of diverse kinds. That [the names of] the fathers were carved on precious stones of exactly the same kind clearly signifies that the hearts of all the fathers are filled with one and the same faith in God, the

---

1 Phil. 3:14

2 Bede had also interpreted gems as representative of diverse virtues in the earliest of his biblical commentaries, where he commented on the jewels that form the foundations of the holy city in Rev. 21:19-20; cf. *In Apoc.* 3, 21 (*PL* 93: 197B-203B), especially the reference to the stones on the high priest's rational (203A). For Bede's sources in that passage, see Kitson (1983). Eight of the twelve stones in the rational of Exod. 28:17- 20 are also mentioned in Rev. 21:19-20, and Bede may have considered it unnecessary to expound the meaning of the individual stones here since he had already done so at considerable length in the earlier commentary.

3 Gregory the Great, *Reg. past.* 2, 2 (*SC* 381: 178, 22-8)

very same charity, and a common hope of heavenly life; but that they were written on stones of diverse kinds figuratively indicates that when the aforesaid faith, hope and charity of the saints have been well established, they will shine with a manifold and varied grace of good works.

Now on the rational there were four rows, and each of them consisted of three stones. What is being suggested to us by means of a type, except that we ought to hold fast to unfeigned faith in the Holy Trinity by [exercising] what are known as the four principal virtues? For surely the priest has four rows of gems on his breast when everything that he thinks has been made circumspect by prudence, constant by fortitude, excellent by justice, and free from every evil by temperance.[1] But the rows also have three gems when the same prudence, fortitude, justice, and temperance have been sanctified by faith in the Holy Trinity. Since our life in the present time consists of right faith and action, the priest aptly bears four rows of gems on his breast, so that he may be distinguished in his action, and there are three gems in each row, so that along with his works he may be pure in the sincerity of his faith. As a result, to everyone who sees him he will always exhibit both the confession of a true faith and the examples of good action, so that by imitating his right faith and action they may themselves also merit to be made members of the High Priest.

In the variegated beauty of the stones, we are certainly able to apprehend not only the multiform brilliance of the priest's action and thought, but also the charisms of spiritual virtue and the miracles of healing. Concerning them, the Lord himself says to his apostles, *'Cure the sick, raise the dead, cleanse the lepers, cast out demons,'*[2] and again, *'And these signs will follow those who believe: in my name they will cast out demons; they will speak in new tongues; they will pick up serpents, and if they drink any deadly thing, it will not hurt them.'*[3] But whether they designate the one or the other or both, rightly is twelve the number [of stones] that is commanded to be made on the rational, so that we may learn that the deeds and miracles of those who follow in the unity of apostolic faith and charity are the only ones accepted by God. There may be others who speak in tongues; there may be others who distribute all their property to the poor; there may be others who hand over their bodies to be burned; but if they do not have the unity of catholic charity, it profits them nothing.[4]

[105]

---

1 Jerome, *Ep.* 64, 20, 3 (*CSEL* 54: 611, 10-12)
2 Matt. 10:8
3 Mark 16:17-18
4 1 Cor. 13:1-4

Rightly also were the two onyx stones on the superhumerale engraved with [the names of] the same number of twelve fathers, so that they might signify that the doctrine and faith of the apostles would be for the benefit of both peoples, that is, Jews and Gentiles. This accords with that which the Lord promises openly to the spiritual Jerusalem (that is, to his Church) when he says, *'For you will make your way to the right and to the left, and your descendants will inherit the nations.'*[1]

Now since onyx is alleged to be red in colour (that is to say, sparkling like fire and encircled with white bands[2]), who does not see that it designates either the ardour of charity or the light of knowledge, accompanied by the band of chastity? The priest wears the names of the fathers inscribed on stones of this sort whenever he is following after[3] the righteous who have gone before by devoting continual zeal to charity, chastity, humility in teaching, and other works of virtue. And [he wears] them on both shoulders so that anyone who is present, whether Jew or Gentile, may regard in the teacher that brilliance of truth and piety through which [the observer] also will advance to better things.

28:22-5 And on the rational you shall make chains linked to one another, of the purest gold, and two rings of gold, which you shall put at the top of the rational, on either side; and the golden chains you shall join to the rings that are on its edges. And the ends of the chains themselves shall be joined together with the two hooks on either side of the superhumerale, which is facing towards the rational. This was the design of the work, as far as we can make it out: there were two hooks placed at the two corners at the top of the superhumerale, and there were two rings opposite them, on the two corners at the top of the rational, *from which* hung *the two golden chains.*[4] When it was time [for the priest] to get dressed, these [chains] were inserted into the hooks *that protruded from the edges of the superhumerale*—as it is written more clearly later on—*in such a way that the superhumerale and the rational were bound together.*[5] Up to this point the upper connection of these [two vestments] has been described; now there follows what Scripture adds concerning the lower [connection], which was underneath the armpits:

28:26 You shall also make two rings of gold, which you shall put on the top parts of the rational, and on the borders that are opposite the

---

1 Isa. 54:3
2 Isidore, *Etymol.* 16, 8, 3 (ed. Lindsay, vol. 2)
3 *exsecutus*, a well-attested MS variant for *expectatus*, 'eagerly awaited'
4 Exod. 39:17
5 Exod. 39:17-18

[106]   **superhumerale and look toward its back.** When it says, **and on the borders that are opposite the superhumerale,** this does not mean 'on the borders of the superhumerale', but rather 'on the borders of that other thing, which are opposite the superhumerale'—that is, on the borders of the rational, which are obviously the borders opposite the superhumerale. For opposite those rings that were on the highest and lowest edges of the rational there were other similar rings also on both sides of the superhumerale, to which they were joined by binding ribbons. Concerning these [other rings] there is subsequently added:

28:27 **And also another two rings of gold, which are to be put underneath, on each side of the superhumerale, that faces toward the lower joining, so that it may be fitted with the superhumerale.** It says, **that faces toward the lower joining,** because it had already spoken about the upper joining which was above the shoulders. It is clear that the difference between these joinings was that the upper one was fashioned with little chains, but the lower one with binding ribbons. Hence there is openly added:

28:28 **And the rational shall be fastened by its rings to the rings of the superhumerale with a blue ribbon, so that the fabricated joining may be maintained, and the rational and the superhumerale may not be separated from one another.** Now we must not suppose that both garments came to an end at the same point. The rational, which measured a span in length as also in width, was just barely long enough to cover the chest, but the superhumerale reached all the way to the girdle,[1] as is shown much more clearly later on, where it is written: *They met each other both in front and behind; in this way the superhumerale and the rational were bound together, being fastened to the sash and securely connected with rings which were joined with a blue ribbon, lest they should slip loose and be moved away from one another.*[2]

These things were spoken according to the letter concerning the connection of the superhumerale and the rational. But since, as we have said more than once, the superhumerale pertains to the consummation of good works and the rational signifies purity of thought, the connection that unites them to each another rightly indicates figuratively that industriousness of mind with which the understanding and the faith of faithful teachers is joined together with action. For **the fabricated joining** is maintained, so that **the**

---

1 'girdle' = *cingulum*; following the example of the text of Exodus, Bede uses this term interchangeably with *balteus* = 'sash'.
2 Exod. 39:18-19

rational and the superhumerale may not be separated from one another, because the ruler excels just as much in his eruditon as in his zeal
for works, so that nothing that he knows he ought to do will be left
unfinished, and nothing that he seems to be doing rightly will be deprived
of the excellence of its rectitude due to his carelessness of heart. Surely the
garments of the high priest fall down and are moved away from one another   *[107]*
if an inferior custody over the heart defiles the beauty of good work, or if
the integrity of perfect action does not follow the chastity of pure thought.
In order to keep them from being separated from each another, the priest
has on the rational two little chains of the purest gold; that is to say, he has
the continuation of pure and unfeigned love fixed firmly in his heart, and it
never allows his hand or his tongue to be out of conformity with pure reason.

It is appropriate that there are two [of these little chains], so that he may
advance properly in both the observance of divine service and the relief of
the needs of the brethren. And the work of charity is aptly expressed by
little golden chains, because just as one little chain is woven from many
golden strands, so is charity perfected from the exercise of many different
virtues. Assuredly, the Apostle describes these strands when he says,
*Charity is patient; it is kind; charity is not envious or false or puffed up; it
is not ambitious; it does not seek its own advantage; it is not provoked to
anger; it does not think evil; it does not rejoice over injustice, but rejoices
in the truth,*[1] and so forth.

Let [the priest] also have rings of gold from which those chains may hang;
that is, let him have the perpetual memory of eternal and never-ending
brightness in the heavenly homeland, for it is only by means of this memory
that continuous bonds of charity are able to remain in us. Let him have two
hooks protruding out from the corners of the superhumerale, into which the
chains may be inserted; that is, in the very beginning of every good action
let him have a firm intention of pleasing God, which is ready to be supported
and held together in everything by the love of God and neighbour in such
a way that whatever may occur, whether good fortune or bad, the most
salutary bond of pious devotion may never be undone. For surely this is
what it means for the priest to have on both shoulders hooks that receive
the little chains of the rational: for him to be zealously fixed on pleasing
God in prosperous and adverse circumstances alike, and for him to be
strengthened in this zealous intention by love for [God] himself, and for the
neighbour as well. Accordingly, the hooks of the superhumerale are inserted
into the little golden chains that are brought over from the top parts of the
rational when as soon as the rational mind tastes something according to

---

1 1 Cor. 13:4-6

the inner light of charity, eagerness to do good works willingly embraces it and takes it up; otherwise, before very long the most beautiful garment of the rational accidentally slides away from the priest's breast, unless the hook of good work to hold it together hastens to grasp it.

[108]   The two garments of the priest must also be joined together by blue ribbons that must be put into place to assist the little chains; that is, the superhumerale and the rationale are tied together by very strong bands of heavenly desire which are put into the golden rings. This is the case when, having perceived the light of the eternal homeland, we sigh for that ineffable glory and, so that we may be deemed worthy to enter therein, strive to serve the Lord in the tabernacle of the present Church in such a way that our faith is always in harmony with our life, and our work with our profession.

Farther on, when the priest is being dressed, it is indicated more clearly that the superhumerale was drawn together by a sash, for it says, *And over it he put the humerale, and drawing it tight with the sash, he fitted it to the rational.*[1] Who does not see that the guardian of good works is continence? Concerning that most faithful virtue, the Lord also says in the gospel, *'Let your loins be girded and let your lamps be burning,*[2] which is to say, 'Let your loins be girded through continence and let your lamps be burning through the exercise of virtues.'[3]

28:29 **And Aaron shall bear the names of the sons of Israel in the rational of judgement upon his breast when he goes into the sanctuary, as a memorial before the Lord for ever.** It is indeed always necessary for the priest to carry the memory of the fathers within his breast, but most especially at the time when he is going up to the altar to minister before the Lord. In that place where the ministry is more sacred, he should heed the examples of the saints that much more diligently, by cleansing himself with all zeal and adorning himself with all industriousness of mind and body, so that by proving to be an assiduous imitator of those [examples] he may show himself fit for divine eyes. Moreover, Aaron carries the names of the sons of Israel upon his breast as a memorial before the Lord for ever when every faithful leader never ceases to be concerned for those over whom he has been appointed, but is continually eager to strengthen their life by exhorting, reproving, and consoling them, and to commend them to the Lord with frequent prayers, that they may be strengthened and protected.

---

1 Lev. 8:7-8
2 Luke 12:35
3 Gregory the Great, *Hom. in evang.* 13, 1 (*PL* 76: 1123D-1124A); cf. Bede, *In Luc.* 4 (*CCSL* 120: 256, 992-5).

28:30 **And in the rational of judgement you shall put Doctrine and Truth, which shall be on Aaron's breast when he goes in before the Lord.** Whether engraved on it in writing or put into it as a sacrament, by name only, the reason that Doctrine and Truth were in the rational of judgement was so that when the high priest was clothed with that same vestment he might remember that by receiving the priesthood he had been consecrated for investigating the study of doctrine and truth, and not for conducting and examining secular business. As a result, he would take care that the external type shining forth on his vestment should be expressed interiorly in his heart. Moreover, Doctrine and Truth were put in the rational   *[109]* so that it might be clearly figured that this vestment not only clothed the high priest of the law but also foretold the high priest of the gospel, which could be the Lord himself of whom it is written, *For the law was given through Moses; grace and truth came through Jesus Christ,*[1] or perhaps his apostles, or maybe even all the heralds of that same grace and truth.

28:30 **And he shall wear the judgement of the children of Israel on his breast in the sight of the Lord always.** The priest wears the judgement of the children of Israel on his breast in the sight of the Lord when he examines his subjects' *cases in accordance with the mind of the inner Judge alone, so that he allows nothing of his own* lowliness *to be mixed with that which he dispenses as a result of his being set in a divine office.*[2]

6.   THE TUNIC OF THE SUPERHUMERALE

28:31 **And you shall make the tunic of the superhumerale all of blue.** It speaks of **the tunic of the superhumerale,** much of which was covered by the superhumerale, in distinction from the inner tunic, which was linen. In like manner, it makes mention of these [tunics] above, when it says, *And these will be the vestments that they shall make: a rational and a superhumerale, a tunic and a close-fitting linen garment.*[3] Thus the inner tunic was linen (or fine twisted linen, which is generally acknowledged to be the noblest kind of linen), but the outer tunic was all of blue, with nothing of any other colour being allowed at all. The uniformity of its appearance clearly teaches what sort of life ought to be characteristic of a priest: that is, he should be unceasingly intent upon heavenly desires alone, and (in the

---

1 John 1:17

2 Gregory the Great, *Reg. past.* 2, 2 (*SC* 381: 178, 38-41); Bede has *humilitatis* ('lowliness') where Gregory had *humanitatis* ('humanity').

3 Exod. 28:4

words of the Apostle) he should have his conversation in heaven,[1] eagerly expecting from there the coming of his Saviour.

Surely this tunic reached to the feet, as did the fine twisted linen one also; for this reason both of them were called *poderis*[2] in Greek. In this way it was shown that nothing low or sordid should remain in the life of a priest, but in everything that he does all his members should be covered from head to foot with the grace of virtues, as though they were most resplendent with the colour of the sky.

Moreover, the priest is vested in a tunic all of blue and reaching to the ankles as a reminder that all those who wish to be saved must not only make a beginning of heavenly work but must also persevere in it unto the end. For surely to be vested with a blue tunic unto the feet is to devote oneself to good works until the end of this life, as the Lord commands and promises, *'Be faithful until death, and I will give you the crown of life.'*[3] And because the only way that we can attain the perfection of good action through untiring resolution is if we have our intention fixed on a heavenly reward from the beginning, rightly is it added concerning the same tunic:

[110]   **28:32 In the middle of it there shall be an opening on top for the head, with a border woven all around it, as is customarily made on the outer edges of garments, so that it may not be easily torn.** The opening for the head in the blue tunic has a border that is very strong and woven out of itself so that it may not be easily torn[4] when it is proved that the beginning of our good action is based on the strong foundation of godly fear and well-protected against all assaults of the ancient enemy. For surely a border of this sort clothes and adorns the neck of the priest all around when it gives the ruler a very great confidence in speaking and preaching heavenly things to his subjects, inasmuch as he has not only lived rightly throughout the course of his life, but has also begun with rectitude from the very start, in accordance with the examples of the blessed prophets Samuel, Jeremiah, and John [the Baptist], who from their very infancy were filled with the grace of the Holy Spirit and set apart for the order of teachers.[5] And since the voice is indeed [located] in the neck, it is quite appropriate for the neck to depict the ability to speak.

Now when the border of the opening for the head was being commanded to be made woven all around, aptly was it immediately added, **as is**

1 Phil. 3:20
2 The Greek word ποδήρης literally means 'reaching to the feet'.
3 Rev. 2:10
4 Jerome, *Ep.* 64, 14, 1 (*CSEL* 54: 600, 10-12)
5 1 Sam. 1:11, 27-8; Jer. 1:4-5; Luke 1:13-17

customarily made on the outer edges of garments. For just as works are figured by the vestments, it is not unsuitable for the completion of works to be figured by the outer edges of the vestments. Or perhaps the outer edges of the vestments are those final acts of solicitude with which all the faithful, when we are being constrained to finish this life, strive more intently than usual to cleanse ourselves of the stain of every evil, making expiation[1] with fear and trembling. As a result, when we are led before the strict Judge we shall not be cast out on account of the unclean garment of our vices and be thrown into eternal darkness,[2] but shall instead appear clothed *as God's chosen ones, holy and beloved, with mercy, kindness, humility, modesty, and patience in the inmost parts, . . . and above all these . . . charity, which is the bond of perfection.*[3] For this is truly the wedding garment that our King and Judge is pleased to find on his spouse, that is, on the Holy Church.

But the blue tunic of the priest has a woven border on the opening for the head, as is customarily made on the outer edges of garments, when there is one illustrious teacher who begins the work of virtue with a high degree of perfection, although another one hardly ever attains to it, though he labours for a very long time; or when there is one who serves at every hour with great fear while walking humbly with the Lord his God in accordance with the word of the prophet,[4] while another is hardly capable of having that [111] much fear even when he is about to die and enter into the last judgement before his Lord. But since the complete perfection of the priest is comprised of works and the teaching of truth, in accordance with blessed Luke's comment that in writing his gospel he had composed a treatise concerning the things *that Jesus began to do and to teach,*[5] rightly is there added:

28:33 **And all around the lower hem of the same tunic you shall make pomegranates, as it were, of blue, and purple, and scarlet twice dyed, with bells mixed in between.** Surely there are pomegranates, as it were, and bells made all around the lower hem of the tunic when the priest attains to a way of life that is devoted to God with so much excellence that nothing else is seen in him but the splendour and the grace and the manifold flowering (if I may put it that way) of good works, and nothing other than their sweetest sound is heard from him when he opens his mouth. For since in a pomegranate there are many seeds on the inside covered by one rind on the outside, rightly does the pomegranate designate the multifarious

1 'making expiation' = *procurantes*
2 Matt. 22:2-13
3 Col. 3:12, 14
4 Mic. 6:8
5 Acts 1:1

exercise of virtues, which is protected on every side by the single rampart of charity.

Now it happens that the image of these pomegranates was imprinted with blue and purple and scarlet twice dyed, and (as we find out later on[1]) with fine twisted linen also; the variety of virtues is quite often suggested by these four colours. And bells are mixed in between these [pomegranates] when the priest's work is never inconsistent with the sound of the word that he speaks and the sound of his tongue never disagrees with the rectitude of his work, even when he is plagued by adversities. Here there is pleasingly added:

28:34 **In such a way that there shall be a golden bell and a pomegranate, and another golden bell again and a pomegranate.** Golden bells are surely inserted into the blue tunic of the high priest and placed around on every side when his every word resounds with the clarity of heavenly light and when that same sound is also commended to the minds of his hearers by its sublimiity, just as though it were firmly fixed in the blue tunic of works. And there are two pomegranates around every bell and two bells around every pomegranate when everything that he says is confirmed by his good actions and thereby fixed the more firmly in the hearts of his hearers, and when everything that he does, in so far as it accords with reason, is proclaimed in the distinct sound of a word. There properly follows:

28:35 **And Aaron shall be vested with it in the exercise of his ministry, so that the sound may be heard when he goes into the sanctuary in the sight of the Lord, and when he comes out, so that he may not die.** *Surely the priest dies if no sound is heard from him when he goes in or comes out of the sanctuary, because he arouses the wrath of the hidden Judge against himself if he approaches without the sound of preaching.*[2] If we are willing to pay attention to those words of Josephus in which he says that there were [*112*] seventy-two pomegranates on the tunic of the high priest and the same number of bells,[3] [we shall find that] this is consistent with the figures of the mysteries. In the same way that [the high priest] was ordered to bear the apostolic number on the shoulder and the breast, he also had the number of the seventy-two disciples distributed around his feet.[4] For just as the

1 Exod. 39:22

2 Gregory the Great, *Reg. past.* 2, 4 (*SC* 381: 190, 52-4)

3 Bede has in fact derived the information that follows not from Josephus' description of the tunic in *Ant. Jud.* 3, 7, 4 (ed. Blatt, 238, 19-21), but from Jerome, *Ep.* 64, 14, 2 (*CSEL* 54: 600, 12-13). This is a rare instance in which Bede derived an allegorical meaning from a non-biblical source, contrary to a principle he was to express several years later in *De templo* 2 (*CCSL* 119A: 193, 73-6). See Holder (1989a), 129-31.

4 Luke 10:1

number of the twelve apostles marked the beginning of the episcopal rank, it is apparent that the seventy-two disciples, who were also sent out by the Lord to preach the word, signify in their selection the lesser rank of priesthood which is now called the presbyterate. For the same reason, it is appropriate that these [seventy-two] were figured in the last part of the priestly vesture, as those [twelve] had been in the first. For it was fitting that the type of those who were to occupy a higher rank in the body of the High Priest (that is, in the Church of Christ) should have a higher place in the typic clothing of the high priest.

But if anyone also wishes to interpret the numbers in these same two orders mystically, [then we might say that] Aaron bore twelve precious stones on his breast in order to signify that there would come a time in which the faith of the Holy Trinity would be preached to the human race in all four parts of the world. Or perhaps, as we have also explained above,[1] he carried twelve precious stones (that is, three groups of four) in order to advise all teachers that they should always possess both the works of righteousness which are chiefly comprehended in the four virtues along with faith in the truth of the Trinity, and that they should also urge their disciples to possess the same.

He also bore seventy-two golden bells with the same number of pomegranates, that he might mystically show that the same faith and the same working of righteousness were going to lead the whole world from the darkness of error into the true light. For three days and nights contain seventy-two hours, and during the course of seventy-two hours this visible sun of ours circles every part of the world three times in succession as it sheds its light up above and down below. Aptly, then, was this the number of bells and pomegranates of diverse colours placed on the high priest's tunic, teaching figuratively that Christ the Sun of righteousness[2] was going to illuminate the entire world and bestow upon it the gift of true faith, which lies in the acknowledgement and confession of the Holy Trinity, and also the gift of good works, which are found in the flowering and the splendour of the various virtues.

Of course we can also understand that in the number of the twelve precious stones of the rational there is being figuratively expressed that the same Sun of righteousness is going to fill all our times and all regions of our world with his light, after the pattern of the mundane sun which is accustomed to traverse the circuit of the zodiac and to go around the entire world during the course of twelve months. For the fact that each of the four

[113]

---

1 Bede, *De tab.* 3, 5 (*CCSL* 119A: 104, 443-52)
2 Mal. 4:2

rows on the rational contains three stones corresponds to the sequence of the yearly cycle, which is divided into four seasons of three months each. Now in the Scriptures the entire year is designated as the time of our salvation, in which we strive for an eternal reward. As the Saviour himself bears witness, he was sent in accordance with the saying of Isaiah to preach the acceptable year of the Lord and the day of recompense.[1] The psalmist also sings to him concerning the same year, saying, *'You bless the crown of the year with your goodness.'*[2] For in the present time he gives them the goodness of right faith and working, and on the day of recompense he will give the crown of everlasting blessing.

7.   THE GOLDEN PLATE

28:36-8 You shall also make a plate of the purest gold, on which you shall engrave with engraver's work, 'Holy to the Lord'. And you shall tie it with a blue ribbon, and it shall be upon the turban, hanging down over the forehead of the high priest. This golden plate on the forehead of the high priest, on which was engraved 'Holy to the Lord' (or 'The Holy of the Lord', as it is related farther on[3]) was holier than his other garments, and rightly so, because just as the divine power stands out above everything that it has created, so was it necessary that its name should stand out higher by surmounting the other garments and adornments of the high priest, and sanctify them all (as it were) by occupying a prominent position on his forehead. Now this signifies the very pledge of our profession which we bear on our forehead,[4] each of us saying with the Apostle, *May I never boast except in the cross of our Lord Jesus Christ.*[5] And rightly was this the only thing in the vesture of the high priest that was made completely of gold, so that it might show forth the purity of the hearts in which we ought to recollect the mysteries of our redemption, or the purity of the bodies upon which they ought to be worn. Or perhaps the priest wears 'The Holy of the

---

1 Isa. 61:2; Luke 4:19

2 Ps. 65:11 (64:12)

3 Exod. 39:29 (Vulg.)

4 The repeated signing of the cross on the foreheads of those enrolled for baptism was a conspicuous feature of the catechumenal rites of the Roman liturgy, as was the twofold signing of the cross with chrism (once by a presbyter and once by the bishop) on the foreheads of the newly baptized; see the Gelasian Sacramentary 1, 26-44 (ed. Wilson, 34-87) and the *Ordo Romanus XI* 1-105 (ed. Andrieu, 2: 417-47). Cf. the early ninth-century Irish Stowe Missal fol. 46v-59 (ed. Warner, 32: 24-33), which has only one post-baptismal anointing (by a presbyter), but also calls for the sign of the cross to be made upon the right hand of the newly baptized.

5 Gal. 6:14

Lord' inscribed in gold on his forehead so that he might mystically suggest
that we should venerate and embrace the passion of our Lord and Saviour
through which we have been redeemed in such a way that we recognize in
it the brightness of the divine majesty through which we were created, and
which it is equally necessary for us to confess. Furthermore, [the high priest
was suggesting] that we confess the death of the humanity assumed by [our
Lord] in such a way that we acknowledge that the same humanity immediately rose again from death unto eternal glory.

Now 'The Holy of the Lord', which is ordered to be engraved on the
plate, signifies his holy and venerable name, which among the Hebrews is
accustomed to be written with four vowel letters, that is, with *ioth*, *he*, *vav*,
and *he*; the interpretation of these sounds is ineffable in their language,[1] not
because it cannot be spoken but because it cannot be comprehended by the
understanding or the intellect of any creature. And since there is nothing
that can worthily be said concerning [his name], on that account is it quite   *[114]*
rightly said to be ineffable, in accordance with that [saying] of the Apostle,
And the peace of God which surpasses all understanding;[2] the psalmist also
says, *Great is the Lord, and greatly to be praised, and of his greatness there
is no end.*[3]

Properly was the same name of the Lord inscribed on the forehead of the
high priest with four letters, in order to signify the same number of parts of
the Lord's cross which we were going to bear on our foreheads, that is, the
upper, the lower, the right, and the left. Moreover, we bear 'The Holy of
the Lord' engraved in gold on our foreheads when we are purged of the
uncleanness of the vices which we inherited from our first parent [Adam],
and receive in ourselves the image and likeness of our Creator, in which we
have been created. We do not conceal in secret the fact that we have received
it, but we openly make it known to everyone by word and deed, in
accordance with that [saying] of the Apostle: *Just as we have borne the
image of the earthly [man], let us also bear the image of the heavenly
[man].*[4] He explains this even more clearly when he speaks to the Colos-
sians, saying, *But now you must also put away all anger, indignation,
malice, blasphemy, filthy speech from your mouth. Do not lie to one*

---

1 Jerome, *Ep.* 64, 17, 1 (*CSEL* 54: 604, 16-18). In Hebrew the Tetragrammaton is actually
comprised of four consonants; Jerome simply says that it is written 'in four letters'. Bede may
have been confused about this due to his lack of firsthand knowledge of Hebrew, on which
see Sutcliffe (1935).

2 Phil. 4:7

3 Ps. 145:3 (144:3)

4 1 Cor. 15:49

another, since you have stripped yourselves of the old man with his deeds, and have put on the new, which is being renewed in knowledge according to the image of the one who created him.[1] In the Apocalypse, John also writes of this [inscription], namely, 'The Holy of the Lord', saying, *I saw the Lamb standing on Mount Zion, and with him were one hundred forty-four thousand who had his name and his Father's name written on their foreheads.*[2] Once again, in describing the brightness of the heavenly homeland, he says, *And the throne of God and of the Lamb will be in it, and his servants will serve him, and they will see his face, and his name will be on their foreheads.*[3] Consequently, since all of those who follow the Lamb (that is, all the faithful) ought to have this same most sacred and venerable name on the very forehead of their profession, how much more necessary must it be for those chosen for leadership of the Lord's flock, having received the priesthood and the spiritual office of teaching, to exhibit in themselves an example of virtue for all?

Now the plate containing 'The Holy of the Lord' is tied to the turban of the high priest with a blue ribbon when we are greatly strengthened in our faith by the hope for heavenly rewards which is designated by [the colour] blue. Therefore, we shall strive all the more intently to keep undefiled that which we know to be the only way of salvation, [which we can understand as] either the sacraments of our redemption or the image and likeness of our Creator and Redeemer.

[115]   We shall speak about the figure of the turban later on, in its own proper place. But because a priest ought to be so industrious that he is able to correct and chastise the sins of the people by his exhortation, rebuke, and admonition, and so deserving before God that he is able to wash them away with his prayers, rightly is there added:

28:38 **And Aaron shall bear the guilt of those things that they will offer and sanctify among the children of Israel in all their gifts and offerings.** Surely the high priest bears the guilt of his subjects (that is, he bears it away and removes it) when his teaching calls them to repent of their transgressions, or when he procures the favour of the righteous Judge toward those who are penitent by making supplication for his grace. And he does this in the gifts and offerings that they will offer and sanctify to the Lord when he absolves the penitent from the guilt of the evil deeds they have previously committed, for the sake of the fruits worthy of repentance[4]

---

1 Col. 3:8-10
2 Rev. 14:1
3 Rev. 22:3-4
4 Matt. 3:8; Luke 3:8

(that is, the alms and the other works of righteousness) which they will produce. All these things are to be carried out in this way by divine institution, as has been mystically figured in the vesture of the high priest and also openly taught in the words of Sacred Eloquence.

Sadly, the actions of certain ones who preside [in the Church] are far different from this. They are willing to accept—and even to demand!— gifts and offerings from the people, but they do not bother to labour on their behalf, that their guilt may be carried away and rebuked and pardoned. The only justification they have for taking temporal gifts from their subjects is that they have guided them away from error by preaching about eternal goods and have led them back to the way of truth, in imitation of the first teachers in the Holy Church, who confidently said to those from whom they were receiving temporal support, *If we have sown spiritual things among you, is it too much if we reap your material things?*[1] But because anyone who presides or any minister of the word, whether he is preaching or making supplication to the Lord, can only be effectual in his labours on his subjects' behalf if his soul is always endowed with the memory of the Divine Name, there follows:

28:38 **And the plate shall always be on his forehead, in order that the Lord may be kindly disposed toward them.** The Lord will be kindly disposed toward the children of Israel if the plate with the name of the Lord will always be on Aaron's forehead, because when the teacher faithfully subjects himself to the divine service with a pure mind, then those who are subject to his example and who wait upon his counsel are also themselves fired with zeal to live rightly, and to merit the grace of the internal Observer.

8.   THE FINE LINEN TUNIC, THE TURBAN,
      AND THE SASH

28:39 **And you shall bind the tunic with fine linen.** This is the inner tunic, which above is called *a close-fitting linen garment.*[2] We have already explained above the reason that it was called 'a close-fitting linen garment' or commanded to be bound with fine linen.[3] Now we should add that *soldiers are accustomed to have linen garments called 'camisias' which are fitted to their limbs and bound close to their bodies in such a way that whether they are on the march or in battle they are ready to throw a javelin,*   *[116]*

---

1 1 Cor. 9:11
2 Exod. 28:4
3 Bede, *De tab.* 3, 3; 3, 6 (*CCSL* 119A: 98, 201-4; 109, 638-49)

hold a shield, or brandish a sword wherever necessity demands;[1] we read that when Joab killed Amasa he was wearing something of this sort, namely, a close-fitting garment that was as long as the rest of his attire.[2] *Accordingly, the priests also wore this tunic when they were prepared for the ministry of God, so that clothed in vestments of simple beauty they could run with quickness.*[3]

Because this tunic, like the blue one, reached to the feet, it too was called in Greek *poderis*, that is, a long robe reaching to the ankles.[4] The mystical significance of this is clear, for we have already agreed that linen or fine linen signifies the continence and chastity of our body, in accordance with what we have frequently explained above. Priests have a close-fitting linen garment or a tunic of fine linen when they never weaken or mentally waver in their intention to remain continent, but maintain it with such constancy that the concupiscent flesh never makes war against the spirit, or the spirit against the flesh.[5] They have a close-fitting linen garment when their soul longs and faints for the courts of the Lord so completely that their heart and their flesh are mutually allied with one another, rejoicing together in the living God.[6]

This linen [tunic] is not only a close-fitting garment but also a *poderis*, that is, one that hangs down to the feet, when continence is not imposed upon any one member by force but is rather accomplished with the willing cooperation of the whole body. For surely this linen garment ought to bind the hands and arms of the priest, lest they should do anything that is not suitable; the breast, lest it should think something vain; the belly, lest it should presume to make a glutton of itself by seeking pleasures beyond the limit set by God; the members located beneath the belly, lest they should mar the beauty of the entire priestly vesture by being lascivious; the knees, lest they should become stiff from their constancy in prayer; the legs and feet, lest they should run toward evil. Therefore, let the priest first be clothed with a close-fitting linen garment, so that he may restrain his body from wicked deeds and his mind from improper thoughts; then let him also receive a blue [tunic], so that after the salutary discipline of continence he may beautify both body and soul alike by the practice[7] of spiritual virtues.

---

1 Jerome, *Ep.* 64, 11, 2 (*CSEL* 54: 598, 10-13)

2 2 Sam. 20:8

3 Jerome, *Ep.* 64, 11, 2 (*CSEL* 54: 598, 13-15)

4 'a long robe reaching to the ankles' = *talaris*. The Greek word ποδήρης literally means 'reaching to the feet'.

5 Gal 5:17

6 Ps. 84:2 (83:3)

7 *habitu*, which can also mean 'garment' or 'vesture'.

But since four of the five bodily senses (sight, hearing, taste, and smell) are proper to the head and the last (touch) is common to the whole body, this tunic of which we have been speaking properly designates both the conti- *[117]* nence and the righteousness of touch. Consequently, the innocence that we are supposed to preserve in the other four senses, or the sanctification of them that we are supposed to seek, is figuratively shown in the vesture of the high priest when it is said:

28:39 **And you shall make a fine linen turban.** Surely the turban,[1] which is also called a head-dress[2] or mitre,[3] covers and adorns the head of the high priest so that he may be admonished by this garment to consecrate all the senses of his head to God, lest his eyes should look at vanity,[4] or his ears take up a reproach against his neighbour[5] by willingly listening [to the same], or his mouth be filled with vileness and his tongue frame deceit;[6] lest his heart should be weighed down with intoxication and drunkenness,[7] or his sense of smell embrace the couch of a harlot perfumed with myrrh, aloes, and cinnamon.[8] On the contrary, let his eyes be looking at equity;[9] let his ears be inclined to hear the words of prudence;[10] let the eloquences of the Lord be sweeter in his throat than honey and the honeycomb;[11] as long as breath remains in him, let him neither speak iniquity nor depart from his innocence.[12] And with regard to the fifth sense, which is common to the whole body, let him be careful to fulfill that prophetic [command]: *'Depart, depart, go out from there; touch no unclean thing.'*[13] As the Apostle admonishes, *Let us cleanse ourselves from every defilement of the flesh and of the spirit, making sanctification perfect in the fear of God.*[14]

Now Josephus explains how this turban was made when he says: *And upon the head he wears a cap in the manner of a little skull-cap or helmet, which is stretched over the top of the head and extends slightly beyond the*

---

1 *tiara*
2 *cidaris*
3 *mitre*
4 Ps. 119:37 (118:37)
5 Ps. 15:3 (14:3)
6 Ps. 50:19 (49:19)
7 Luke 21:34
8 Prov. 7:17
9 Ps. 17:2 (16:2)
10 Prov. 1:2 (1:3); 5:1
11 Ps. 119:103 (118:103)
12 Job 27:3-5
13 Isa. 52:11
14 2 Cor. 7:1

middle of the crown. It is made in such a way that it appears to be of woven linen, for its wrapped bands are joined together repeatedly so that it cannot easily slip off.[1] This same Josephus relates that over this cap there was added another larger veil which covered *the entire surface of the head, adjusted perfectly lest it should fall off as the priest was working around the sacrifices;*[2] however, he does not indicate what colour it was. These things have to do with the turban of the lesser priest, but concerning that of the high priest he testifies in this way: *Now the high priest has a cap made in the same fashion as that of the rest of the priests, and another one stitched with blue embroidery. Encircled around it there is a golden crown made with three* tiers, *upon which there sprouts in the middle of the forehead something like a certain small golden calyx, similar to that of the plant that among us is called* 'thistle', *which the Greeks call* 'henbane'.[3] A little later he added descriptions of the marvelous variety [of its appearance], saying, *Now it has a flower similar to that of a plantain, and round about the whole crown it is engraved with these flowers, from the back of the head to both temples. It does not have this on the forehead, however; instead, there is a plate of gold on which the name of God is inscribed with the sacred letters.*[4]

[118]

Holy Scripture seems to be silent about these things concerning the second veil and the golden crowns of the high priest. Subsequently, it did briefly make mention of the crowns, saying, *They also made the tunics with woven work, for Aaron and his sons, and the mitres with their little crowns of fine linen,*[5] but it did not say from what material they were made. For when it says, *and the mitres with their little crowns of fine linen,* it would be possible for us to understand that both of them had been made from fine linen, if Josephus had not indicated that the crowns were of gold. When the temple was still standing and the ceremonies of the law were still being celebrated, it was very easy for [Josephus], since he was of priestly descent, to learn all about the priestly mode of dress, not merely by reading about it, but by seeing it [for himself].

But whether the little crowns were of fine linen or of gold, since it is agreed that they were made with the mitres, let us speak briefly concerning the figurative meaning. The priests have mitres of fine linen with little crowns because they keep their sight, hearing, taste, smell, and touch in the

1 Josephus, *Ant. Jud.* 3, 7, 3 (ed. Blatt, 238, 9-12)
2 Ibid. (ed. Blatt, 238, 13-14)
3 Ibid., 3, 7, 6 (ed. Blatt, 240, 16-19). Bede has *vicibus* ('tiers') where the Cassiodorian Josephus reads *versibus* ('turns'), and *achano* ('thistle') where it has *accaro* (probably the plant known as yellow flag).
4 Ibid. (ed. Blatt, 240, 6-8)
5 Exod. 39:27-8 (39:25-6)

loveliness of chastity, in order that in return for keeping them so they may hope to receive *the crown of life that God has promised to those who love him*.[1] For if anyone is so zealous for continence or good works as to neglect to seek the rewards of eternal recompense in return for them, that person may indeed appear to have a fine linen mitre on his head, but he does not have little crowns, for although he certainly displays the image of virtue before humans, he does not acquire the reward of virtue with the Lord. Consequently, either the little crowns were of gold, signifying the brightness of everlasting light, or else they were of fine linen, figuratively announcing that immortality of our body which is to be everlasting. And rightly does the priest wear crowns added on top of his fine linen clothes, so that in his own continence he may be continually meditating upon eternal rewards, and also at the same time, in his preaching of continence or of good works, he may be promising the same joys of heavenly blessedness to his hearers. For if he were to impose the weight of labour apart from the hope of reward, he would be rendering the sweet yoke of Christ bitter for his hearers, and the light burden hard to bear.[2] But when the Lord was commanding that the turban was to be made, he added:

28:39 **And a sash of embroidery work.** Farther on, it is written more clearly what the sash was to be made of: *But the girdle they made of fine* [119] *twisted linen, blue, purple, and scarlet twice dyed, with embroidery work.*[3] As Jerome writes from Josephus, *This girdle was woven all around, after the manner of a snake's skin which it casts off when it has grown old, in such a way that you might even consider it a pouch. Now it was woven with a scarlet, purple, and blue woof and a fine linen warp, for beauty and for strength; it was so artfully decorated with weaving that you might think the diverse flowers and gems had not been woven by the hand of an artisan, but rather affixed onto it;* and it had *a width of four inches.*[4] It was the high priest in particular who made use of this girdle to bind both the blue tunic and the superhumerale, for subsequently it is openly said concerning the joining of the superhumerale and the rational: *They met each other both in front and behind in such a way that the superhumerale and the rational were bound together, being fastened to the sash and securely connected with rings which were joined with a blue ribbon, lest they should slip*

---

1 Jas. 1:12

2 Matt. 11:30

3 Exod. 39:29 (39:28)

4 Jerome, *Ep.* 64, 12, 1-2 (*CSEL* 54: 598, 19 - 599, 8). Of the eight quotations or clear parallels to this work in *De tabernaculo*, this is the only instance where Bede cites Jerome by name. It seems likely that he does so in order to point out that Jerome took the notion of comparing the girdle to a snake's skin from Josephus, *Ant. Jud.* 3, 7, 2 (ed. Blatt, 237, 18-20).

loose and be moved away from one another.[1] Now there is no doubt that the sash or girdle with which the superhumerale was bound was placed around the blue tunic, which was also called 'the tunic of the superhumerale'. For surely everything that has been said up to this point pertains to the vesture of the high priest; from here on, consequently, his sons' sashes are described together with the rest of their garments, when it is said that:

28:40 **For Aaron's sons you shall then prepare linen tunics and sashes and turbans, for glory and for beauty.** It does not state whether their sashes were to be made of embroidery work also, or of only one colour; therefore, we must first speak about the sash of the high priest. It was made of those four colours that are most noble and acceptable to God, because it was appropriate for the high priest to have the kind of [sash] that would ensure that he was always girded with the ornament of every virtue. Aptly did the high priest go forth girded with the variegated adornment of shining colours, because just as it is necessary for anyone else to be girded with industriousness in regard to continence, lest the flesh should ever disturb that person's inner peace of mind by fighting against the spirit, in the same way it is obligatory for the high priest and teacher of the faithful to be encircled with the very glory of virtues, once his every lustful impulse of soul or body has been tamed. For only in this way will *righteousness be the girdle around his loins, and faith the belt around his reins,*[2] in accordance with the example of that flower which came forth from the root of Jesse,[3] that is, of the Lord and Saviour.

Now from the things that we have previously explained it is easy to understand what the linen tunics and the sashes and the turbans that were ordered to be made for glory and for beauty for the sons of Aaron commend to us in internal glory and beauty. Surely priests have linen tunics when *[120]* they dedicate their whole body to the splendour of chastity, and they gird their tunics with sashes when they look all around that same chastity with a vigilant custody of the mind, lest their consciousness of it should leave them indolent toward the exercise of good works, or lest they should diminish the merit of their chastity by boasting of it. For if someone clothed with a tunic reaching to the ankles tries to walk without a sash, the tunic will slip down and leave room for the wind and cold to come in upon the unprotected body; also, it may well impede the feet, so that the person's ability to walk is hindered, or even trip them up and become a cause of stumbling. In the same way, there is no doubt that the chastity of the flesh

---

1 Exod. 39:20-1 (39:18-19)
2 Isa. 11:5
3 Isa. 11:1

often deprives some people of chastity of the heart, because the slower they are to devote themselves to good works, the less do they perceive that the keeping of chastity has no value unless it is augmented by other good things; nevertheless, when joined with good deeds it will procure great glory for the one who possesses it. Accordingly, chastity of the flesh profited nothing to the foolish virgins who were without the light of inner purity when the bridegroom came.[1]

But let the sons of Aaron be girded with linen tunics, so that they may have chastity of the flesh. Let the priests be girded with sashes, lest chastity itself should become slack and careless, opening the way for the wind of self-exaltation to blow upon the soul, and causing charity to grow cold because of an increase of iniquity.[2] For [chastity] must not be allowed to impede the progress of good works by boasting in its presumption, nor to become soiled with earthly concupiscence and cheapened so that it obstructs the path of virtue and ultimately compels its own maker to stumble by being haughty. And when they have been girded [with sashes] let the priests also receive turbans on their heads, so that after the vigilant and circumspect keeping of corporeal chastity, they may also maintain the keeping and care of their vision, hearing, taste, and smell in a manner that is acceptable to God.

28:41 And with all these things you shall vest Aaron your brother, and his sons with him, and you shall consecrate all their hands, and sanctify them, so that they may exercise the office of priesthood before me. Aaron and his sons were to be vested with all these things, with the distinction, however, that he himself was to make use of them all, but his sons only of the last three. These were specifically ascribed to them by name when it was written, *For Aaron's sons you shall then prepare linen tunics and sashes and turbans, for glory and for beauty.*[3]

9.   THE UNDERGARMENTS

There follows:
28:42-3 You shall also make linen undergarments to cover the nakedness of their flesh, from the loins to the thighs. And Aaron and his sons shall use them when they shall go into the tabernacle of the testimony, or when they come near the altar to minister in the sanctuary, or they will be guilty of iniquity and die. This pertains to both of   *[121]*

---

1 Matt. 25:1-12
2 Matt. 24:12
3 Exod. 28:40

them at once (that is, to Aaron and to his sons as well), as the words themselves clearly indicate. And thus it happens that Aaron himself is clothed with all eight of the vestments that are mentioned (namely, the linen undergarments, the linen tunic, the blue tunic, the superhumerale, the rational, the sash, the turban, and the plate of gold), but his sons make use of only four of them (that is, the undergarments, the close- fitting linen garment, the sash, and the turban). Since we have discussed the others above, it is appropriate [to say that] these undergarments, which are commanded to be made to cover the indecency of the flesh, designate that part of chastity which holds one back from desiring the bond of marriage. Without it, no one can assume the priesthood or be consecrated for the ministry of the altar, that is, unless he will either remain a virgin or dissolve the covenant of union that he has contracted with his wife.[1] Clearly, God's law does not enjoin this kind of virtue upon anyone as a necessary obligation, but it is rather to be offered voluntarily to the Lord with devotion. For he himself says of it, *'Not everyone receives this word;*[2] nevertheless, soon afterwards he invites to it those who are able, saying with kindly exhortation, *'Let anyone who is able to receive it, receive it.'*[3] And a little later on, he promises those who will leave wives or other kinsfolk and the entanglements of this world for his sake[4] that they will receive a hundredfold reward in this life, *and in the world to come life everlasting.*[5]

Therefore, it is right to acknowledge a distinction: Moses is not ordered to vest Aaron and his sons with this garment, as he did with the previous ones. Concerning them, it says, **And with all these things you shall vest Aaron your brother, and his sons with him;** but [here] it says, **You shall make linen undergarments to cover the nakedness of their flesh.** 'They themselves', it says, 'should cover the nakedness of their flesh. You shall make linen undergarments for the high priest and his sons; you shall teach them the rule of chastity; you shall tell those who are to serve in the priesthood that they must abstain from the embrace of a wife. However, you shall not impose the yoke of this sort of continence upon any of them by force, but if any wish to be priests and to serve at the ministry of the altar, let them of their own free will cease to be servants of wives.' Once they have reached a conclusion and agree that they will be ministers of the

---

1 On Bede's teaching regarding clerical celibacy, see Carroll (1946), 241-2. For the history of the celibacy requirement in the early church, see Gryson (1970), Frazee (1972), and Conchini (1990).
2 Matt. 19:11
3 Matt. 19:12
4 Matt. 19:29
5 Mark 10:30

sanctuary and the altar by undertaking the intention of continence, they will have the assistance of the divine law. For just as it gives the priests copious instructions about how they ought to live and how they ought to teach by placing other suitable vesture upon them, rejoicing in their voluntary devotion it also adds the adornment appropriate for the priesthood of wisdom, patience, clemency, spiritual zeal, humility, mercy, fear of the [122] Lord, and the other similar ornaments without which they would be guilty of iniquity and die. For if anyone who is living wantonly presumes to usurp the priestly office for himself, his soul shall surely incur most certain death. Spiritually, this meaning is also confirmed by the following words which are added a little later. [1]

10. THE FOUR COLOURS ONCE AGAIN, FROM WHICH THE VESTMENTS [WERE MADE], AND THE FOUR ELEMENTS AND THE CONSECRATION OF THE PRIESTS

29:4-9 **And when you have washed the father and his sons with water, you shall clothe Aaron with his vestments, that is, with the linen garment and the tunic, and the superhumerale and the rational, which you shall bind together with the sash; and you shall set the turban on his head, and the holy plate upon the turban, and you shall pour the oil of unction upon his head; and by this rite shall he be consecrated. You shall bring his sons also, and you shall clothe them with the linen tunics, and gird them with a sash, Aaron and his children, and you shall put mitres upon them. And they shall be priests to me by a perpetual ordinance.** Since nothing else is commanded here concerning the undergarments received from Moses, it is clearly apparent that Aaron and his sons first clothed themselves with this kind of vestment and then went in to be washed, clothed, anointed, and consecrated at the hand of Moses.

Here we should also note that Moses first washed with water those whom he was intending to consecrate and then placed the vesture of sacred rank upon them, because it is doubtless necessary for anyone who is to be promoted to the office of the altar to wash himself at the time of dedication with an extraordinarily great flow of tears, or compunction. The cleaner he is when he comes to receive the rank, the more perfectly will he bring to completion what has been received. However, it may be possible to understand this bath as referring to baptism in the sacred font, if it should be necessary for someone who is elected to the priesthood to be washed in the

---

1 Bede does not quote the text of Exod. 29:1-3 here, but his commentary on 29:4-9 includes a discussion of the previous verses.

water of baptism then for the first time, for the remission of sins; nor was the Apostle objecting to ordination of such men when he said, *Do not* ordain *a neophyte, or he may be puffed up with pride and fall into the judgement of the devil.*[1]

But as soon as he has been clothed with the sacred vestments the high priest is then anointed with the oil of unction, so that the consecration may be made perfect through the grace of the Holy Spirit. This does not imply that it is possible for us to have any of the previously mentioned garments of virtue apart from the grace of God, but it is even more necessary for the Lord to bestow the assistance of grace when someone either rises to a higher rank or comes to preside over the guidance of a very great number [of souls].

Meanwhile, we should note that while it is asserted here in the Book of Exodus that Aaron is to be clothed with eight vestments, in Leviticus it appears that a ninth is added also, namely the sash with which the linen tunic is girded before the blue one is put on. For thus is it written: *And when [123] he had washed them, he vested the high priest with the linen under-tunic, girding him with the sash and putting the blue tunic on him, and over it he put the humerale, which he fitted to the rational by binding it with the girdle.*[2] But how and when this was done is clearly evident from those things that we have explained concerning the figure of the intellectual vestments.

But since, following the sayings of the fathers, we have briefly touched on these things concerning the priestly vesture, we suppose that we should also note that those four selected colours from which it was made are well suited to be compared with the four elements of the world: fine linen or linen with earth, because it comes forth from it; purple with water, because it is produced with dye from snails of the sea; blue and scarlet with air and fire, on account of the similarity of colour; and the scarlet was twice dyed because fire is endowed with the twofold power of giving light and setting ablaze. Therefore, the Hebrews say that the high priest carried the figure of all the elements in his vesture, because when he offered sacrifice he was under an obligation to pray not for Israel alone, but also for the whole

---

1 1 Tim. 3:6. The most prominent example of someone chosen for ordination prior to baptism was Ambrose of Milan (*c.*339-97), who was elected bishop while still a catechumen; see Paulinus, *Vit. Ambr.* 7 (*PL* 14: 29B), a work certainly known to Bede, as he used it in writing *De temp. rat.* 66 (*CCSL* 123B: 513, 1514-16).

2 Lev. 8:6-8

world.[1] Nor would it be inconsistent with these things if we should make bold to add that every individual human being contains the figure of all the elements: fire, in the heat [of the body]; air, for its sustenance; water, in its fluids; earth, in the very solidity of its members. For this same reason, Greek natural science refers to the human being as a 'microcosm', that is, a 'little world'.[2]

If you are also wondering what the gold that was in the same vesture might signify according to this understanding, you can understand it to be the inner person's power of reasoning. Hence also was 'The Holy of the Lord' properly written in [gold], because only through this [power of reasoning] can anyone ascend to the knowledge of our Creator. For the Apostle says that it is here, in the inner person, that Christ dwells in our hearts through faith.[3] Therefore Scripture shows us the high priest of the Old Testament clothed in this fashion, so that the high priest of our time may realize that he is obligated to intercede for the whole human race, and especially for those who have come to know the truth and who bear the sign of that faith on their foreheads.[4] As the Apostle admonishes and says, *First of all, then, I implore that supplications, prayers, intercessions, and thanksgivings be made for all people, for kings and for all who are in high station.*[5]

But if we understand the high priest whom Moses consecrates as the Lord Saviour, it is by right that he carries in his vesture a figure of the whole world, and of a human being as well. For, as the Apostle says, he himself is *the brightness of the glory and the figure of the substance* of God the Father, *and he upholds all things by his powerful word.*[6] He is *the Lamb of God who takes away the sins of the world;*[7] he is *a priest forever,*[8] bright with every adornment of holiness. He did not merit to receive this [holiness]   [124] through laborious exercise when he was born in flesh, but he received it

1 Jerome, *Ep.* 64, 17, 2 (*CSEL* 54: 605, 6-16). A cosmological interpretation of the vestments of the high priest is suggested in Wisd. 18:24 and developed by Philo (unknown to Bede) in *De vit. Mos.* 2, 16, 133- 5 (*LCL* 6: 512-14) and *De spec. leg.* 1, 17, 97 (*LCL* 7: 152-4), and by Josephus in *Ant. Jud.* 3, 7, 7 (ed. Blatt, 242, 2-12). On cosmological symbolism in Philo and Josephus, see Daniélou (1957). For the Christian appropriation of this exegetical approach, see Holder (1993).

2 Jerome, *In Eccles.* 9, 13-15 (*CCSL* 72: 331, 328-9); *In Ezech.* 1, 1, 6-8 (*CCSL* 75: 12, 237-86); cf. also Aldhelm, *De virg. (pros.)* 3 (*MGH AA* 15: 230, 26 - 231, 1)

3 Eph. 3:16-17

4 As above in the comment on Exod. 28:36-8 in *De tab.* 3, 7 (*CCSL* 119A: 113, 797-8), this is a reference to the signing of the cross on the foreheads of candidates for baptism and the newly baptized.

5 1 Tim. 2:1-2

6 Heb. 1:3

7 John 1:29

8 Ps. 110:4 (109:4)

altogether at the same time through the prevenient grace of the Holy Spirit when he became incarnate in the Virgin's womb. Pleasingly commending the intercession of his priesthood on our behalf, the Apostle says: *But because he continues forever, he has an everlasting priesthood, whereby he is also able to save forever those who approach God through him, since he always lives to make intercession for us.*[1] And in like manner commending the garments and ornaments of his virtues, [the Apostle] added: *For it was fitting that we should have such a high priest, holy, blameless, undefiled, separated from sins, and made higher than the heavens.*[2] He truly had on his head a golden plate upon which was engraved 'The Holy of the Lord', because he comes in the name of the Father, saying, *'I am in the Father and the Father is in me,*'[3] and *'Whoever has seen me has seen the Father also.*'[4]

Up to this point the heavenly oracle has been designating what sort of vesture Aaron and his sons ought to have. Now, what follows next explains that the proper manner of consecration which is to be used in dedicating [Aaron and his sons] as well as the tabernacle with all its furnishings is to offer the Lord a calf, and two rams, and wheat bread that is not only unleavened but also sprinkled with oil, or even covered with an application of oil of unction.[5] Figuratively, all of these things doubtless indicate either devotion to good works and purity of faith or the grace of divine illumination, which is the only proper means of consecrating priests. For who does not know that the sacrifice of those animals and [the sprinkling of] their blood designate the death of our Lord and the sprinkling of his blood, through which we are set free from sins and strengthened for good works? And the Apostle explains that the unleavened bread contains a mystery of the Saviour when he says, *Therefore let us keep the feast, not with the old leaven, nor with the leaven of malice and evil, but with the unleavened bread of sincerity and truth.*[6]

Now the cakes and wafers were sprinkled or covered with oil so that we might be admonished to have works that are not only restrained from the leaven of malice and evil but also made worthy in the divine eyes with the richness of charity. Or perhaps we offer the Lord cakes sprinkled with oil

---

1 Heb. 7:24-5

2 Heb. 7:26; Bede's reading *segregatus a peccatis* ('separated from sins') in this quotation from the Vulgate, instead of the more usual *segregatus a peccatoribus* ('separated from sinners') is a variant found also in the Codex Amiatinus, which was produced at Wearmouth-Jarrow at the end of the seventh century.

3 John 14:10

4 John 14:9

5 Exod. 29:1-3

6 1 Cor. 5:8

at our consecration when in everything we do our hearts grow rich in devotion through the inner grace of the Holy Spirit, and we offer wafers covered with oil when we also publicly display the spiritual things we do as a reliable example of [right] living for others. Our consecration is doubtless brought to completion through these offerings when with the Lord's assistance we seek to make ourselves worthy of sanctity through good works and pure thoughts. After these instructions for the consecration [125] of Aaron and his sons have been completed,[1] Scripture returns to impart some further directions for making the altar of incense, on which the same Aaron was supposed to burn incense daily.

11. THE ALTAR OF INCENSE

30:1-2 **You shall also make an altar of acacia wood for the burning of incense. It shall be one cubit long and another wide (that is, square), and two cubits high.** If that altar of holocaust concerning which we have spoken above[2] designates in a general way the life of the righteous who daily crucify their flesh with its vices and desires[3] and are accustomed to offer themselves to God as a living sacrifice,[4] what else could this altar made for the burning of incense specifically signify, other than the life of those who are perfect?

Not without reason was the flesh of animals burned on the first [altar] and incense burned as an offering on the second. For [animal sacrifices] figure those persons who do not walk according to the desires of the flesh but instead dedicate all their bodily senses to the Lord's will (as it were) by offering themselves to him as a sacrifice through the fire of the Holy Spirit, while [incense] depicts a type of those who with a greater perfection of mind offer nothing to the Lord but prayers of longing, having completely quenched all the charms of the flesh and laid them to rest. For nothing that is of the flesh assails [the perfect], and they are not conscious of any sin whereby they are disturbed or made to be afraid, but with a profusion of sweet tears they long to come and appear before the face of God.[5]

For this reason, the altar [of incense] was aptly placed inside, in the vicinity of the veil and the ark, and the [altar of holocaust] outside, in front of the tabernacle, because [those who crucify the flesh] doubtless shine in

---

1 Exod. 29:10-45

2 Bede *De tab.* 2, 11 (*CCSL* 119A: 76, 1361-3); cf. *De templo* 1; 2 (*CCSL* 119A: 176, 1185-8; 224, 1277-80)

3 Gal. 5:24

4 Rom. 12:1

5 Ps. 42:3-4 (41:3-4)

the sight of the Holy Church as an example of virtue for everyone, while [the perfect] who burn with a higher desire draw especially near to the contemplation of future blessedness, even though they remain in the body. Aptly is [the altar of holocaust] commanded to be covered with bronze and [the altar of incense] with gold, for bronze is more resonant than all other metals and lasts for a very long time, but when compared to something made of bronze, gold is as superior in splendour as it is inferior in sound. Hence rightly does the bronze altar, upon which the flesh of victims was burned and their blood poured out, bear the type of those who have overcome the pleasures of the flesh and sacrificed them (as it were) to God; with perseverance they finish the way of truth which they have begun once and for all, and in the word of preaching they also repeatedly tell out to their neighbours that this is the [way] in which they should be walking. The golden altar, however, is aptly compared to those who are more fully illuminated with the grace of heavenly brightness but are less open about telling others of the inner pleasures they taste in secret, and less able to give utterance by declaring how much they have been interiorly refreshed with sweetness in the hidden face of God. Aptly also was the altar of incense as superior in the shining of its metal as it was smaller in size, because the holier persons in the Church are always fewer [than the rest].

[126]

Both altars are aptly commanded to be made of the same acacia wood, which is, as we have said, similar to whitethorn and incorruptible,[1] because the hearts of all the elect ought to be fortified with one firmness of unfeigned faith, that they may be prepared to receive the fire of love and to offer the libation of virtues to God. For the Apostle speaks to everyone in general, the small with the great, saying, *Let us cleanse ourselves from every defilement of the flesh and of the spirit, making sanctification perfect in the fear of God,*[2] which is to say in other words, 'Let us cut off and remove from ourselves the thorns of vices and the pricking stings of titillation which the earth of our heart or our body has been accustomed to sprout forth in us as a result of the sin of the first transgression, and let us vigorously cultivate our inner self and our outer self as well, as though we were trimming ourselves with some two-edged axe and pruning ourselves thoroughly, that we may become worthy to offer the sacrifice of virtues in the presence of our Creator by receiving the fire of the Holy Spirit.' And aptly was it one and the same fire, not two different ones, that consumed victims on the first altar and incense on the other, because there is doubtless one

---

1 Bede, *De tab.* 1, 3; 2, 5 (*CCSL* 119A: 13, 324-7; 59, 690-3)
2 2 Cor. 7:1

Spirit who quickens the minds of all the faithful with the various gifts of grace.

Now the altar of incense was square, being one cubit long and another wide, but two high. As we said in the exposition of the altar of holocaust, length pertains to the longsuffering of patience, width to the amplitude of love, and height to the sublimity of hope, through which we are able to rejoice with an honest mind in the endurance of temporal labours and in the joy of love.[1] Both the length and the width of the altar are one cubit when all the men who are highest and most perfect in the Church bear temporal evils patiently, looking for nothing else but an eternal reward, and charitably expend as many of their possessions as possible on their neighbours' behalf.

Similarly, the altar of incense was rightly ordered to be made square in its length and width, because *charity is patient and it is kind,*[2] that is, patient so that it may endure the injury inflicted by the neighbour, and kind so that it may endure adversities along with the neighbour, discharging the duties of charity and kindness even when it takes effort to do so. For this suggests that these virtues are so closely allied with one another in the spirits of the perfect that they are as capable of loving the brother as they are of bearing   *[127]*
with him, and just as able to withstand his troublesomeness through patience as to show him goodwill through the kindness of their own love. And it is two cubits high because the elect hope that they will receive a twofold reward for themselves in the life to come, that is, one [reward] of rest for their souls when they will strip off this corruptible and mortal body to enter the heavenly kingdom, and another when they will regain that same body incorruptible and immortal, and rejoice more perfectly in the presence of their Creator, so as to fulfill the promise of the prophet who says, *They shall possess a double portion in their land; everlasting joy shall be theirs.*[3]

30:2-3 Horns shall project out from [the altar of incense], and you shall overlay it with the purest gold, its grate as well as its sides and horns. In the Scriptures it is often the custom for horns to designate the eminence of faith and of the virtues with which we ought to strike out against and overcome the hostile advances of our ancient enemy,[4] joining the prophet in saying to the Lord, *'Through you we will fight against our enemies with the horn.'*[5] As it is sometimes the custom, on the other hand, for the word 'horns' to indicate the armies of the vices that endeavour to

---

1 Bede, *De tab.* 1, 4; 2, 11 (*CCSL* 119A: 13, 343 - 14, 347; 76, 1367 - 77, 1373)
2 1 Cor. 13:4
3 Isa. 61:7
4 i.e., the devil
5 Ps. 44:5 (43:6)

fight against us, he then explained whose horn he had spoken of subduing, saying, *'And through your name we disdain those who rise up against us.'*[1] The Lord concisely joined both of these [meanings] together when he said through the prophet, *'And all the horns of sinners I will cut off, but the horns of the righteous shall be exalted.'*[2] Hence it is properly decreed in the law that the only animals which are clean and suitable to be eaten by the people of God are those that have horns. For it is well known that those animals that chew the cud and divide the hoof are also those that have horns,[3] so that it is mystically disclosed that the only people who can be incorporated into a spiritual union with the Church of God are those who by the strength of their faith prove that they are unconquered in their battles with the vices.

Now horns project directly out from the altar of incense when the elect do not exhibit works of virtue before humans, only for the sake of appearance, but perform them with a fixed and unmoveable devotion [which comes forth] from the inner root of the mind. Hypocrites, on the other hand, are like horns borrowed from someone else; although they have the appearance of godliness, they deny its power.[4] They aptly correspond to the crow decked out with the flying wings of a peacock, which one of Aesop's fables describes as having no reason to boast of its beauty; in fact, the blazing jealousy of the peacocks eventually deprives [the crow] of all use of its wings, and of life itself.[5]

Now the altar is overlaid with the purest gold when the perfect each shine with the true light of inner wisdom, when in everything that they do they show forth the splendour of charity just as if it were the glory of their everyday clothing, when it is evident to everyone who either sees them or hears them that the memory of eternal brightness is always in them, and when they make it clear that they are thinking about the kingdom of God and his righteousness, seeking that before everything else.[6]

The grate of the altar, as well as its sides and horns, is properly ordered to be covered with gold, seeing that the grate was inside, in the middle of

[128]

---

1 Ps. 44:5 (43:6)
2 Ps. 75:10 (74:11)
3 Lev. 11:1-3; Deut. 14:4-7
4 2 Tim. 3:5
5 'all use of its wings' = *omni pennarum virtute*; literally, 'every strength of the wings'. Versions of this fable are recounted about a jackdaw and various kinds of birds in Babrius, 72 (*LCL*: 88-90); about a jackdaw and a peacock in Phaedrus, 1, 3 (*LCL*: 194-6); and about a crow and some unspecified birds in Horace, *Ep.* 1, 3 (*LCL*: 272, 8-20). Jerome recalls the crow adorned in colours not its own in *Ep.* 108, 15, 1 (*CSEL* 55: 325, 16-17). None of these would seem to be Bede's source, however, for none of them states that the characters are a crow and some peacocks, and in none of them is the crow said to lose its life.
6 Matt. 6:33

the altar, to support the incense which was being prepared, but the sides were visible on the outside, and the horns, which were also visible outside, protruded out above the top [of the altar]. Now the grate is gilded when the grace of Christ shines in our inner self through faith. The sides are gilded when the same grace of the Lord's love spreads itself out externally through good works. And the horns are gilded when the confidence of fortitude gleams everywhere with the splendour of light within; with this [confidence] the righteous have learned how to bear with the adversaries of the truth bravely through patience, or to refute and correct them prudently through wisdom. And because such persons as these have every right to say, *I have fought the good fight, I have finished the race, I have kept the faith; for the rest, there is reserved for me a crown of righteousness,*[1] there is rightly added:

30:3 **And you shall make for it a crown of gold all around.** Surely a crown of gold is all around the altar of incense when the saints anticipate eternal rewards on account of the good things that they remember themselves to have done. And the crown is properly made all around the altar to show that everything they have done is worthy of a heavenly reward, and there is nothing left in such people that needs to be cleansed in the purgatorial fire after their release from the flesh.[2] Moreover, the altar of incense has a crown of gold all around even in those who are lesser in merit. Although they do not dare to testify openly that there is assuredly reserved for them the reward for the good fight and for keeping the faith, nevertheless, everything that they do is done with the intention of pleasing God, and in hope of obtaining the same heavenly reward. There follows:

30:4-5 **And two golden rings under the crown on each side, so that the poles may be put into them and the altar may be carried. And the poles you shall also make of acacia wood, and overlay them with gold.** In accordance with what we have explained above in relation to the altar of holocaust, the ark, and the table,[3] these rings with which the altar was carried can be suitably understood as the books of the four gospels, through whose faith and doctrine the saints are raised up above earthly thoughts so that they may be carried through the desert of this everyday life and conveyed to the heavenly homeland by their progress in good works. In the former instance it was clear that four rings were being enjoined to be made,

---

1 2 Tim. 4:7-8

2 For Bede's understanding of the purgatorial fire, which he derived largely from Gregory the Great, see Carroll (1946), 178-80, and Le Goff (1984), 102-3, 112-6. On the emergence of the doctrine of purgatory in Latin Christianity, see Le Goff (who maintains that purgatory was not understood in a spatialized way until the twelfth century) and Atwell (1987).

3 Bede, *De tab.* 1, 4; 1, 6; 2, 12 (*CCSL* 119A: 15, 419-20; 24, 773-4; 83, 1619-22)

two on one side and two on the other, in this case, however, it is only implied that four is the number of them that are to be made, two rings on each side. To be sure, the number of the evangelists is more openly evident in the former instance, but in this case something else containing a spiritual mystery very much related to the love of God and neighbour is also present. For the altar is surrounded with golden rings on every side because the hearts of the elect are strengthened everywhere by the love of God and neighbour. This [love] is properly compared to rings, because even though prophecies will eventually be made void, knowledge will be destroyed, and tongues will cease, it will never come to an end.[1]

[129]

Now there are two rings on each side because both of the commandments of charity are distinguished by a twofold virtue. Charity toward God is perfected through sincerity of faith and purity of life, *for without faith it is impossible to please God,*[2] and *faith without works is dead.*[3] The prophet sums up both of these [truths] in one little verse when he says, *'But my righteous one lives by faith,'*[4] openly suggesting that the only way that anyone will enter into life is by combining works of righteousness with true faith. In the same way, brotherly love also consists of a twofold virtue, namely of patience and of kindness, as the Apostle bears witness when he says that *charity is patient and it is kind.*[5] For this reason the Lord also says, *'Forgive, and you will be forgiven; give, and it will be given to you.'*[6] That is, he teaches about patience as the forgiving of debts and about the grace of kindness as the giving of the necessities [of life]; the one, so that we may bravely bear misfortunes from our neighbours, and the other, so that we may joyfully share our good fortune with our neighbours. The altar, therefore, has two rings on each side when the saints are surrounded with a twofold perfection of charity, for honouring their Creator and for caring for and serving the neighbour as well. Bars overlaid with gold are put into these rings so that the altar may be carried when these [saints] prepare an opening in the mind to receive the brightest sayings of the fathers who have gone before them, through which they are lifted up higher and higher above earthly things and transported to the love of eternal blessings. In the words that follow, it is also mystically designated that they deserve to draw near to heavenly things in spirit, for it says:

---

1 1 Cor. 13:8
2 Heb. 11:6
3 Jas. 2:26
4 Bede quotes from Heb. 10:38, although his reference to 'the prophet' shows that he recognizes the original source as Hab. 2:4.
5 1 Cor. 13:4
6 Luke 6:37-8

30:6 **And you shall place the altar in front of the curtain that hangs before the ark of the testimony, in front of the propitiatory with which the testimony is covered, where I will speak to you.** As we explained in its proper place,[1] the ark designates the Lord Saviour, and the curtain that hung before the ark designates heaven itself, into which the Lord entered when he conquered death *so that he may now appear in the presence of God on our behalf,* as the Apostle says.[2] The altar stands in front of the curtain that was hung before the ark when the righteous direct their every intention to entering the kingdom of heaven. It stands in front of the propitiatory with which the ark is covered when they draw near to the vision of their Creator with purity of mind, and when they have a life in heaven,[3] quite closed off from the body.

[130]

12. THE INCENSE TO BE BURNED ON [THE ALTAR OF INCENSE]

30:7-8 **And Aaron shall burn sweet-smelling incense upon it; in the morning when he dresses the lamps, he shall burn it, and when he sets them up in the evening.** It is well known that incense or *thimiama*[4] represents the way of prayer, for the psalmist says, *'Let my prayer be directed as incense in your sight,'*[5] and in the Apocalypse John saw that the saints had *golden bowls full of aromatic spices,*[6] which he immediately explained by adding, *which are the prayers of the saints.* And since Aaron, as we have said above,[7] designates both the High Priest himself in particular (that is, the Lord Saviour) and also the priests of our line, Aaron shall burn sweet-smelling incense upon this altar in the morning when the Lord himself incites the hearts of the faithful to the sweetness of prayer, having newly illuminated them with the radiance of his grace, or when those who share in his priesthood stimulate the faithful by diligently exhorting them to pray before the face of their Creator.

Now the priest burns incense not only in the morning but also in the evening. For incense is burned in the morning so that whenever we are

---

1 Bede, *De tab.* 1, 3; 2, 8 (*CCSL* 119A: 13, 321-2; 71, 1137)
2 Heb. 9:24
3 Phil. 3:20
4 *incensum sive thimiama*; Bede indicates that the two words for 'incense' used in the Vulgate are equivalent terms, one derived from the Latin verb *incendo* ('to kindle') and the other a transliterated form of the Greek θυμίαμα.
5 Ps. 141:2 (140:2)
6 Rev. 5:8
7 Bede, *De tab.*, 1, 1; 3, 1 (*CCSL* 119A: 7, 81; 95, 104-5)

disposed to begin a good deed with God's inspiration we will invoke his help in order to bring it to completion, and it is burned in the evening so that when we have finished the things that we began so well we will return prayers of thanks to the one who has given us everything that we have received. Or perhaps it is because in the morning and at sunrise we clearly see everything around us in all directions, but when evening comes we are left in the dark, with unsure vision, and therefore require light from a lamp in order to see whatever we wish [to see]. Thus, in so far as we are now able to distinguish the sacraments or the sayings of our Redeemer plainly, even in accordance with the limits of human reason, it is as if we are seeing them in the daytime. Whenever human reason is insufficient, however, and we can only follow the authority of Holy Scripture, then the eye of our understanding is in the dark, as if it were night, but the lamp of God's Word assists our feet,[1] lest we should accidentally stumble and deviate from the way of truth. For this reason, when Peter is talking about the sacrament of faith in the Lord, he says, *And we have the firmer prophetic message. You do well to attend to it as to a lamp shining in a dark place, until the day dawns and the morning star rises in your hearts.*[2]

[131]

Therefore, it is properly said, **And Aaron shall burn sweet-smelling incense upon it; in the morning when he dresses the lamps, he shall burn it, and when he sets them up in the evening.** Aaron burns incense upon the altar in the morning when the Lord sets the hearts of the faithful on fire for the grace of compunction by means of those hidden truths which they are already able to understand. He burns it in the evening when he sets up the lamps when [the Lord] uses even those things that they are not yet capable of grasping, but which they do not hesitate to accept as holy and divine, to fashion them for the love of the things of heaven, where all secrets are brought to light. And he burns sweet-smelling incense when they receive the divine touch of sudden compunction which moves them to devote themselves sweetly to nothing but tears and prayers. Now there properly follows:

30:8 **He shall burn an everlasting incense before the Lord throughout your generations,** because it is doubtless necessary that the soul should not turn away from prayer and lamentation to idle words or deeds. Even when its prayer is finished, it should maintain the same vigour of devotion that it assumed in prayer, in accordance with the example of Hannah, of whom it

---

1 Ps. 119:105 (118:105)
2 2 Pet. 1:19

was said that after she had prayed, *her countenance was no longer changed in diverse things.*[1]

30:9 **You shall not offer upon it incense of another composition.** Later in this book the spices from which this incense was to be composed are specified by name: stacte, and onycha, galbanum of pleasing fragrance, and the purest frankincense.[2] It is obvious that all of these signify the eternal goods which we ought to seek from the Lord before anything else. Consequently, upon the altar of gold they were not supposed to offer incense of any composition other than that which the Lord had decreed, because when we pray we ought to seek from the Lord nothing other than that which he himself has commanded and has promised to give us, and we ought to believe nothing concerning him other than that which he himself has taught.

Neither victim nor libation was to be offered upon it.[3] All these things pertain to the exterior altar, since they designate the life of those who are just beginning, and of those who are still making progress. For the life of those who are perfectly righteous is so sublime that it is impossible to find in it anything that they need to sacrifice to the Lord. It is common knowledge that libations of wine sometimes designate the great power of spiritual grace, whether it be the cup of doctrine, or the chalice of the passion, or the intoxification of love that surpasses all things, or the reception of the Holy Spirit itself, or something of that sort. However, whenever libations of wine are offered along with the flesh of victims,   *[132]* according to a tropological exposition they must surely designate the sanctity of those who still have some carnal desires which are opposed to the purity of the spirit, and which ought to be burned on the altar of the heart by the fire of the Holy Spirit. But those who are perfectly righteous can say, *'My heart and my flesh have failed; you are the God of my heart and the God who is my portion forever.*[4] It is as if they have ceased the libations [poured out upon] victims, which pertain to the bronze altar set outside, and offer to the Lord nothing but the spices of heavenly desire on the golden altar within. Since they are already quite confident about the remission of their sins, they mourn only on account of their delayed entrance into the eternal kingdom, and they water their couch every night with sweet streams of tears.[5] There is now properly added concerning this altar:

---

1 1 Sam. 1:18
2 Exod. 30:34
3 Exod. 30:9
4 Ps. 73:26 (72:26)
5 Ps. 6:6 (6:7)

30:10 And once a year Aaron shall make intercession upon its horns with the blood of the sin offering. Surely our High Priest offered his own blood for the sins of the whole world once in a year. That was the year in which, as he himself says through Isaiah, he came *to preach the acceptable year of the Lord,*[1] referring thereby to this entire period of time in which he has deigned to join the Church to himself. In the holy font, he has also given each believer a bath in the mystery of his own blood once for all, to break the bonds of sin. The difference between the figures is pleasing in every way. The high priest is commanded to make intercession upon the horns of the altar with the blood of the offering once a year, but to burn sweet-smelling incense upon it daily, because our Lord and Saviour daily renews his faithful by enkindling in them the grace of inner compunction, but he redeemed them once for all when he overcame death by the sacrifice of his blood. Therefore, the faithful themselves, who are accustomed to wash away their daily sins with daily prayers and tears, rejoice that in the sacrament of his passion they have been set free from all their sins once for all.

[The Lord] makes intercession upon the horns of the altar, because he not only prayed for human beings while he himself lived among them, but he also intercedes for us now that he is seated at the right hand of the Father in heaven.[2] And since he dwells in the hearts of the elect through faith, he is rightly said to be making intercession when he arouses them to prayer. Moreover, Aaron makes intercession upon the horns of the altar when the Lord commends his own elect to the Father by recalling the virtuous deeds that they have done. Accordingly, as if he is holding the horns of the altar of gold, he speaks of the disciples' devotion: *'Those whom you gave me from the world were yours, and you gave them to me, and they have kept* [133] *your word. Now they have come to know that everything you have given me is from you.*[3] He also makes intercession for them, adding, *'I am asking on their behalf; I am not asking on behalf of the world, but on behalf of those whom you gave me, because they are yours.*[4] And because the Lord frequently takes pity on our infirmity on account of the merits and the intercessions of noble men, there is rightly added:

30:10 And he shall make atonement upon it throughout your generations. It shall be most holy to the Lord. Aaron makes atonement upon the altar of incense when the Lord is appeased toward us on account of the

---

1 Bede quotes from Luke 4:19, where Jesus was himself quoting Isa. 61:2.
2 Rom. 8:34
3 John 17:6-7
4 John 17:9

righteousness of the saints whom we ask to be our intercessors and patrons. Accordingly, when Hezekiah was besieged by enemies and was calling upon him for help, [the Lord] said, *'I will defend this city and save it, for my own sake and for the sake of my servant David.'*[1] In the same way, when Moses was interceding on behalf of the sinful people he too invoked the memory of the fathers and said, as if he were endeavouring to appease the Lord by making intercession upon the horns of the altar, *'Let your anger cease, and be appeased toward the wickedness of your people. Remember Abraham, Isaac, and Israel, your servants, to whom you swore by your own self, saying, "I will multiply your descendants like the stars of heaven."'*[2]

Perhaps it would be possible for us to interpret these altars in another way as well. The bronze altar, on which the flesh of victims was burned and their blood was poured out, we might understand as the whole Church of this present time, in which there is no one who has lived on earth for even one day who is without sin, no one who has not been born according to the flesh through the sin of Adam's transgression, no one who does not need to be reborn in Christ, no one whose spirit does not need to be cleansed by fire. The golden altar, however, can signify the Lord himself, who derived true flesh from Adam in such a wonderful and ineffable manner that he was truly free from the sin of Adam's flesh, just as the two altars were made from one and the same kind of wood, but they were not both covered with gold. Only spices were burned on this altar, nothing fleshly being offered upon it, because when the Lord poured forth prayers or tears[3] he was not doing this on account of his own errors, for he had none,[4] but rather for the sake of our salvation. For just as the ark which was set within the curtain signifies the God-man sitting at the right hand of Majesty on high, so might the same Mediator between God and humankind[5] be figuratively expressed by the altar which was set outside the curtain but near to its entrance. Among human beings he lived in the manner of humans, but with the power of his divinity he penetrates the innermost parts of heaven.

The altar of incense stood in the sanctuary where the lampstand and the table were also, because *the Word was made flesh and dwelt among us.*[6] The ark stood within the curtain, because after his passion and resurrection the same Lord Jesus *was taken up into heaven, and sat down at the right* [134]

---

1 2 Kgs. 19:34
2 Exod. 32:12-13
3 Heb. 5:7
4 Heb. 4:15; 1 John 3:5
5 1 Tim. 2:5
6 John 1:14

hand of God.[1] Aaron makes intercession upon the horns of this altar with the blood of the sin offering and makes atonement upon it when the priests, who are praying on behalf of God's people or on account of their own ignorance and that of the people, are confident that they will be helped by [God's] only-begotten Son and saved by the sacrament of his passion, as the Apostle reminds us when he says, *Through him, then, let us always offer a sacrifice of praise to God, that is, the fruit of lips that confess his name.*[2] It would also be appropriate to understand this as applying to all the elect members of the High Priest, who pray to the Father in spirit and in truth.[3] For that which was said, **It shall be most holy to the Lord,** is more applicable to him than to this altar, since when he was about to be born into the world the archangel spoke concerning him to the Virgin Mother: *'The Holy Spirit will come upon you, and the power of the Most High will overshadow you; therefore the one to be born will be holy; he will be called Son of God.'*[4]

Having described the making of the altar of incense to this extent, we still have to deal with the description of the bronze basin in which the priests washed their hands and feet when they were about to enter into the tabernacle. But first there is set forth one commandment of the Lord that it is fitting for us to touch upon briefly and to expound according to our ability.

13.   THE RANSOM FOR THEIR SOULS THAT THE PEOPLE
       [SHALL GIVE] WHEN THEY ARE COUNTED

There follows:

30:11-13 **And the Lord spoke to Moses, saying: When you take the sum of the children of Israel according to their number, they shall each give a ransom for their souls to the Lord, so that no plague may come among them. And this is what each one who is registered shall give: half a shekel according to the standard of the temple (a shekel is twenty obols), half a shekel shall be offered to the Lord.** David forgot about this precept when he numbered the people, and thus he brought a plague upon those people by numbering them.[5] In the spiritual sense, the sum of the children of Israel designates the sum of all the elect whose names are written in heaven.[6] They each give a ransom for their souls to the Lord when they

1 Mark 16:19
2 Heb. 13:15
3 John 4:23
4 Luke 1:35
5 2 Sam. 24:1-15
6 Luke 10:20

show him the obedience of diligent service in good works; otherwise, a
plague will come among them when they have been counted, because
eternal vengeance doubtless awaits those who belong to the number of the
faithful in name only and refuse to offer the Lord the perfected works of
faith. It is said of such persons that they *will not give God their price, nor
the ransom for the redemption of their souls.*[1] For, as Solomon says, *a man's*   *[135]*
own wealth is the redemption of his soul;[2] this might be temporal wealth
which one distributes and gives to the poor so that one's righteousness may
endure forever,[3] or it might be spiritual wealth in the form of the righteousness that one has attained by taking pity on the poor, or by doing other good
things.

Now **each one who is registered shall give half a shekel**, which is ten
obols. It is quite appropriate for us to understand this as as a reference to
nothing else but the observance of the Decalogue of the law. For anyone
who is able to understand it rightly has come to realize that it contains all
the fullness of both faith and works, as well as the promise of a future
reward. Accordingly, the first three [commandments] deal with the love of
God, and the seven that follow deal with the love of neighbour, as the
Apostle also bears witness: *Love is the fullness of the law.*[4] But we should
not fail to mention another sacrament which is also contained in the number
ten. For among the Hebrews the first letter of the name Jesus is *ioth*, among
the Greeks it is *iota*, and both of these peoples use that letter as the number
ten. Those who believe in Jesus Christ offer ten obols as a ransom for their
souls to the Lord because on their foreheads and in their profession they
display the sign of his name, which begins with the number ten.[5] And
perhaps it was on account of this sacrament that the Lord declared in the
gospel that not one iota could pass away from the law,[6] because the rebellion
of the unfaithful can destroy neither the power of the Decalogue which [that
letter] contains, nor the faith in his name which it mystically signifies.

---

1 Ps. 49:7-8 (48:8-9)

2 Prov. 13:8

3 Ps. 112:9 (111:9)

4 Rom. 13:10

5 Another reference to the custom of signing candidates for baptism and the newly baptized
with the sign of the cross of their foreheads; see Bede's comments above on Exod. 26:36-8
and 29:4-9 in *De tab.* 3, 7; 3, 10 (*CCSL* 119A: 113, 797-8; 123, 1185-7). Presumably the sign
of the cross was considered to be the sign of Jesus' name because it was often administered
with the words, 'In the name of the Father, and of the Son, and of the Holy Spirit,' though it
is possible that Bede is thinking here of the chi-rho monogram of the Greek title 'Christ', which
has the shape of a cross.

6 Matt. 5:18

30:14 **Each one who is reckoned among the number, from twenty years old and upward, shall give a ransom.** The law was written in five books, the gospel in four, and four times five makes twenty. The number twenty, therefore, signifies the joining together of the two testaments. Consequently, those from twenty years old are reckoned among the number of the people, because the only ones worthy of the fellowship of the elect are those who are assisted by the grace of the gospel to fulfill the decrees of the law (spiritually understood) in accordance with their own measure and capacity, and who expect eternal rewards in heaven according to the promises of that same grace.

30:15 **The rich shall not give more than half a shekel, and the poor shall give no less,** for the same law of the Decalogue, through which they love God and neighbour, is imposed upon all, whether they are perfect and have many merits, or immature and still making progress in virtue.

30:16 **And you shall take the money collected from the children of Israel and consign it to the use of the tabernacle of the testimony, so that it may be their memorial before the Lord, and he may have mercy** *[136]* **on their souls.** The money taken from the children of Israel is brought before the Lord as their memorial when our Creator and Judge eternally remembers every single good thing that we do, so that he may deign to have mercy on us for the sake of the fruits of those good works that we have offered to him. That same money is reserved for the use of the tabernacle when the good deeds of the righteous serve to strengthen the character and the conduct of the faithful who follow them in Christ; by asserting that they are all less important, they are acknowledging that they are the sort of people who have learned how to reign with the Lord.

Perhaps we should note that the aforementioned money was not to be given according to the reckoning of the crowd but according to the standard of the temple. For the standard of the temple is the system of divine law, which the Lord commands to be kept in his Church and to be observed by everyone to whom he promises eternal rewards in the future. Otherwise, if there are any who endeavour to serve God according to the principle of human will, their offering will be rejected and thrown away, for they have not offered the money of their devotion according to the standard of the temple, and they will be smitten with the plague of the ultimate punishment.

14. THE BRONZE BASIN

30:18-20 You shall also make a bronze basin with its own stand for washing, and you shall put it between the tabernacle of the testimony and the altar. Water shall be put into it, and Aaron and his sons shall wash their hands and feet in it when they are about to go into the tabernacle of the testimony, and when they are about to come near to the altar. In the first instance, we can understand this basin (or flanged bowl, as it is called further on[1]) to be the water of baptism, in which all those who enter the doors of the Church must bathe in order to be cleansed. It was put between the tabernacle of the testimony and the altar of holocaust, and the priests were commanded to wash themselves in it twice a day (that is, morning and evening) when they were going to the altar of incense to offer to the Lord. We, however, are not supposed to be washed in the water of baptism more than once; consequently, the basin commends to us that washing of compunction and of tears which is required of us at all times, and especially when we draw near to minister at the heavenly mysteries.

The altar of holocaust, upon which the flesh of victims was burned for the Lord, designates the extinction of carnal desires through the fire of the Holy Spirit. The altar of incense, however, signifies the purity of those in whom the charms of the flesh have been completely put to rest and the struggle with the vices has been peacefully resolved; in the pure expectation and desire of entering heaven they pour out tears of love. Rightly, therefore, is the basin in which the priests wash when they enter the tabernacle and *[137]* burn incense to the Lord put behind the altar of holocaust. For there are two different kinds of tears and compunction.[2] At first, all those who are converted to the Lord must shed tears in begging forgiveness for the sins which they have committed, and they must continue to do this for a long time, until they have made [their tears] complete by complementing them with fruits worthy of repentance. Once they are quite confident that they have received the forgiveness of sins, they can then pray with longing desire for the coming of the time when they will merit to see the face of their Creator among the most blessed choirs of angels.

Those who live in accordance with truth are never without tears, for they are always enduring either the prolongation of this life or the delay of the other. Of this [life], they say, *'Woe is me, that my sojourning is prolonged,*

---

1 The Vulgate refers to the basin as a *labrum* in Exod. 30:18, but in Exod. 38:8 the word *labium* ('flanged bowl') is used instead.

2 Gregory the Great, *Moral.* 24, 6, 10-11 (*CCSL* 143B: 1194, 1 - 1196, 40); *Hom. in Ezech.* 2, 10, 20-1 (*CCSL* 142: 395, 531 - 396, 574)

that I must live among the inhabitants of Cedar,[1] (that is, with those who
live in the shadows of error and wickedness which are signified by the name
Cedar[2]). They are already sighing for the joys of perpetual light and saying,
'I have led a life that is very wearisome, for I thirst as much for the heavenly
homeland as I loathe the proximity of the wicked persons among whom I
dwell as a stranger,' for they speak again of that other [life]: *'My soul has
thirsted for the living God. When shall I come and appear before the face
of God?'*[3] Surely the words that follow indicate that they cannot bear this
thirst without tears: *'My tears have been my bread day and night.'*[4] It is as
if they were saying openly, 'The longer I am delayed from seeing the face
of God for which I thirst so ardently, the more sweetly am I refreshed with
the bread of the tears that I pour out in memory of him.' Therefore, the altar
of holocaust suggests the tears of those who repent of the sins that they have
committed, but the altar of incense expresses the weeping of those who
rejoice over the good works that they have done with the Lord's help, and
long for the rewards that they confidently expect to receive as recompense
from the Lord. This sort of weeping is undoubtedly superior, in the same
way that the golden [altar] was obviously preferable to the first [altar] of
bronze, and the holy of holies containing the ark of the Lord was preferable
to the first tabernacle, in which there stood the lampstand and the table of
the Lord.

The basin, in which those who were going in to the altar of incense
washed themselves was put behind the altar of holocaust, because *no one
attains to the highest place all of a sudden.*[5] Instead, as one increases in
merit one must first win the war against vice, and then make humble
supplication to one's Creator with tears of compunction, so that one is able
to shed sweet tears for the sake of entrance to the kingdom, even as one
formerly shed bitter tears out of fear of punishment.

Now the stand on which that basin was set is quite aptly understood as
that same desire for the kingdom and the heavenly life, because the perfect
and noblest men undoubtedly wash themselves daily in the font of tears.

[138]   By sighing for the joys of inner peace, they can at least enjoy a foretaste of
that which they are not yet able to see perfectly. For the tears of the perfect
are figured in this bath which was put between the tabernacle and the altar,
as the very words in which it is described bear witness: **Water shall be put**

---

1 Ps. 120:5 (119:5)
2 Jerome, *Nom.* (*CCSL* 72: 63, 6-7)
3 Ps. 42:2 (41:3)
4 Ps. 42:3 (41:4)
5 Gregory the Great, *Hom. in Ezech.* 2, 3, 3 (*CCSL* 142: 238, 53-4)

into it, and Aaron and his sons shall wash their hands and feet in it. It was not just anyone from among the people who was commanded to wash there, but the high priest himself and his sons (that is, the priests of the lesser rank), because just as the lives of great men are more perfect, so also is their compunction usually expected to be more sublime.

We do not mean to imply that it is only ministers of the altar who either can or should possess the virtue of this kind of compunction, for we are mindful of the words with which the blessed apostle Peter speaks to all the faithful concerning the cornerstone which is Jesus Christ,[1] saying, *And, like living stones, let yourselves be built up into spiritual houses, to be a holy priesthood, to offer spiritual sacrifices.*[2] And there is also what John says in the Apocalypse: *Blessed and holy are those who share in the first resurrection. Over these the second death has no power, but they will be priests of God and of Christ.*[3] Therefore we admonish all the faithful to be known by the mystical name of priests, inasmuch as they are members of Christ, that is, of the eternal Priest. The blessed apostle Paul also shows them what kind of victims they ought to offer, saying, *I beseech you, brethren, by the mercy of God, to present your bodies as a living sacrifice, holy and acceptable to God.*[4] Consequently, Moses did not set up this bath for the ministers of the sacred altar alone, but also for all the perfect in whatever rank they may be stationed, for the law of God preached the healing grace of compunction to all the faithful in general.

If we wish to understand the person of Aaron as the great High Priest himself, the Lord and Saviour, it is apparent that he too washed with the water of this basin before he went in to offer at the altar. On account of his love for us, he also shed tears before he burned the incense of his own most holy body on the altar of the cross for our salvation, as was made known in the widely-celebrated resuscitation of Lazarus.[5] And there is properly added:

30:20-1 **To offer on it incense to the Lord, lest by chance they should die.** Surely those who have been chosen for the ministry of the altar should fear the spiritual and eternal death of the soul if they fail to render the incense of prayers of God. They should fear death if they presume to go in to the sacred mysteries without the distinctive washing of compunction, or to

---

1 Eph. 2:20
2 1 Pet. 2:5
3 Rev. 20:6
4 Rom. 12:1
5 John 11:35

[139]   handle the holy things of the Lord with hands that are unclean. Consequently, let them wash their hands and feet in the water of the bronze basin,
and then let them come near to the altar. Let them wash their actions and
their movements with tears; then let them put forth their hands to touch the
mysteries of Christ, and let them set their feet to walking in the courts of
the Lord.

I believe that this precept applies equally to those who are about to be
made clean by receiving the same sacraments. First, they must sift, winnow,
and refine their thoughts and actions with very prudent care; then let them
go forth to participate in the sacraments of faith. Otherwise, they will
deserve to hear that [saying] of the Apostle, *For all who eat and drink in
an unworthy manner, eat and drink judgement against themselves, not
discerning the body,*[1] that is to say, they have in no way used a prudent and
attentive mind to distinguish the food of living bread from the commonness
of ordinary food. It is quite useful to understand these things concerning
the basin and the entrance to the altar in this way also; however, that altar
primarily signifies the internal votive offerings of spiritual prayers. But we
must consider more carefully that which is added in conclusion:

30:31 **It shall be an everlasting law for him, and for his descendants
throughout their generations.** The basin and the altar that Moses made
have been destroyed, and the priesthood that he established has been
replaced by the new priesthood of the Church. Even so, the law of the
spiritual bath and incense, which was signified by means of a type through
the incense of that altar and the water of that basin, nevertheless continues
to be everlasting in the life of the faithful. In the same way, there are many
other things that the law commands to be made, or that it predicts must be
done or celebrated forever, which have in fact ceased to be observed
according to the letter. However, they will never cease to be observed
spiritually by the saints in accordance with the typic understanding, for the
one who comes not *to abolish the law, but to fulfill it* bears witness that *not
one iota, not one stroke, will pass from the law until all is accomplished.*[2]

For, in all humility, we too belong[3] among those descendants of whom
it was said that **it shall be an everlasting law for him, and for his
descendants throughout their generations.** We are not born of the lineage
of Aaron, but we have believed in him in whom Aaron also, with the saints
of that age, believed. Concerning him, it was promised to Abraham that *in*

---

1 1 Cor. 11:29
2 Matt. 5:17-18
3 literally, 'For our humility also belongs'

your descendants all the families of the earth shall be blessed.[1] Isaiah makes mention of these families when he says, *All who see them shall acknowledge them, that these are the descendants whom the Lord has blessed.*[2]

1 Acts 3:25; cf. Gen. 22:18
2 Isa. 61:9

SELECT BIBLIOGRAPHY

PRIMARY SOURCES

Adam of Dryburgh, *De tripartito tabernaculo*, ed. in *PL* 198.

Aldhelm, *De virginitate (prosa)*, ed. R. Ehwald, *MGH AA* 15 (Berlin, 1919); transl. M. Lapidge and M. Herren, in *Aldhlem: The Prose Works* (Cambridge and Totowa, N.J., 1979).

Amalarius of Metz, *Liber officialis*, ed. J. M. Hanssens, in *Amalarii episcopi opera liturgica omnia*, 2 (*Studi e Testi* 139; Vatican City, 1948-50).

Andrew of Saint Victor, *In Exodum*, ed. C. Lohr and R. Berndt, *CCCM* 53 (Turnhout, 1986).

Augustine, *De civitate Dei*, ed. B. Dombart and A. Kalb, *CCSL* 47-8 (Turnhout, 1955); the same ed. with transl. by G. E. McCracken, W. M. Green, D. S. Wiesen, P. Levine, E. M. Sanford, and W. C. Greene, *LCL*, 7 vols. (London and Cambridge, Mass., 1957-72); also ed. E. Hoffmann, *CSEL* 40, 2 vols. (Vienna, 1899-1900); transl. H. Bettenson (*Penguin Classics*; Harmondsworth, 1972); also transl. M. Dods, *NPNF*, 1st ser., 2 (Buffalo, 1887; reprinted Grand Rapids, 1956); D. B. Zema, G. G. Walsh, G. Monahan, and D. J. Honan, *FOTC* 8, 14, and 24 (New York, 1950-4).

_____, *De consensu evangelistarum*, ed. F. Weihrich, *CSEL* 43 (Vienna, 1904); transl. S. D. F. Salmond, *NPNF*, 1st ser., 6 (New York, 1888; reprinted Grand Rapids, 1956).

_____, *De doctrina christiana*, ed. J. Martin, *CCSL* 32 (Turnhout, 1962); also ed. G. M. Green, *CSEL* 89 (Vienna, 1963); transl. D. W. Robertson, Jr. (New York, 1958); also transl. J. F. Shaw, *NPNF*, 1st ser., 2 (Buffalo, 1887; reprinted Grand Rapids, 1956); J. J. Cavigan, *FOTC* 2 (New York, 1947).

_____, *De Genesi ad litteram*, ed. J. Zycha, *CSEL* 28, 1 (Vienna, 1894); transl. J. H. Taylor, *ACW* 41-2 (New York, 1982).

————, *De sermone domini in monte*, ed. A. Mutzenbecher, *CCSL* 35 (Turnhout, 1967); transl. D. J. Kavanagh, *FOTC* 11 (New York, 1951); also transl. J. J. Jepson, *ACW* 5 (Westminster, Md., 1948); W. Findlay, revised by D. S. Schaff *NPNF*, 1st ser., 6 (New York, 1888; reprinted Grand Rapids, 1956).

————, *Enarrationes in psalmos*, ed. D. E. Dekkers and J. Fraipont, *CCSL* 38-40 (Turnhout, 1956); transl. A. C. Coxe, *NPNF*, 1st ser., 8 (New York, 1888; reprinted Grand Rapids, 1950).

Babrius, *Aesopic Fables*, ed. and transl. B. E. Perry, *LCL* (London and Cambridge, Mass., 1965).

Bede, *De schematibus et tropis*, ed. C. B. Kendall, *CCSL* 123A (Turnhout, 1975); transl. G. H. Tanenhaus, in *Quarterly Journal of Speech* 48 (1962), 237-53; reprinted in *Readings in Medieval Rhetoric*, ed. J. M. Miller et al. (Bloomington, 1973).

————, *De tabernaculo*, ed. D. Hurst, *CCSL* 119A (Turnhout, 1969).

————, *De temporum ratione*, ed. C. W. Jones and T. Mommsen, *CCSL* 123B (Turnhout, 1977).

————, *De templo*, ed. D. Hurst, *CCSL* 119A (Turnhout, 1969).

————, *De temporibus*, ed. C. W. Jones and T. Mommsen, *CCSL* 123C (Turnhout, 1980).

————, *Epistola ad Albinum*, ed. C. Plummer, in *Venerabilis Baedae opera historica*, 1 (Oxford, 1896; reprinted 1946, 1956).

————, *Epistola ad Ecgbertum Episcopum*, ed. C. Plummer, in *Venerabilis Baedae opera historica*, 1 (Oxford, 1896; reprinted 1946, 1956); transl. D. H. Farmer, in *Ecclesiastical History of the English People, with Bede's Letter to Egbert and Cuthbert's Letter on the Death of Bede* (*Penguin Classics*; London, 1990); also ed. and transl. J. E. King, *LCL* 2 (Cambridge, Mass. and London, 1930).

————, *Epistola ad Plegvinam*, ed. C. W. Jones, *CCSL* 123C (Turnhout, 1980).

_____, *Historia abbatum*, ed. C. Plummer, in *Venerabilis Baedae opera historica*, 1 (Oxford, 1896; reprinted 1946, 1956); transl. D. H. Farmer, in *The Age of Bede* (*Penguin Classics*; Harmondsworth, 1983); also ed. and transl. J. E. King, *LCL* 2 (Cambridge, Mass. and London, 1930).

_____, *Historia ecclesiastica gentis Anglorum*, ed. and transl. B. Colgrave and R. A. B. Mynors (Oxford, 1969; reprinted with corrections, 1991); also transl. L. Sherley-Price, revised by R. E. Latham (*Penguin Classics*; Harmondsworth, 1968; reprinted London, 1990); also ed. and transl. J. E. King, *LCL*, 2 vols. (Cambridge, Mass. and London, 1930).

_____, *Homiliae evangelii*, ed. D. Hurst, *CCSL* 122 (Turnhout, 1965); transl. L. T. Martin and D. Hurst, 2 vols. (*Cistercian Studies Series* 110-11; Kalamazoo, 1991).

_____, *In Apocalypsin*, ed. in *PL* 93.

_____, *In Cantica Canticorum*, ed. D. Hurst, *CCSL* 119B (Turnhout, 1983).

_____, *In Esram et Neemiam*, ed. D. Hurst, *CCSL* 119A (Turnhout, 1969).

_____, *In Marcum*, ed. D. Hurst, *CCSL* 120 (Turnhout, 1960).

_____, *In principium Genesim*, ed. C. W. Jones, *CCSL* 118A (Turnhout, 1967).

_____, *In Habacuc*, ed. J. E. Hudson, *CCSL* 119B (Turnhout, 1983).

_____, *In Lucam*, ed. D. Hurst, *CCSL* 120 (Turnhout, 1960).

_____, *In primam partem Samuhelis*, ed. D. Hurst, *CCSL* 119 (Turnhout, 1962).

_____, *In Regum Librum XXX quaestiones*, ed. D. Hurst, *CCSL* 119 (Turnhout, 1972).

_____, *Liber hymnorum, rhythmi, variae preces*, ed. J. Fraipont, *CCSL* 122 (Turnhout, 1965).

_____, *Vita sancti Cuthberti prosaica*, ed. and transl. B. Colgrave (Cambridge, 1940); also transl. J. F. Webb, in *The Age of Bede* (*Penguin Classics*; Harmondsworth, 1983).

Biblia Sacra iuxta vulgatam versionem, ed. R. Weber, 2 vols. (Stuttgart, 1969; 2nd ed., 1975).

Cassiodorus, *Expositio in psalmorum*, ed. M. Adriaen, *CCSL* 97-8 (Turnhout, 1958); transl. P. G. Walsh, *ACW* 51-3 (New York, 1990-1).

_____, *Institutiones*, ed. R. A. B. Mynors (Oxford, 1937); transl. L. W. Jones, *An Introduction to Divine and Human Readings* (New York, 1946).

Cyprian, *Ad Fortunatum*, ed. R. Weber, *CCSL* 3 (Turnhout, 1972); transl. R. J. Deferrari, *FOTC* 36 (New York, 1958); also transl. R. E. Wallis, *ANF* 5 (Buffalo, 1886; reprinted Grand Rapids, 1951).

Epiphanius, *De XII gemmis*, ed. G. Dindorf, in *Epiphanii episcopi Constantiae opera*, 4, 1 (Leipzig, 1862).

Eucherius of Lyons, *Formulae spiritalis intelligentiae*, ed. C. Wotke, *CSEL* 31 (Vienna, 1894).

Gelasian Sacramentary, ed. H. A. Wilson, *Liber sacramentorum Romanae ecclesiae* (Oxford, 1894); baptismal rites transl. E. C. Whitaker, in *Documents of the Baptismal Liturgy* (London, 1970).

Glossa ordinaria, in *Biblia Latina cum Glossa ordinaria: Facsimile Reprint of the Editio Princeps, Strassburg, c.1480*, ed. K. Froehlich and M. T. Gibson (Turnhout, 1992).

Gregory the Great, *Homiliae in evangelia*, ed. in *PL* 76; transl. D. Hurst (*Cistercian Studies Series* 123; Kalamazoo, 1990).

_____, *Homiliae in Ezechielem*, ed. M. Adriaen, *CCSL* 142 (Turnhout, 1971); also ed. (with French transl.) C. Morel, *SC* 327, 352, 360 (Paris, 1986-90); transl. T. Gray (Etna, Calif., 1990).

_____, *Moralia in Iob*, ed. M. Adriaen, *CCSL* 143, 143A, 143B (Turnhout, 1979-85); to date only Books 1-16 have appeared in a new ed. (with French transl.) by R. Gillet, *SC* 32, 212, 221 (Paris, 1952-1975; 2nd ed. of vol. 32, 1975); transl. in *Library of Fathers of the Holy Catholic Church* 18, 21, 23, 31 (Oxford, 1844-50).

_____, *Regulae pastoralis liber*, ed. (with French transl.) C. Morel, *SC* 381-2 (Paris, 1992); transl. H. Davis, *ACW* 11 (Westminster, Md., 1950); also transl. J. Barmby, *NPNF*, 2nd ser., 12 (New York, 1895; reprinted Grand Rapids, 1952).

_____, *Registrum epistularum*, ed. D. Norbert, *CCSL* 140-140A (Turnhout, 1982); to date only Books 1-2 have appeared in a new ed. (with French transl.) by P. Minard, *SC* 370-1 (Paris, 1991); selections transl. J. Barmby, *NPNF*, 2nd ser., 12-13 (New York, 1895-8; reprinted Grand Rapids, 1952).

A. W. Haddan and W. Stubbs (eds.), *Councils and Ecclesiastical Documents Relating to Great Britain and Ireland*, 3 vols. in 4 (Oxford, 1869-78).

Horace, *Epistulae*, ed. and transl. H. R. Fairclough, *LCL* (Cambridge, Mass., 1926; revised ed., 1929).

Irenaeus, *Adversus Haereses*, ed. (with French transl.) F. Sagnard, A. Rousseau, B. Hemmerdinger, C. Mercier, and L. Doutreleau, *SC* 34, 100, 152-3, 210-11, 263-4, 293-4 (Paris, 1952-82); transl. A. Roberts and W. H. Rambaut, *ANF* 1 (New York, 1885; reprinted Grand Rapids, 1950); to date only Book 1 has appeared in a new transl. in progress, by D. J. Unger with revisions by J. J. Dillon, *ACW* 55- (New York, 1992-).

Isidore, *Etymologiae*, ed. W. M. Lindsay (*Scriptorum classicorum bibliotheca Oxoniensis*; Oxford, 1911).

_____, *Quaestiones in Exodum*, ed. in *PL* 83.

Jerome, *De nominibus hebraicis*, ed. P. de Lagarde, *CCSL* 72 (Turnhout, 1959).

_____, *Epistulae*, ed. I. Hilberg, *CSEL* 54-6 (Vienna, 1910-18); also ed. (with French transl.) J. Labourt (Paris, 1949-63).

_____, *Quaestiones hebraicae in Genesim*, ed. P. de Lagarde, *CCSL* 72 (Turnhout, 1959).

_____, *In Ecclesiasten*, ed. M. Adriaen, *CCSL* 72 (Turnhout, 1959).

_____, *In Esaiam*, ed. M. Adriaen, *CCSL* 73 and 73A (Turnhout, 1963).

_____, *In Ezechielem*, ed. F. Glorie, *CCSL* 75 (Turnhout, 1964).

_____, *In Habacuc*, ed. M. Adriaen, *CCSL* 76A (Turnhout, 1970).

_____, *In Ioelem*, ed. M. Adriaen, *CCSL* 76 (Turnhout, 1969).

_____, *In Matthaeum*, ed. D. Hurst and M. Adriaen, *CCSL* 77 (Turnhout, 1969); also ed. (with French transl.) E. Bonnard, *SC* 252, 259 (Paris, 1977-9).

John Cassian, *Collationes*, ed. M. Petschenig, *CSEL* 13 (Vienna, 1886); also ed. (with French transl.) E. Pichery, *SC* 42, 54, 64 (Paris, 1955-9; reprinted 1967-71); selections transl. C. Luibheid, *Classics of Western Spirituality* (New York, 1985); also transl. E. C. S. Gibson, *NPNF*, 2nd ser., 11 (Oxford and London, 1894; reprinted Grand Rapids, 1952).

Josephus, *Antiquitates Judaicae*, Latin version of Books 1-5 ed. F. Blatt in *The Latin Josephus* (*Acta Jutlandica* 30; Copenhagen, 1958); Greek text ed. and transl. H. St. J. Thackeray, *LCL*, 6 vols. (London and New York, 1926).

Ordo Romanus XI, ed. M. Andrieu, in *Les ordines romani du haut moyen âge*, 2 (Louvain, 1948); transl. E. C. Whitaker, in *Documents of the Baptismal Liturgy* (London, 1970).

Origen, *Homiliae in Exodum*, ed. W. A. Baehrens, *GCS* 29 (Leipzig, 1920); also ed. (with French transl.) M. Borret, *SC* 321 (Paris, 1985); transl. R. E. Heine, *FOTC* 71 (Washington, D.C., 1982).

Paulinus, *Vita sancti Ambrosii*, ed. in *PL* 14; transl. J. A. Lacy, *FOTC* 15 (New York, 1952).

Peter of Poitiers, *Allegoriae super tabernaculum Moysi*, ed. P. S. Moore and J. A. Corbett, in *Publications in Mediaeval Studies* 3 (Notre Dame, 1938).

Peter of Celle, *De tabernaculo I* and *De tabernaculo II*, ed. G. de Martel, *CCCM* 54 (Turnhout, 1983).

Peter Comestor, *Historia scholastica*, ed. in *PL* 198.

Phaedrus, *Aesopic Fables*, ed. and transl. B. E. Perry, *LCL* (Cambridge, Mass. and London, 1965).

Philo, *De specialibus legibus*, ed. and transl. F. H. Colson, *LCL* 7 (Cambridge, Mass. and London, 1937).

_____, *De vita Mosis*, ed. and transl. F. H. Colson, *LCL* 6 (Cambridge, Mass. and London, 1935).

Pliny, *Naturalis historia*, ed. and transl. H. Rackham, W. H. S. Jones, and D. E. Eichholz, *LCL*, 10 vols. (Cambridge, Mass. and London, 1938-52).

Rabanus Maurus, *In Exodum*, ed. in *PL* 108.

Richard of Saint Victor, *Benjamin major*, ed. in *PL* 196; transl. G. A. Zinn (*Classics of Western Spirituality*; New York, 1979).

_____, *Expositio difficultatum suborientium in expositione tabernaculi foederis*, ed. in *PL* 196.

_____, *Nonnullae allegoriae tabernaculi foederis*, ed. in *PL* 196.

Stowe Missal, ed. G. F. Warner, Henry Bradshaw Society 31-2 (London, 1906-15); baptismal rites transl. E. C. Whitaker, in *Documents of the Baptismal Liturgy* (London, 1970).

Vergil, *Aeneid*, ed. and transl. H. R. Fairclough, *LCL*, 2 vols. (Cambridge, Mass. and London, 1916; revised ed., 1934-5).

Vita Ceolfridi, ed. C. Plummer as *Historia abbatum auctore anonymo*, in *Venerabilis Baedae opera historica*, 1 (Oxford, 1896; reprinted 1946, 1956); transl. D. S. Boutflower (Sunderland, 1912); also transl. D. Whitelock, in *English Historical Documents*, 1 (London and New York, 1955; 2nd ed., 1979).

SECONDARY WORKS

J. J. G. Alexander, *Insular Manuscripts: 6th to the 9th Century* (*A Survey of Manuscripts Illuminated in the British Isles*; London, 1978).

T. L. Amos, 'Monks and Pastoral Care in the Early Middle Ages', in *Religion, Culture, and Society in the Early Middle Ages: Studies in Honor of Richard E. Sullivan*, ed. T. F. X. Noble and J. J. Contreni (*Studies in Medieval Culture* 23; Kalamazoo, 1987), 165-80.

R. R. Atwell, 'From Augustine to Gregory the Great: An Evaluation of the Emergence of the Doctrine of Purgatory', *Journal of Ecclesiastical History* 38 (1987), 173-86.

R. N. Bailey, 'Bede's Text of Cassiodorus' Commentary on the Psalms', *Journal of Theological Studies* n.s. 34 (1983), 189-93.

M. P. L. Barrows, 'Bede's *Allegorical Exposition of the Canticle of Canticles*: A Study in Early Medieval Allegorical Exegesis', unpublished Ph.D. dissertation, University of California at Berkeley, 1963.

J. Blair and R. Sharpe (eds.), *Pastoral Care Before the Parish* (*Studies in the Early History of Britain*; Leicester, 1992).

G. Bonner, *Saint Bede in the Tradition of Western Apocalyptic Commentary* (Jarrow Lecture, 1966).

_____ (ed.), *Famulus Christi: Essays in Commemoration of the Thirteenth Centenary of the Birth of the Venerable Bede* (London, 1976).

G. H. Brown, *Bede the Venerable* (*Twayne's English Authors Series* 443; Boston, 1987).

P. Brown, 'Pelagius and His Supporters: Aims and Environment', *Journal of Theological Studies* n.s. 19 (1968), 83-114.

R. L. S. Bruce-Mitford, *The Art of the Codex Amiatinus* (Jarrow Lecture, 1967); reprinted in *Journal of the Royal Archaeological Association* 32 (1969), 1-25.

J. A. Burrows, *The Ages of Man: A Study in Medieval Writing and Thought* (Oxford, 1988).

M. T. A. Carroll, *The Venerable Bede: His Spiritual Teachings* (*Catholic University of America Studies in Mediaeval History* n. s. 9; Washington, D.C., 1946).

A. Chavasse, 'La discipline des scrutins, à Rome, du cinquième au huitième siècle', *Recherches de science religieuse* 35 (1948), 325-81.

_____, 'La discipline romaine des sept scrutins prèbaptismaux', *Recherches de science religieuse* 48 (1960), 227-40.

M.-D. Chenu, *La théologie au douzième siècle* (Paris, 1957).

C. Cochini, *Apostolic Origins of Priestly Celibacy*, transl. N. Marans (San Francisco, 1990).

G. Constable, 'Monasteries, Rural Churches, and the *cura animarum* in the Early Middle Ages', *Settimane di Studio del Centro Italiano di Studi sull'Alto Medioevo* 28 (1982), 1: 349-89.

K. Corsano, 'The First Quire of the Codex Amiatinus and the *Institutiones* of Cassiodorus', *Scriptorium* 41 (1987), 3-34.

F. M. Cross, 'The Priestly Tabernacle', *Biblical Archaeologist Reader* 1 (1961), 201-28.

C. Cubitt, 'Pastoral Care and Conciliar Canons: The Provisions of the 747 Council of *Clofesho*', in Blair and Sharpe (1992), 193-211.

J. Daniélou, *The Angels and Their Mission*, transl. D. Heimann (Westminster, Md., 1957; reprinted 1987).

_____, 'La symbolisme du temple de Jerusalem chez Philon et Josèphe', in *Le symbolisme cosmique des monuments religieux* (*Serie Orientale Roma* 14; Rome, 1957), 83-90.

E. Dassmann, 'Die Bedeutung des Alten Testaments für das Verständnis des kirchlichen Amtes in der frühpatristischen Theologie', *Bibel und Leben* 11 (1970), 198-214.

H. de Lubac, *Exégèse médiévale: les quatre sens de l'Écriture*, 2 vols. in 4 pts. (Paris, 1959-64).

B. de Margerie, *Introduction à l'histoire de l'exégèse*, 4 vols. to date (Paris, 1980-).

A. Dondeyne, 'La discipline des scrutins dans l'église latine avant Charle-magne', *Revue d'histoire ecclésiastique* 28 (1932), 5-33, 751-87.

B. Fischer, 'Codex Amiatinus und Cassiodor', *Biblische Zeitschrift* n.f. 6 (1962), 57-79.

J. D. C. Fisher, *Christian Initiation: Baptism in the Medieval West* (*Alcuin Club Collections* 47; London, 1965).

S. Foot, '"By Water in the Spirit": The Administration of Baptism in Early Anglo-Saxon England', in Blair and Sharpe (1992), 171-92.

_____, 'The Parochial Ministry in Early Anglo-Saxon England: The Role of Monastic Communities', in *The Ministry: Clerical and Lay*, ed. W. J. Sheils and D. Wood (*Studies in Church History* 26; Oxford and Cambridge, Mass., 1989), 43-54.

C. A. Frazee, 'The Origins of Clerical Celibacy in the Western Church', *Church History* 41 (1972): 149-67.

R. E. Friedman, 'Tabernacle', in *Anchor Bible Dictionary*, ed. D. N. Freed-man (New York, 1992), 6: 292-300.

M. Gibson, 'The Place of the *Glossa ordinaria* in Medieval Exegesis', in *Ad Litteram: Authoritative Texts and Their Medieval Readers*, ed. K. E. Emery, Jr. and M. D. Jordan (Notre Dame, 1992), 5-27; re-printed in her *'Artes' and Bible in the Medieval West* (Aldershot, Hamp. and Brookfield, Vt., 1993).

R. Gryson, *Les origines du célibat ecclésiastique du premier au septième siècle* (Gembloux, 1970).

J. W. Halporn, 'Pandectes, Pandecta, and the Cassiodorian Commentary on the Psalms', *Revue Bénédictine* 90 (1980), 290-300.

A. G. Holder, 'Allegory and History in Bede's Interpretation of Sacred Architecture', *American Benedictine Review* 40 (1989a), 115-31.

_____, 'Bede and the Tradition of Patristic Exegesis', *Anglican Theological Review* 72 (1990), 399-411.

_____, 'The Mosaic Tabernacle in Early Christian Exegesis', *Studia Patristica* 25 (1993), 101-6.

_____, 'New Treasures and Old in Bede's *De tabernaculo* and *De templo*', *Revue Bénédictine* 99 (1989b), 237-49.

_____, 'The Venerable Bede on the Mysteries of Our Salvation', *American Benedictine Review* 42 (1991), 140-62.

P. Hunter Blair, 'From Bede to Alcuin', in Bonner (1976), 239-60.

_____, *Northumbria in the Days of Bede* (London, 1976).

_____, *The World of Bede* (Cambridge, 1970; reprinted London, 1990).

N. R. Ker, Review of M. L. W. Laistner and H. H. King, *A Hand-List of Bede Manuscripts*, in *Medium Aevum* 13 (1944), 36-41.

P. v. D. Krabben, 'Beda als Bron van *Van den Gheesteliken Tabernakel*', *Ons Geestelijk Erf* 9 (1935), 382-7.

C. Jenkins, 'Bede as Exegete and Theologian', in Thompson (1935), 152-200.

C. W. Jones, 'Some Introductory Remarks on Bede's Commentary on Genesis', *Sacris Erudiri* 19 (1969-70), 115-98.

B. Judic, 'La Bible miroir des pasteurs dans la *Règle pastorale* de Grégoire le Grand', in *Le monde latin antique et la Bible*, ed. J. Fontaine and C. Pietri (*Bible de tous les temps* 2; Paris, 1985), 455-73.

P. Kitson, 'Lapidary Traditions in Anglo-Saxon England: part II, Bede's *Explanatio Apocalypsis* and related works', *Anglo-Saxon England* 12 (1983), 73-123.

M. L. W. Laistner, 'The Library of the Venerable Bede', in Thompson (1935), 237-66; reprinted in *Intellectual Heritage of the Early Middle Ages*, ed. C. G. Starr (Ithaca, 1957), 93-116.

M. L. W. Laistner and H. H. King, *A Hand-List of Bede Manuscripts* (Ithaca, 1943).

J. Le Goff, *The Birth of Purgatory*, transl. A. Goldhammer (Chicago, 1984).

W. Liebeschuetz, 'Pelagian Evidence on the Lost Period of Roman Britain?', *Latomus* 26 (1967), 436-47.

_____, 'Did the Pelagian Movement Have Social Aims?', *Historia* 12 (1963), 227-41.

T. W. Mackay, 'Bede's Biblical Criticism: The Venerable Bede's Summary of Tyconius' *Liber regularum*', in *Saints, Scholars, and Heroes: Studies in Medieval Culture in Honour of Charles W. Jones*, ed. M. H. King and W. M. Stevens (Collegeville, 1979), 1: 209-31.

R. A. Markus, 'Pelagianism: Britain and the Continent', *Journal of Ecclesiastical History* 37 (1986), 191-204.

_____, 'Gregory the Great's *rector* and His Genesis', in *Grégoire le Grand: Actes du Colloque de Chantilly (15-19 septembre, 1982)*, ed. J. Fontaine, R. Gillet, and S. Pellistrandi (Paris, 1986), 137-46.

L. T. Martin, 'Bede's Structural Use of Wordplay as a Way to Teach', in *From Cloister to Classroom: Monastic and Scholastic Approaches to Truth*, ed. E. R. Elder (*Spirituality of Western Christendom* 3; Kalamazoo, 1986), 27-46.

H. Mayr-Harting, *The Coming of Christianity to Anglo-Saxon England* (London, 1972; 2nd ed., 1977; 3rd ed., 1991).

J. McClure, 'Bede's *Notes on Genesis* and the Training of the Anglo-Saxon Clergy', in *The Bible in the Medieval World: Essays in Memory of Beryl Smalley*, ed. K. Walsh and D. Wood (*Studies in Church History*, Subsidia 4; Oxford, 1985), 17-30.

P. Meyvaert, 'Bede and the Church Paintings at Wearmouth-Jarrow', *Anglo-Saxon England* 8 (1979), 63-77.

_____, 'Bede the Scholar', in Bonner (1976), 40-69; reprinted in his *Benedict, Gregory, Bede and Others* (London, 1977).

J. Morris, 'Pelagian Literature', *Journal of Theological Studies* n.s. 16 (1965), 26-60.

J. N. L. Myres, 'Pelagius and the End of Roman Rule in Britain', *Journal of Roman Studies* 50 (1960), 21-36.

G. Olsen, 'Bede as Historian: The Evidence from His Observations on the Life of the First Christian Community at Jerusalem', *Journal of Ecclesiastical History* 33 (1982), 519-30.

C. Plummer, *Venerabilis Baedae opera historica*, 2 vols. (Oxford, 1896; reprinted 1946, 1956).

A. Quacquarelli, *Il triplice frutto della vita cristiana: 100, 60 e 30 (Matteo XIII - 8, nelle diverse interpretazioni)* (Rome, 1953).

R. Ray, 'Bede and Cicero', *Anglo-Saxon England* 16 (1987), 1-15.

_____, 'What Do We Know about Bede's Commentaries?', *Recherches de théologie ancienne et médiévale* 49 (1982), 5-20.

P. Siniscalco, 'Le età del mondo in Beda', *Romanobarbarica* 3 (1978), 297-332.

B. Smalley, Review of M. L. W. Laistner and H. H. King, *A Hand-List of Bede Manuscripts*, in *Journal of Theological Studies* 45 (1944), 228-31.

E. F. Sutcliffe, 'The Venerable Bede's Knowledge of Hebrew', *Biblica* 16 (1935), 301-6.

A. Thacker, 'Bede's Idea of Reform', in *Ideal and Reality in Frankish and Anglo-Saxon Society: Studies Presented to J. M. Wallace-Hadrill*, ed. P. Wormald, D. Bullough, and R. Collins (Oxford, 1983), 130-53.

_____, 'Monks, Preaching and Pastoral Care in Early Anglo-Saxon England', in Blair and Sharpe (1992), 137-70.

A. H. Thompson (ed.), *Bede: His Life, Times, and Writings: Essays in Commemoration of the Twelfth Centenary of His Death* (Oxford, 1935; reprinted New York, 1966).

B. Ward, *The Venerable Bede (Outstanding Christian Thinkers Series*; London, 1990).

G. G. Willis, *Further Essays in Early Roman Liturgy (Alcuin Club Collections* 50; London, 1968).

A. Willmes, 'Bedas Bibelauslegung', *Archiv für Kulturgeschichte* 44 (1962), 281-314.

N. Wright, 'Bede and Vergil', *Romanobarbarica* 6 (1981), 361-79.

INDEX OF BIBLICAL QUOTATIONS
AND ALLUSIONS

INDEX OF PATRISTIC AND CLASSICAL SOURCES

TRANSLATED TEXTS FOR HISTORIANS
Published Titles

Gregory of Tours: Life of the Fathers
Translated with an introduction by EDWARD JAMES
Volume 1: 176pp., 2nd edition 1991, ISBN 0 85323 327 6

The Emperor Julian: Panegyric and Polemic
Claudius Mamertinus, John Chrysostom, Ephrem the Syrian
edited by SAMUEL N. C. LIEU
Volume 2: 153pp., 2nd edition 1989, ISBN 0 85323 376 4

Pacatus: Panegyric to the Emperor Theodosius
Translated with an introduction by C. E. V. NIXON
Volume 3: 122pp., 1987, ISBN 0 85323 076 5

Gregory of Tours: Glory of the Martyrs
Translated with an introduction by RAYMOND VAN DAM
Volume 4: 150pp., 1988, ISBN 0 85323 236 9

Gregory of Tours: Glory of the Confessors
Translated with an introduction by RAYMOND VAN DAM
Volume 5: 127pp., 1988, ISBN 0 85323 226 1

The Book of Pontiffs *(Liber Pontificalis to AD 715)*
Translated with an introduction by RAYMOND DAVIS
Volume 6: 175pp., 1989, ISBN 0 85323 216 4

Chronicon Paschale 284-628 AD
Translated with notes and introduction by
MICHAEL WHITBY AND MARY WHITBY
Volume 7: 280pp., 1989, ISBN 0 85323 096 X

Iamblichus: On the Pythagorean Life
Translated with notes and introduction by GILLIAN CLARK
Volume 8: 144pp., 1989, ISBN 0 85323 326 8

Conquerors and Chroniclers of Early-Medieval Spain
Translated with notes and introduction by KENNETH BAXTER WOLF
Volume 9: 176pp., 1991, ISBN 0 85323 047 1

Victor of Vita: History of the Vandal Persecution
Translated with notes and introduction by JOHN MOORHEAD
Volume 10: 112pp., 1992, ISBN 0 85323 127 3

The Goths in the Fourth Century
by PETER HEATHER AND JOHN MATTHEWS
Volume 11: 224pp., 1991, ISBN 0 85323 426 4

Cassiodorus: Variae
Translated with notes and introduction by S.J.B. BARNISH
Volume 12: 260pp., 1992, ISBN 0 85323 436 1

The Lives of the Eighth-Century Popes *(Liber Pontificalis)*
Translated with an introduction and commentary by RAYMOND DAVIS
Volume 13: 288pp., 1992, ISBN 0 85323 018 8

Eutropius: Breviarium
Translated with an introduction and commentary by H. W. BIRD
Volume 14: 248pp., 1993, ISBN 0 85323 208 3

The Seventh Century in the West-Syrian Chronicles
introduced, translated and annotated by ANDREW PALMER
including two seventh-century Syriac apocalyptic texts
introduced, translated and annotated by SEBASTIAN BROCK
with added annotation and an historical introduction by ROBERT HOYLAND
Volume 15: 368pp., 1993., ISBN 0 85323 238 5

Vegetius: Epitome of Military Science
Translated with notes and introduction by N. P. MILNER
Volume 16: 182pp., 1993, ISBN 0 85323 228 8

Aurelius Victor: De Caesaribus
Translated with an introduction and commentary by H. W. BIRD
Volume 17: 264pp., 1994, ISBN 0 85323 218 0

Bede: On the Tabernacle
Translated with notes and introduction by ARTHUR G. HOLDER
Volume 18: 224pp., 1994, ISBN 0 85323 378 0

Caesarius of Arles: Life, Testament, Letters
Translated with notes and introduction by WILLIAM E. KLINGSHIRN
Volume 19: 176pp., 1994, ISBN 0 85323 368 3

For full details of Translated Texts for Historians, including prices and ordering information, please write to the following:

All countries, except the USA and Canada: Liverpool University Press, PO Box 147, Liverpool, L69 3BX, UK *(tel* 051-794 2235, *fax* 051-708 6502).

USA and Canada: University of Pennsylvania Press, Blockley Hall, 418 Service Drive, Philadelphia, PA 19104-6097, USA *(tel* (215) 898-6264, *fax* (215) 898-0404).